Golfing
the
Virginias

Golfing
the
Virginias

Rob Armstrong

PELICAN PUBLISHING COMPANY
Gretna 1999

*The word "Pelican" and the depiction of a pelican are
trademarks of Pelican Publishing Company, Inc., and are
registered in the U.S. Patent and Trademark Office.*

Library of Congress Cataloging-in-Publication Data

Armstrong, Rob
    Golfing the Virginias / Rob Armstrong.
       p.   cm.
    ISBN: 1-56554-273-8 (alk. paper)
    1. Golf—Virginia—Directories. 2. Golf—West Virginia-
-Directories. 3. Golf courses—Virginia—Directories. 4. Golf
courses—West Virginia—Directories.   I. Title.
GV982.V57A76 1999
796.352′06′8755—dc21   99-12558
                                                                    CIP

Course maps by Scott Lockheed

Printed in Hong Kong
Published by Pelican Publishing Company
1000 Burmaster Street, Gretna, Louisiana 70053

For Barbara
with love and thanks

CONTENTS

ACKNOWLEDGMENTS

This has been an enormous undertaking that has involved hundreds of people: those who offered advice and counsel; those who helped facilitate my research; those who took the time to play the various golf courses with me or to offer their expertise on the courses, design, construction, history, and highlights; and the countless people in pro shops across Virginia and West Virginia who were kind, patient, and helpful. There are simply too many to name them all.

Foremost, I am indebted to my wife, Barbara, who played as many of these golf courses with me as time and the demands of her law practice would allow. In addition, she suffered through my long absences and then cheerfully and expertly applied her knowledge of the game and her considerable editing skills to the rough versions of the manuscript. As always, my father and mother were there with love and support; it was Murray and Freda Armstrong who first put a golf club in my hand and encouraged me to write from an early age.

The people at Pelican Publishing have been spectacular. They are among the best in the book world. I am especially grateful to my publisher, Dr. Milburn Calhoun, for having enough faith and confidence to undertake a second book with me. Editor in Chief Nina Kooij is nothing less than brilliant—a gifted, diligent, patient professional who does a huge amount of the work and gets too little of the credit. My thanks also to Patrick Davis, Lynda Moreau, and Frank McGuire.

Golf people are a special breed. Scores of golf people devoted far more time and effort to helping me than was required. At the various golf courses and resorts, my sincere gratitude to Joe Stevens, Rob Mahan, Jim Bradley, Howie Barrow, Glen Byrnes, Tom Lernihan, Sue Donald, Francis Fenderson, Ben Thompson, William Luce, Lynn Polizos, Michael Thomas, Jeff Winters, Kenny Clark, Chris McLean, Marc Glickman, Billy McBride, Paula Hank, Hagen Giles, Townley Aide, Dick Moore, Karen Waialea, Frank Sluciak, Bob Benning, Bud Harold, and Jill Vanden Heuvel.

Thanks also to my friends, colleagues, and golfing associates who lent me their wisdom, experience, advice, support, and humor, including: Jim Babcock, Bob Palmer, Dave Newsom, Bob Stevenson, Bob Schieffer, Jamie Dupree, Dan and Tina Tate, Ray Lustig, Mary Hager, Toby Marquez, Bob and Nancy Finan, Alex and Mea Gillies, Sheila Vidamour, Tom and Marjorie Taylor, and the great people at McLean Photo Lab and Irving's Camera Shop.

INTRODUCTION

Virginia and its younger sibling, West Virginia, are inextricably linked. They were once one. They were rent apart by the same internal dispute that divided the country and cast brother against brother in the War between the States. Together they were the cradle of American democracy, home to Washington, Jefferson, Madison, Mason, the Lees; apart, as separate and equal members of the union, they remain kindred spirits. For those who love the game of golf, there are few places that offer as many and such varied examples of the sport at its best as in this relatively limited geographical area.

The Old Dominion is replete with golf courses of virtually every type—from the championship courses of Williamsburg to delightful and demanding mountain courses such as Cascades at The Homestead (arguably one of the best two or three golf courses in the country), the Olde Mill, and Devils Knob at Wintergreen. West Virginia adds to the mix with a variety of mature, veteran tracks (such as the Speidel Course at Oglebay Park, George Cobb's masterpiece at Glade Springs, and Cacapon) and testing new courses (such as Gary Player's grueling Hawthorne Valley and Locust Hill). There are public, daily-fee, and resort golf courses in the two states to please golfers of every skill level and to accommodate almost every budget.

While golf has long been popular in the Virginias, the 1980s and '90s saw a veritable golf boom. New golf-course construction and expansion has reached record levels in Virginia and West Virginia. Not only were existing facilities enlarged, improved, or redesigned, but new courses were built and new golf communities and golf resorts burst on the scene. Places that were once farmland, untouched mountain slopes, and even swamps were hewn and caressed into golf courses. Big-name designers have been lured to ply their trade, producing such wonderful new layouts as Raspberry Falls (a sand-laden monster created by Gary Player), Augustine (an awesome challenge by Rick Jacobson, once part of the Nicklaus group), and Lee's Hill (a splendid test crafted by Ed Ault). Such highly reputed designers as Robert Trent Jones Sr. and family, Jack Nicklaus, Ellis and Dan Maples, and the Dyes have all contributed to golf here.

The history of golf in the Virginias began around the dawn of the twentieth century. There were only a few private clubs with golf courses in Virginia and none in West Virginia before 1900. Back then golf was quite a novelty everywhere in North America. The sport itself predates the American Revolution in its earliest forms in Scotland and had migrated to parts of England and Ireland long before the U.S. Civil War. The first known golf club anywhere was founded in Edinburgh,

Scotland, in 1744; the Royal and Ancient Golf Club at St. Andrews was born in 1754. The first golf club in the United States was named after St. Andrews and located among pleasant, picturesque hills in the village of Hastings-on-Hudson in New York's Westchester County. It opened in 1888.

The Homestead resort in Hot Springs, Virginia, boasts the oldest tee in continuous use in the United States, dating to 1892. West Virginia's legendary and luxurious Greenbrier resort started planning its first nine-hole layout in 1910. In the summer of 1927, Bobby Jones himself presided over the opening of a charming little nine-hole course in the Blue Ridge Mountains at the Shenandoah Valley Hotel in New Market, Virginia; it is now a part of today's Shenvalee Resort. The Crispin course in Wheeling's Oglebay Park opened in 1928.

In the early part of the twentieth century, the skill and ability of such wonderful professional golfers as Harry Vardon and Bobby Jones piqued the interest of a small but growing number of sports fans and helped expand the popularity of the game. Even though golf remained a relatively minor pastime, resorts and hotels that catered to the rich were eager to increase their own attractiveness to their patrons by offering the sport.

Golf was a diversion for the very wealthy—and mostly wealthy white men at that. Most average citizens could neither afford the cost of golf clubs nor the tariff charged to join private clubs or play the few resort-type courses available. Many people were arbitrarily excluded because of race or religion; golf privileges were routinely denied to African Americans, Jews, Asians, and women. In fact, golf was highly restrictive on racial, religious, social, and sexual grounds until

the late 1960s (and in a few isolated cases into the 1970s and '80s). Mercifully, the issues of ethnicity and gender have for the most part disappeared in the golf world, although change was often grudging and painfully slow.

The sometimes-gloomy history of the game, like the sometimes-unfortunate history of the nation, must not be overlooked or diminished. The issues of slavery and states' rights caused West Virginia to break away from Virginia in 1863. The political differences between the rural, mountainous, and remote western part of Virginia and the more urban and cultured eastern and central part of the common-wealth had been festering for a substantial period before the Civil War. The split was not much of a surprise.

For its part, Virginia was the home of the legendary Confederate general and leader Robert E. Lee, and Richmond served for a time as the capital of the Confederacy. Ironically, there is a deep-rooted belief among Virginians that the Old Dominion was the birthplace of the Union to begin with. After all, native son Thomas Jefferson penned the Declaration of Independence; George Washington led the Revolutionary Army and was the father of his country; James Madison was the architect of the Constitution; and Patrick Henry thundered before the House of Burgesses, "Give me liberty or give me death!"

Today, golf developers have managed to amalgamate the rich history of the region with some of the country's finest golf courses. You can walk the streets of Colonial Williamsburg and Jamestown after you've played Kingsmill's River Course or the Gold Course at the Golden Horseshoe. You can stroll the campus of the University of Virginia or visit

Monticello, the home of Thomas Jefferson, the man who designed and built both masterpieces, after you've tested your golfing skills at Wintergreen's Stoney Creek or Devils Knob. As you contemplate your club selection or drink in the scenery at Augustine, you know you're on the spot where George Washington's father, Augustine, built the first smelter in 1727. The skeleton of Locust Hill—the plantation house that was the site of a Civil War skirmish in Charles Town, West Virginia—is in play beside the 11th green at the course that bears its name. The bullet holes are still visible in the bricks. Lee's Hill, Ed Ault's brilliant course, sits in the shadow of the knoll on which Robert E. Lee bivouacked his troops in the winter of 1862-63.

Some of the magnificent new designs that demand attention include the two Williamsburg-area courses owned by South Carolina's Legends Group, Royal New Kent and Stonehouse, both designed by former Tom Fazio associate Mike Strantz; the brilliantly laid out Colonial Golf Course; Virginia Oaks in the Washington, D.C., area of northern Virginia; and Hawthorne Valley, south of Elkins, West Virginia.

From the Atlantic coast to the Shenandoah Valley to the Appalachian Mountains, Virginia and West Virginia offer a bounty for golfers. This book recognizes that every golfer employs a different set of criteria by which he or she rates a golf course. For some, the test is difficulty and challenge; for others, it is the aesthetics of the place; for still others, it's how well they might play a particular course; and for some, it boils down to value for their dollar. The Virginias offer something for every golfer.

Not every course represented here is a "championship" layout; some will hold little interest to low-single-digit-handicap golfers other than for an ego boost, while mid- to high-handicappers will come away singing the praises of the course. In fact, several courses, such as northern Virginia's Brambleton, have been profiled specifically because they are so good for those learning the game or honing their skills. Some courses have taken special pains to accommodate women, and those cases are noted. Others are simply tremendous bargains and warrant attention for that reason. Some great golf courses are too difficult to be enjoyable for the high-handicap player or the less-skilled weekend golfer. Those, too, have been labeled as such. After all, while it's nice to be able to say you've played one of the great golf courses in the world, it's embarrassing to have to say you lost a dozen balls in the process or were escorted off the course by the ranger and given your money back for playing too slowly.

People who live in Virginia and West Virginia clearly have a wide assortment of public, daily-fee, and resort courses from which to choose. Visitors can pick a place and stay for a while or move around to sample the offerings.

Along with the abundance and high quality of the daily-fee and resort golf courses, Virginia and West Virginia also offer visitors a wide array of hotels, motels, restaurants, and resorts either in proximity to virtually every course or featuring golf courses as part of their package of amenities. Some serve dual purposes. Wintergreen and the Canaan Valley, for example, are ski resorts in the winter and golf havens in the summer. The Homestead and The Greenbrier are among the country's most famous and prestigious resorts. Colonial Williamsburg draws tourists and golfers from all over the world. And many of the golf courses of northern Virginia present wonderful opportunities for a side trip into the nation's capital.

There is something for virtually every taste, pocketbook, and level of golfing ability.

More than seventy golf courses were played in the preparation of *Golfing the Virginias* in an effort to find and highlight the best daily-fee and resort facilities in the two states. Not all made the cut. Some fell short because they simply lacked challenge. Others were rejected because of consistently substandard playing conditions or poor course maintenance. A few were omitted because the volume of play made five- and six-hour rounds the norm and the rangers or marshals made no discernable effort to monitor play and move the action along.

What has emerged is a snapshot of golf in an area that is becoming increasingly popular for the sport. As we go to press, new golf courses are both on the drawing board and under construction; some existing facilities are expanding. In a book such as this, time stands still when it goes to press, but the reality is that in the Virginias the business and the pleasure of golf is a constant work in progress.

Golfing
the
Virginias

A treelined fairway leads to Algonkian's 15th green, which is guarded by water and sand.

ALGONKIAN GOLF COURSE

47001 Fairway Drive, Sterling, Virginia (Take Route 7, Leesburg Pike, west to Cascades Parkway north for about 3 miles to clubhouse.)

(703) 450-4655

Architect: Ed Ault   Year opened: uncertain (early 1960s)

Course rating/Slope rating:

Blue - 73.5/125	White (Women) - 72.1/127
White (Men) - 72.1/123	Gold - 74.1/113

There is a little murkiness in the history of Algonkian Golf Course. The name is not the original, and its lineage is a little cloudy because time has fogged individual memories and some of the documentation fails to clarify the picture.

What we do know is that in the late 1950s or early '60s, the Potomac Electric Power Company, known as PEPCO around the Washington, D.C., area, undertook to build a private golf course for the use of its employees and their families. The well-known and popular golf-course designer Ed Ault and his company were hired to draw up the plans. A blueprint in the files of Jill Vanden Heuvel, the manager of Algonkian Regional Park, shows that the plan was completed in 1961, but a separate notation indicates that it was not approved until three years later. Somewhere in that time period, the golf course was finally built and opened for play.

In May 1975, the Northern Virginia Regional Park Authority bought the golf course and turned the private club into a public facility. What exists today is a superbly designed golf course that is a challenge to golfers of virtually every level of ability. It also is a tremendous bargain and one of the only such high-quality, low-priced facilities in easy proximity to the nation's capital. Although it is always crowded on weekends, it is fairly accessible on weekdays. Even on the busiest days the staff is adroit at keeping play moving.

The course is well managed and maintained. The tees and fairways are well groomed. The bunkers receive regular attention. The greens are deliberately kept moderately slow. What Ed Ault did in his design was to work with two highly diverse pieces of property—one fairly flat, dry, and open and the other hillier, watery, and heavily forested. The result is almost two separate golf courses. Typically, Ault likes big greens and challenging approaches. He also likes length, which he more than ably achieves in this par-72 track that measures more than 7,000 yards from the back tees.

The front side opens with a lovely, short par-four dogleg left, followed by a straight par five. These are the only two holes on the outgoing side to have water anywhere in the vicinity of play. The long par-four 3rd provides a preview of what is to come, both in terms of length and subtle difficulty. The straight 3rd is well treed down both sides, and the big green demands an accurate approach, more often than not with a long iron or even a fairway wood.

17

The par-three 5th requires a very big tee shot. For many women it verges on being a two-shot hole, measuring 185 yards from the forward tees. Men must carry at least 200 yards to hit the putting surface. The one-shot 5th is followed by the toughest hole on the course, a long par-five dogleg left that features towering old trees down the left side to the corner of the dogleg and then to the green. Cutting the dogleg over the trees requires a massive shot that more often finds itself punished with a woodsy landing than rewarded by coming to rest in the fairway. There is ample room straight ahead to hit a big drive and put your second in range for a short chip and a birdie try.

The long, tight 9th leads you to the second golf course, the watery, well-treed back nine, which opens with a pair of fine par fours. The long 10th plays downhill, and the even longer 11th requires you to hit your tee shot dead center and short of the hazard that intersects the fairway in front of the green. The water hazard again comes into play on the par-five 13th. That stream and marshy wetland requires players to consider whether to lay up short of it, leaving a long approach to the green, or to try to clear the hazard on their second shot, leaving a wedge or sand wedge to the putting surface. The 13th is rated the second-most-difficult hole on the course.

A difficult pair of par fours follows. The long 14th plays down a chute of trees. The longer 15th is a dogleg left, with a blind tee shot. The stream that is in play on #11 and #13 again comes into play in front of the green. The 16th is a monstrous par three, more than 200 yards for everybody. "You don't see ten players a day hit it," said a member of the grounds crew waiting for a group to putt out before finishing his job mowing the collar of the green. "And you don't see three guys a week off the back."

Algonkian finishes with the straight par-four 17th that's moderate in length and offers a good scoring opportunity, followed by the demanding 18th, a very solid dogleg-right par five. While a forest hugs the right length of the hole, limiting the prospects of cutting the dogleg, it's quite open on the left. If your tee shot is long enough to provide you with a glimpse of the green around the trees at the bend in the fairway, it's reachable in two.

This is a no-frills golf course. If you're looking for country-club amenities, they simply don't exist. But if you're looking for a fair, challenging round of golf at extremely reasonable prices, this is one of the best bets in the area.

ALGONKIAN

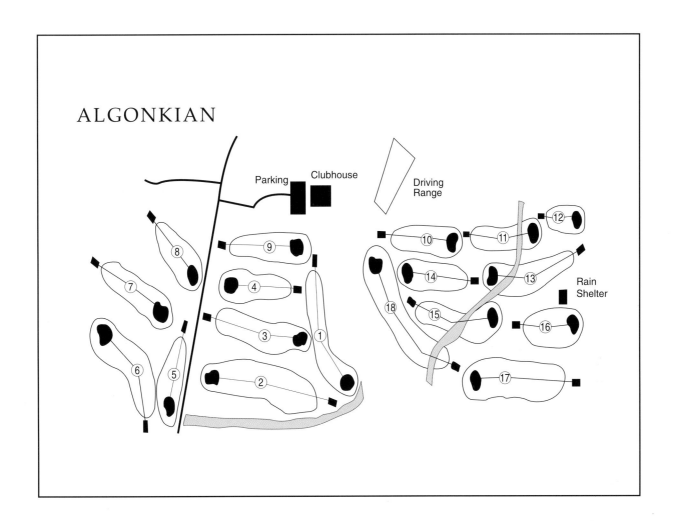

Algonkian

HOLE	Ra	Sl	1	2	3	4	5	6	7	8	9	OUT	10	11	12	13	14	15	16	17	18	IN	TOT
BLUE	73.5	125	345	510	445	410	210	540	415	195	440	3510	390	405	180	525	415	430	235	405	520	3505	7015
WHITE	72.1 (m)/72.1 (w)	123 (m)/127 (w)	339	500	425	395	200	525	400	190	420	3385	375	385	160	505	395	415	215	385	500	3335	6720
GOLD	74.0	113	320	445	330	350	185	450	330	180	315	2905	360	320	145	420	350	350	205	320	420	2890	5795
HCP			13	3	5	9	15	1	11	17	7		14	10	18	2	8	6	16	12	4		
PAR			4	5	4	4	3	5	4	3	4	36	4	4	3	5	4	4	3	4	5	36	72

Golfers are presented with a springtime bouquet from azaleas and dogwoods around the par-four 10th green at Augustine Golf Club.

Augustine Golf Club

HOLE	Ra	Sl	1	2	3	4	5	6	7	8	9	OUT	10	11	12	13	14	15	16	17	18	IN	TOT
BLACK	71.9	130	411	456	401	572	407	199	424	137	406	3413	428	498	441	433	228	305	396	167	501	3397	6810
BLUE	69.8	125	396	432	375	538	381	185	365	123	380	3175	412	477	414	413	204	291	371	143	470	3195	6370
WHITE	67.8 (m)/73.8 (w)	122(m)/134 (w)	357	403	335	503	342	182	339	94	343	2892	372	447	383	387	184	281	349	123	442	2968	5866
PAR			4	4	4	5	4	3	4	3	4	35	4	5	4	4	3	4	4	3	5	36	71
HCP			3	1	13	7	15	9	5	17	11		4	12	2	10	6	18	8	16	14		
RED	65.5 (m)/73.8 (w)	116 (m)/130 (w)	324	380	294	467	311	174	314	90	314	2668	340	426	341	367	167	256	323	109	418	2747	5415
GOLD	65.5 (m)/68.2 (w)	116 (m)/119 (w)	284	289	294	413	291	169	314	90	280	2384	340	355	299	346	143	234	281	91	365	2454	4838

AUGUSTINE GOLF CLUB

76 Monument Drive, Stafford, Virginia (Take I-95 to exit 140, Stafford; go west on
Route 630 about 3½ miles to the Augustine entrance.)
Phone: (540) 720-7374   Fax: (540) 720-6381

Architect: Rick Jacobson   Year opened: 1995

Course rating/Slope rating:

Black - 71.9/130	Red (Men) - 65.5/116
Blue - 69.8/125	(Women) - 70.5/130
White (Men) - 67.8/122	Gold (Men) - 65.5/116
(Women) - 73.8/134	(Women) - 68.2/119

One quick glance at the yardage booklet leaves no doubt for anyone familiar with Jack Nicklaus golf courses that the architect of Augustine Golf Club, Rick Jacobson, has some Nicklaus training in his background. All the earmarks are there: a testing hole with a split fairway, a tricky little short par four, a bounty of man-made difficulties, and bunkers galore. In fact, Jacobson was once a part of the Jack Nicklaus design group.

Playing the course, however, reveals subtle and satisfying differences in the design approaches of the master and the student. Unlike Nicklaus, whose courses often seem to ignore the natural landscape in favor of moving as much earth as possible in a quest to redesign it, architect Jacobson drew upon what nature had laid before him for the foundation and backdrop of Augustine Golf Club. He has embraced the terrain, gently caressing and nurturing it into a magnificent and challenging·golf course.

Augustine sits amid gently rolling hills, ancient trees, natural streams, marshes, and ponds. The trees, water, and hills guarantee that errant shots will be punished, approaches that are off target will be rejected, and failure to get your ball close to the pin on the difficult, undulating greens will result in more three- and four-putt scores than one- and two-putts.

In 1727, when Virginia was an English colony and golf was still an informal game played mostly by Celtic shepherds killing time by batting rounded stones into holes in the ground on the heaths and coastal dunes of Scotland, Augustine Washington, father of future general and president George Washington, built the first furnace to smelt iron in that part of the New World. It is doubtful that he knew anything of "golf," and he certainly could not have envisioned what his rolling tract of Virginia countryside would become.

The opening three holes are stunning, both for their natural splendor and for the shot-making difficulties and the course-management problems they pose. They are among the best opening holes anywhere and provide a lovely prelude to your round at Augustine.

The par-four 1st, with an elevated series of tees and featuring a Nicklaus-style split fairway, starts your round with a choice: a fairway wood or long iron played to the limited landing area to the right or a driver to the left designed to leave a short iron approach to the green. Between the two is a ball-gobbling marsh that rarely yields a ball hit into it. The right front of the tricky green is guarded by a deep kidney-shaped bunker that is best avoided.

The long par-four 2nd—one of Augustine's signature holes and rated the toughest hole on the golf course—tees off across a small inlet, which leads to a lake that runs the entire left length of the hole. The first question to ask yourself is how much, if any, of the water you should challenge with your drive. The same question applies regardless of ability or which set of tees is being played. Trees, hills, deep rough, and a tight out-of-bounds guard the right, which leaves a landing area about as wide as a two-lane road. The hole is a dogleg left, and the tricky green is protected to the left by water and to the right by a steep, unfriendly hill. A short drive can require a lay-up; a drive that's too bold can find the hazard; and a tee shot that's too far right can make the second shot impossible.

Once you've successfully negotiated the opening two holes, you climb a steep hill to the elevated tees of the 3rd. The drive plays across a valley to a landing area atop another substantial hill. (Women have the toughest of the tee shots in that while they get a generous break in distance, compared with the back tees, the ladies drive straight uphill.) Again, an imprecise tee shot will render it impossible to find the long, narrow green on your second. The left side of the flat landing area on the top of the hill is the ideal position from which to approach the green.

The par-five 4th is a solid three-shot hole for all but players who mash the ball like Tiger Woods. It's a double dogleg with more-than-ample trouble in every direction: marsh and water within driving distance, trees, wetlands, tall grass, and bunkers abound. The elevated green is guarded by a pair of yawning bunkers and grassy hillocks. The best advice for everyone is to keep the ball in the short grass.

Once you've completed the 4th, you can breathe a little easier. The par-four 5th features a blind tee shot. The solid par-three 6th will test your long-iron ability. The rest of the outbound nine is less strenuous.

Past the clubhouse, the 10th tee reveals a treacherously narrow fairway that plays down a hill to a little buttonhook green that's protected by marsh and bunkers. In the spring it is one of the most aesthetically pleasing holes on the golf course, with the back of the green framed by blooming azaleas and white dogwoods peeking from among the towering old hardwood trees. The wide, shallow green requires a high, soft approach.

The serpentine par-five 11th is reachable in two for the long hitters, but the fairway is intersected diagonally by a sweep of marshy wetland that is indisposed to giving back golf balls that find their way into the morass. To the right of the steeply pitched and hilly green is a Saharan bunker that will engulf a left-to-right approach shot.

The crescent-shaped 12th hole is rated the second most difficult on Augustine. It's a long par four that plays from a series of marsh-side tees to a two-tiered green up a substantial hill, nestled among trees and strategically placed shrubbery. The tee shot is blind. Three fairway bunkers are designed to catch stray left-to-right shots. Anything left is in jail. Even from the right-center of the fairway, the approach is a challenge. Failure to get your ball onto the same tier as the flag can yield an extraordinary uphill slam or a terrifying downhill roll to get it close.

A demanding par four and long par three lead to tiny *S*-shaped par-four 15th. This is a typical Nicklaus hole, playing only 305 yards from the back tees and a mere 234 yards from the front. But even though it is rated the easiest hole on the golf course, there is more trouble than you can imagine for a mis-directed shot. The bunker on the left will catch a short drive; thoughts of going for the green in one shot must be tempered by the fact that the shallow, elevated green is protected by bunkers directly along the line of flight that a brave drive would take. A mid-iron and a surgically precise wedge are the best tickets to birdies here.

The 16th, 17th, and 18th holes—a long par four, a testing par three, and a tight and demanding par five—provide a highly satisfying conclusion to the round at Augustine.

Be advised that Augustine Golf Club is *not* a course for beginners. It's simply too difficult. For middle- to low-handicap golfers it is a treat, a fair and enjoyable test of the game. It was the brainchild of Japanese developer Tadahiko Nukui, whose goal was to create a country-club setting and top-notch course for the public and daily-fee player. His goal has been surpassed.

Brambleton's par-three #12 requires a tee shot across the lake in front of the green.

Brambleton

HOLE NUMBER	Ra	Sl	1	2	3	4	5	6	7	8	9	OUT	10	11	12	13	14	15	16	17	18	IN	TOT
BLUE	71.4	121	394	397	187	406	362	399	586	173	534	3438	392	360	168	528	378	425	362	192	521	3326	6764
WHITE	69.8	118	378	352	170	394	346	390	538	146	520	3234	376	349	145	511	362	413	347	178	511	3192	6426
PAR			4	4	3	4	4	4	5	3	5	36	4	4	3	5	4	4	4	3	5	36	72
HANDICAP			11	5	15	7	13	3	1	17	9		8	6	18	4	14	2	10	16	12		
RED	72.0	121	361	299	154	348	330	343	465	136	423	2859	358	336	123	432	347	338	332	145	414	2825	5684

BRAMBLETON GOLF COURSE

Ashburn, Virginia (From Route 7, Leesburg Pike west, take the left turn at Route 659 to
Brambleton Park sign.)
Phone: (703) 327-3403

Architect: Hank Gordon   Year opened: 1994

Course rating/Slope rating:
Blue - 71.4/121
White - 69.8/118
Red - 72.0/121

Many times throughout the text of this book, you will see an admonition that certain golf courses are not for beginners or that high-handicap golfers would probably be better off and have a more enjoyable and rewarding golf experience if they played somewhere else. Brambleton Golf Course, the newest entry among courses owned by the Northern Virginia Regional Park System, is a superb place to learn the game and for the high handicapper to hone his or her skills. It is inexpensive. It is well maintained. It is well managed. And while much attention must be given to championship golf courses in a book such as this, some attention must also be paid to golf courses that go out of their way to accommodate beginners and high-handicap players. That in no way suggests that this is anything but a well-conceived layout. Unlike some of the brutally hard courses profiled here that throw two, three, or more major challenges at a player on each hole—water, mounds, sand, and the like—Brambleton tends to offer one significant challenge per hole.

The golf course is generally flat, open, and forgiving, but that is not to say that it does not have ample trouble and challenge, especially for players who are just coming to grips with the degrees of difficulty one can face on a golf course. Golf is a difficult game, and very little can frustrate, demean, and dampen the spirits of a new player more than to be confronted with a golf course that's too hard while being told to play it quickly. This course requires you to move along, but the course itself is a superior test for those in the early stages of learning the game.

It should be added that at 6,764 yards from the back tees, there's enough challenge not to bore a better golfer who wants to improve a part of his or her game or who simply wants an inexpensive and ego-bolstering round of golf. In fact, the four par fives are a very solid test for any player and will improve your accuracy on long shots. All four are more than 500 yards for men and more than 400 yards for women.

The long 7th is the toughest hole on the golf course—not just because of its length, but because it is among the tightest holes on the track. This hole will discourage players from trying shots that exceed their capabilities, because the amount of trouble lurking on both sides is ample. The 9th is more open than the 7th, but it plays to one of the only tiered greens on the course. The 13th is again tight and

25

testing, and the finisher features a water hazard to the right and trees that edge the fairway up to the end of the landing area for your drive.

The par fours offer a fine mix, from the short #2, a dogleg right that requires your tee shot to carry a small creek and plays to one of the better bunkered greens on the course, to the long, tough #15. Water comes into play on #5; fairway bunkers lie in wait for errant shots on #10 and #16; a tiered green tests your putting stroke on #14.

The par threes also offer variety, from the long #3 and even longer #17 to the very attractive little #12. The 12th hole is rated the easiest hole on the course, but it's fun, playing from tiered tee boxes across a pleasant little pond that arcs around the front portion of the green.

Brambleton presents a variety of golfing challenges, but not in the quantity or at a level of severity to make the game unpleasant for players whose skill level is not up to massive numbers of hazards, bunkers, contours, and the like all at one time.

A serious argument could be made that there needs to be more golf courses like this one, on which people can learn the game, experience some of its challenges, and do so in a setting that is pleasant and enjoyable.

BRISTOW MANOR GOLF CLUB

11507 Valley View Drive, Bristow, Virginia (Take I-66 west to exit 44, Route 234 south; go about 4 miles to the exit for Route 28 south; go about 2 miles and turn left at the light onto Bristow Road, Route 619 for about 1½ miles and turn right onto Valley View Drive, Route 611.)
Phone: (703) 368-3558

Architect: Ken Killian   Year opened: 1993

Course rating/Slope rating:
Blue - 73.5/128
White - 71.9/125
Red - 71.7/126

Getting to Bristow Manor Golf Club can test your navigational abilities right from the start. It's easier now that Route 234 is complete, but it's still out in the boonies. It sits southwest of the historic old Virginia town of Manassas, and there's a labyrinth of back roads you must travel to get there. Once you're there, however, you will enjoy a superior golfing experience. Bristow Manor plays to a par 72 for men and a difficult par 73 for women.

A glance across the golf course offers a misleading first impression. As you approach the lovely antebellum clubhouse, the course looks flat and open. The scorecard supports the first visual impression by telling you that it is it not a massively long layout. But all these initial indices fail to reflect that, in reality, this is a tough and exacting golf course that relies on blind shots, tight landing areas, tricky greens, hills, mounds, moguls, abundant water, strategically designed bunkers, and environmentally sensitive wetlands to encourage precise shot making and course management. That is not to suggest that this is some kind of tricked-up monster. Quite to the contrary. Bristow Manor is a fine golf course that has been massaged and sculpted out of a fairly flat, open piece of real estate.

Architect Ken Killian favors big greens with lots of sinews and tiers. They are generally not cut to be lightning fast, but they are difficult to read and present subtle contours as well as the more obvious breaks and bends.

The opening two holes, which play relatively straight and unobstructed from tee to green and offer generous landing areas, create the illusion that you're headed for an easy time of it, but don't let down your guard. You get a good taste of the course's treachery on the little par-three 3rd hole. It's all carry across a small pond to a slippery green that's irregularly shaped. Club selection is paramount. Missing the green makes a bogey or worse a distinct possibility.

The 4th hole is a narrow, nasty, devilish par five—rated the toughest hole on the course for women. The thin fairway is intersected by a stream that is reachable from all tee boxes. The stream is bordered by deep rough on both sides. A massive drive—more than 300 yards from the back tees—will carry it, but most players

27

The Bristow Manor Golf Club overlooks the 9th green.

opt for a fairway wood or long iron to lay up to the rough in front of the water. That sets up a second shot that must avoid the lake on the right near the green and the marshy wetland and trees to the left. The landing area narrows precipitously the closer you play to the green. A mammoth bunker waits beyond the lake in front of the green, and another little sand trap sits to the left.

The par-five 6th hole offers some of the same problems near the green as #4, only the lake is on the left.

The par-four #7 is a brutal dogleg right that will call up your reserves of both skill and nerve. The first decision is how much, if any, of the lake on the right will

you try to carry with your tee shot, but the biggest hitters must beware that a tee shot that's too long can slide through the fairway and into the deep grasses and water in front of the green. Three well-placed bunkers frame the elevated green. The 7th is rated the toughest hole on the course for men; for women, it's a par five that offers superior opportunities for birdies with strategic shot placement.

The 9th is a lovely way to finish the front side. It's a short but tricky little par four, a sharp dogleg left for men and a fairly straight hole for women. Your tee shot plays to a tiny landing area amid trees and hills. The elevated green then is uphill. It is well bunkered on the right

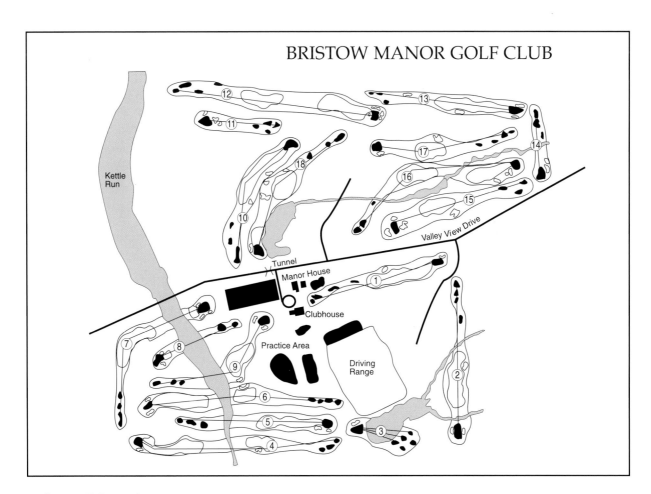

Bristow Manor

HOLE NUMBER	Ra	Sl	1	2	3	4	5	6	7	8	9	OUT	10	11	12	13	14	15	16	17	18	IN	TOT
CHAMP	73.5	128	347	408	162	541	385	517	455	217	394	3426	385	201	538	377	172	379	511	362	419	3344	6770
REG	71.9	125	318	342	142	528	344	504	438	196	375	3187	344	170	518	356	150	370	495	334	389	3126	6313
PAR (m)			4	4	3	5	4	5	4	3	4	36	4	3	5	4	3	4	5	4	4	36	72
HANDICAP (m)			17	5	15	3	11	7	1	9	13		12	14	4	10	18	6	8	16	2		
FOR	71.1	126	231	285	114	492	242	412	400	118	225	2520	295	139	443	289	116	323	427	288	314	2634	5154
PAR (w)			4	4	3	5	4	5	5	3	4	37	4	3	5	4	3	4	5	4	4	36	73
HANDICAP (w)			13	7	15	1	11	3	5	9	17		12	14	4	10	18	8	6	16	2		

and left fronts, and the fairway is pinched in front of the green by a lake on the left and steep hills on the right.

As with the front nine, the back nine opens gently and increases in difficulty as you go. For both men and women the par-five #12 is the second-toughest hole on the side, a long tight ribbon of a hole with a split fairway. The margin for error is minimal on your drive, with trees eagerly waiting to ensnare shots that stray from the short grass. But as difficult as the long shots are—and virtually every player other than maybe Davis Love III or Laura Davies will be required to hit two long shots—the approach to the green leaves almost no room to maneuver. The wide but anorexically thin green is surrounded by grassy mounds, moguls, and unforgiving sand. The green itself is no more than fifteen paces deep in places.

The par-five #16 features a double

29

dogleg. It is the most accessible of the par fives on Bristow Manor for long hitters to reach in two. The tee shot presents the possibility of cutting some of the dogleg right with a left-to-right shot ideally suited to the hole, but note that shots straying to the left will be severely punished. A stream bounded by deep rough and marsh grass intersects the hole about 160 yards from the green. The wide, slightly elevated green is well protected, and the key to scoring is to get your approach shot onto the same side of the green as the flag.

The short par-four #18, a crescent-shaped dogleg left, is a daunting finisher, replete with trouble from tee to green. To the left, reachable from all tees, is a lake that is in play from about midway on the hole right up to the green. In fact, the lake guards the front and left side of the green on your approach. The right side of the fairway is protected by a series of unpleasant hills and three skillfully con-structed bunkers. (Over the last of the bunkers lurks a rocky, marshy hazard that is invisible from the tees.) The ideal landing spot is directly between the biggest of the fairway bunkers and the lake, so something less than a driver should be considered. If your tee shot crests the hill beyond the ideal landing area, it's only about fifteen steps from the lake to the rocky grassland. The irregularly shaped green is sandwiched between the lake on the left and a large bunker to the

right. The 18th is justifiably rated the toughest hole on the back and the second toughest on the entire course. Birdies here are rare, and bogeys, doubles, and worse leave many players shaking their heads as they depart for the clubhouse.

Bristow Manor offers a grand mix of holes and will demand use of almost every club in the bag for virtually every player. Those who complete the eighteen holes within the bounds of their handicaps have registered a rewarding measure of success. Most players will find that they play it better after their initial round, once they've discovered some of the course's secrets and deceptions. In general, the par fours are all very solid, while the par threes offer a variety of lengths and green constructions. But it is the par fives that are the hallmark of Ken Killian's architectural strength.

To his credit, substantial thought and planning went into the design and place-ment of the women's tee boxes. While women get a huge break in terms of length—the red tees play more than 1,500 yards shorter than the championship markers—each women's tee presents a unique and challenging look at the hole ahead. Virtually no hole leaves the impression that women golfers were an afterthought.

CACAPON STATE PARK GOLF COURSE

Berkeley Springs, West Virginia (about 20 miles north of Winchester, Virginia and about 10 miles south of the town of Berkeley Springs, just off Route 522).
Phone: (304) 258-1022

Architect: Robert Trent Jones Sr.   Year opened: 1974

Course rating/Slope rating:
Blue - 72.3/126   White - 70.4/123
Red - 70.8/118

West Virginia has thirty-eight state parks, four of which have their own golf courses. They offer some of the best, most inexpensive golf bargains in the country. In the case of Cacapon State Park—pronounced "kuh-KAY-pun," an American Indian word meaning "sweet waters"—the golf is simply world class. Cacapon is a glorious mountain golf course designed by one of the finest architects ever to practice that profession. The backdrop could be a movie set of mountains, forest, and lakes.

This golf course makes no pretenses about what it is and is not. You make the trek for the golf. Period. It's no frills all the way. If you want opulent locker rooms, a restaurant with Michelin stars, attendants to fetch your clubs or clean them after your round, a drinks wagon navigating the course to offer you refreshments—forget it. But if you want to play an exemplary Robert Trent Jones Sr. golf course for bargain-basement prices, this is it.

Unlike private clubs or upscale daily-fee courses whose owners have deep pockets, financial concerns are very real, and West Virginia is not a particularly wealthy state. The course is supported both from its own revenue and with taxpayer dollars.

But the managers of Cacapon Golf Course have ordered their priorities well, with course maintenance and care at the top of the list. Such luxuries as flowers around the tee boxes and stuccoed restrooms are nonexistent, but for a busy public golf course, the flaws you might expect are few. The fairways and rough are cut with care, and the greens are expertly manicured. After a busy day, some of the bunkers can occasionally use a little attention, but that is unfortunately true at many private country clubs as well. In fact, for the amount of play this course gets, it is almost always in spectacular condition and maintained in championship form.

Make no mistake: this is a mountain golf course. Every hole, every shot is up and down with a profusion of lies and stances that are anything but flat. Add to that the fact that the course features seventy-two sand traps, all of them in Robert Trent Jones Sr. signature fashion, placed artfully and sometimes treacherously. The greens are generally small, in a few cases minuscule, but they are receptive to high, soft approaches. The fairways are generally tight and feature all types of trouble: bunkers, water, trees, rocks, mounds, and deep roughs.

31

The serpentine double green shared by #4 and #8 at Cacapon State Park Golf Course stretches more than 100 yards from edge to edge.

Cacapon

HOLE NUMBER	Ra	Sl	1	2	3	4	5	6	7	8	9	OUT	10	11	12	13	14	15	16	17	18	IN	TOT
BLUE	72.3	126	390	410	520	190	410	380	420	200	560	3480	370	520	380	430	400	190	420	200	550	3460	6940
WHITE	70.4	123	370	385	490	150	375	350	395	180	530	3225	330	480	360	400	370	160	390	175	520	3185	6410
PAR			4	4	5	3	4	4	4	3	5	36	4	5	4	4	4	3	4	3	5	72	
HANDICAP			15	11	5	17	7	13	1	9	3		16	10	6	8	14	12	2	18	4		
RED	70.8	118	310	340	420	120	330	320	350	130	460	2780	290	410	320	350	330	125	340	115	450	2730	5510

It's long, especially for women. In the old-fashioned manner of golf courses designed in the '60s and early '70s, women were not treated with particular charity, and Robert Trent Jones Sr. never enjoyed much of a reputation for catering to women. He favors runway tee boxes, on which all markers are placed on one long strip of tightly mowed grass. Typically, if there is a separate women's tee box, it is not very far from the men's.

In a couple of cases, such as on the par-four #10, the hole actually plays harder, if shorter, for women than for men. The placement of the women's tees mitigates the 40 yards surrendered in length by creating a more severe uphill drive and by exacerbating an already acute dogleg right. The 10th hole is a brilliant short par four, straight uphill for everybody. It's a sharp dogleg right on which even your second shot will only give you a glimpse of the flag and not of the putting surface itself. The green is guarded by bunkers and mounds ready to foil any timid approach that is not high enough or soft enough to find the green itself.

Jones mixes his par fours like a bartender executing the perfect margarita: with just the right proportions of natural and man-made obstacles, stirred gently with the proper measure of length, contour, and unseen trouble. The 5th is a moderate-length dogleg right. Your blind, downhill tee shot plays to a fairway that is canted steeply from right to left. The approach is then back uphill to a tough green. The short #6 and the even shorter, previously mentioned 10th demand far less muscle than exquisite accuracy. Tee-shot placement will determine how close to the pin you can get.

And the long dogleg-left 7th hole, rated the number-one handicap hole, is a brute.

The blind tee shot must be long enough to give you a reasonable look at the uphill green, even though a substantial number of approaches will only be able to see the flag, not the green itself. The fairway bunker to the left must be avoided. But that's only part of the array of difficulties. The green is intersected by a ridge, and it is critical to get your approach on the same level as the flag if you are to have any chance of scoring.

Jones's reputation for artful par threes is enhanced with the four one-shot holes on Cacapon, especially the two on the front side—the 4th and 8th holes—that share a single, serpentine strip of green that stretches more than 100 yards from one side to the other. The 4th hole is tightly treed and plays down to the monster green. Jones also reputedly believed that the only place a golf ball should land safely on a par three is on the putting surface. As a result, when you play a Robert Trent Jones Sr. golf course, you should know that there is little room for error on par threes and often no bailout area at all. Such is the case with Cacapon's #4. Jones is slightly more generous with #8, but it is substantially longer than #4.

On the back side, #12 is a wonderful one-shot hole playing from a set of elevated tees that gives you a glorious panoramic view of the mountains and the well-bunkered, difficult green far below.

One of the best scoring opportunities on the golf course is on the short par-five #11, a risk-reward hole that offers a good opportunity for low numbers. The downhill tee shot must navigate a pair of fairway bunkers and come to rest in the short grass. A shot that drifts left will be jailed among the trees; to the right are inhospitable hills and deep grass. The entrance to the green is constricted by a pair of bunkers that for the most part precludes the possibility of safely running an approach shot onto the putting surface. The other three par fives are long and tough, especially for women. They are all in excess of 400 yards from the red markers and demand accurate tee shots and long lay-ups to score well. The par-five finisher is quintessential Robert Trent Jones Sr. What you see is what you get. No tricks. No gimmicks. It's 560 yards from the tips, 460 yards from the red markers. And the way to score on it is to hit two long, straight shots, an accurate chip, and put it in the hole. Anything else? Well, you guessed it. Missed shots and mental errors will result in big numbers and frustration.

Very few golfers come away from Cacapon State Park with anything but a positive reaction to the golf course. In fact, from golfers whose entire careers have been spent on the public links to coddled country-club players, people return time and again to play this Robert Trent Jones Sr. gem, lured by the scenic beauty and the sheer excellence of the golf course.

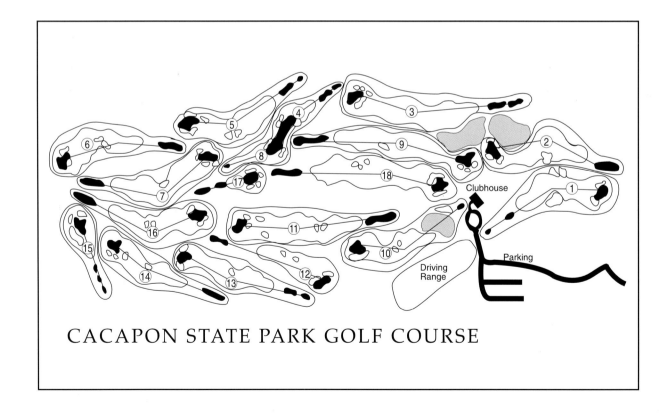

CACAPON STATE PARK GOLF COURSE

CANAAN VALLEY GOLF COURSE

Davis, West Virginia (About 7 miles south of Davis and about 9 miles north of Harman in the Canaan Valley Resort Park.)

Phone: (304) 866-4121

Architect: Geoffrey Cornish   Year opened: 1968

Course rating/Slope rating:
Blue - 73.4/125   White - 70.4/119
Red - 71.8/115

The Canaan Valley Golf Course is a player's course. It rewards good shots and—save for a few trees, bunkers, and ponds—it renders only moderate punishment to shots that stray. It is far from the most difficult golf course in the Virginias, but it is far from easy either. "Fun" and "pleasant" are among the most common descriptions of it. It provides a rewarding and enjoyable golfing experience for players of all handicap levels, although beginners will find it a bit arduous. In addition, it's among the friendliest places anywhere.

Canaan is one of the courses owned by the state park authority of West Virginia, but it is managed by private concerns. The private management company at Canaan Valley has changed over the years, but the golf course has been consistently well maintained for more than a decade.

It's a personal favorite in that my mother and father spent their summers in the Canaan Valley for many years, and whenever my wife and I would visit them, we would play the course. It's like an old friend with a complicated personality of different moods and facets, but always a pleasure to be around.

The golf course tends to be fairly open and forgiving off the tees—although there are some serious exceptions—and the greens are usually pretty receptive to high, soft approaches. It is long, nearly 7,000 yards from the championship tees and playing to a par 72. The holes are far from cookie-cutter designs. The par threes are long and use the course's wonderful elevation changes and water to enhance their difficulty; the par fours offer a nice variety; and the par fives range from the short, easy #3 to the brutal and treacherous #9.

The views are sublime, with panoramas and vistas pleasing to the eye and soothing to the soul. There are mountains on all sides, some revealing the trails and runs enjoyed by skiers in the winter. As the clouds come in and depart, the colors change and intensify; a brooding storm in the distance is the stuff of visual drama. Birds and game are abundant. Deer often venture onto the course to drink from one of the lakes or to graze on the tender grasses of the fairway or rough.

The golf course plays up, down, and around a hill that is at the center of its design. The climb begins with the long, dogleg-left par-four #2 to an elevated green that is invariably farther away than it looks. My father always counseled that it is at least one club longer than it looks on the approach. The short par-five #3, reachable in two shots for even moderately

A twosome of deer look for a lost ball in the pond adjacent to Canaan Valley's par-three 16th green.

long-hitting players, provides the best scoring opportunity on the course. It's a downhill drive and an approach to a wide, shallow green tucked behind a bunker carved out of a ridge.

The picturesque #4 is a long par three that requires a carry-over at least a portion of a pond. There's bailout room in the front and to the right, and the green has a tendency to reject shots that come in too low or too hot into the right-rear bunker. The par-four #5 plays back up the hill to a well-protected, contoured green. The par-three #6 features a steep change in elevation from the tees to the green far below, and club selection is critical.

Two fine par fours follow. The dogleg-left #7 is downhill from the tees and even more steeply downhill to the green. The fairway bunkers on the left must be avoided, although the temptation for long hitters is to try to cut them. A shot that skirts the right of the bunkers will set up a short chip to the green. The long, straight #8 is the best hole on the course, according to Bud Harold, who retired in 1998 after fifteen years as head pro at Canaan Valley: "It's a fair hole. You've got a bunker on the left and trees on the right, and you've got to hit a couple of pretty good shots."

The par-five #9, a severe dogleg left, is lined with tall, imposing trees to the bend of the dogleg that severely diminish the odds of cutting the corner and offer the prospect of wasting a shot if the gamble does not pay off. A lake sits directly in front of the wide, shallow green. It has earned its place as the toughest hole on the golf course. "It's a terrible hole for the average player," Harold said. "Most of them can't hit it far enough to get around the dogleg, so they have to play a safe shot for their second, which means they're shooting three to the water and four to the green." It's far from easy for even the best players. With a smile almost appearing on his weathered face, Bud Harold recalled the West Virginia Open being played there. "We had a few hot shots going for it in two," he said, pointing to the area beyond the trees that guard the dogleg. "A few of them made it. But an awful lot more of them were taking sixes and sevens."

A pair of long par fours open the back nine, with #11 playing straight up that hill again to an elevated green. The long par-three #12 tees off from a hilltop to a green below. The par-five #14 requires a drive that clears a pond on the left and some marshy rough to the right. The approach to the two-tiered elevated green is straight up hill. "The pros would chew it up," Harold said. But for the average player, it's a long, difficult hole. It is critical to a good score that your approach shot land on the same tier as the flag.

The three finishing holes are a superior test of the game. The long par-three #16 features the narrowest green on the course and a lake coming almost up to the putting surface in front. It's a forced carry for everybody. And to make it even more difficult, behind the green there's a big bunker whose presence ensures that if you're long, your recovery shot is from the sand to a tiny thread of green with water on the other side. The par-five #17 features one of the best-protected greens on the course. And #18, a long, straight par four, features an expanse of water from about 100 yards out, almost up to the putting surface. The 18th is considered the toughest hole on the back nine.

The Canaan Valley Golf Course is a thoroughly pleasant, highly satisfying golfing experience at extremely reasonable prices. "It's a very beautiful golf course," said my mother, Freda Armstrong. "And the people couldn't be nicer," added Murray Armstrong, my dad. Far be it for me to disagree with such keen and expert analysis.

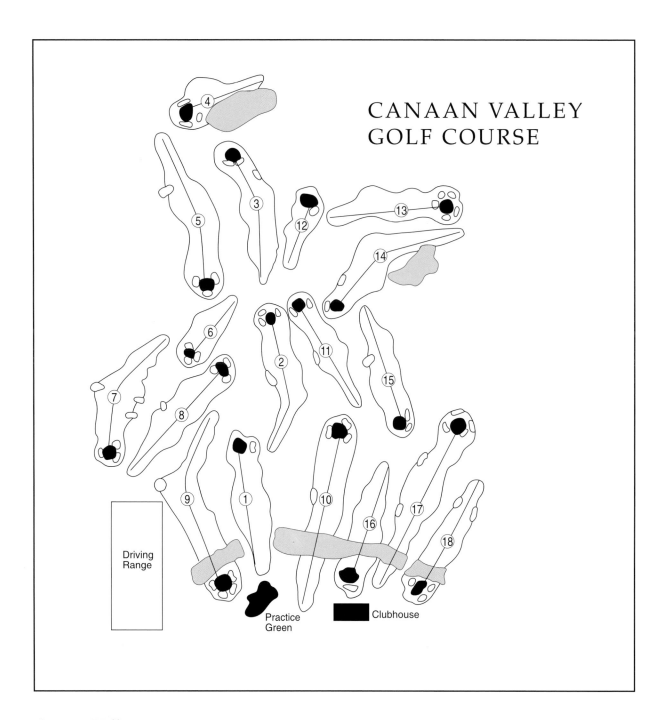

CANAAN VALLEY GOLF COURSE

Driving Range

Practice Green

Clubhouse

Canaan Valley

HOLE NUMBER	Ra	Sl	1	2	3	4	5	6	7	8	9	OUT	10	11	12	13	14	15	16	17	18	IN	TOT
BLUE	73.4	125	390	412	473	214	368	194	383	398	573	3405	402	418	256	350	519	420	233	537	444	3577	6982
WHITE	70.4	119	367	382	454	181	339	179	353	365	556	3176	367	388	196	330	488	383	201	495	412	3260	6436
PAR			4	4	5	3	4	3	4	4	5	36	4	4	3	4	5	4	3	5	4	36	72
HANDICAP			11	4	17	16	9	18	14	6	1		10	3	13	15	7	8	12	5	2		
RED	71.8	115	321	362	398	125	314	144	328	340	528	2860	328	363	145	298	464	361	138	476	387	2960	5820

38

CAVERNS COUNTRY CLUB

Luray, Virginia (Take I-81 exit 264 to New Market and go 14 miles to Route 211 east; the golf course is behind the Luray Caverns.)
Phone: (540) 743-6551

Architect: Mal Purdy   Year opened: 1976

Course rating/Slope rating:
Blue - 71.2/117   White - 69.8/115
Red - 72.4/120

Caverns Country Club is a delightful example of Virginia mountain golf. It is situated on the banks of the Shenandoah River, in the shadow of the Blue Ridge Mountains, on a hilly, wooded tract of land directly behind Luray Caverns. Despite the proximity of the course to one of the state's most visited tourist attractions, only a handful of the thousands of tourists who visit the Luray Caverns each year even know there's a golf course a couple of three woods and a short chip away. It's only marked by a small sign. Golfers who follow the sign's directions discover a pleasant, mature golf course that takes each player from lofty, panoramic heights into refreshing shaded valleys and glens. Flat lies are rare. The greens vary from merely big to huge and require a good eye and a reliable stroke to keep three-putts off your card, although they are generally not cut particularly fast.

Design and construction of this golf course were not rushed. It took architect Mal Purdy and the construction team three years to build Caverns Country Club. What emerged is a well-maintained golf course that will please all levels of players. And while it may be an ego booster for single-digit handicappers, it's no pushover and requires a wide arsenal of shots to score.

The first hole is a lovely, straight par five from which you can glimpse the shimmering waters of the Shenandoah through the trees along its left length. It's tight from tee to green but plays downhill and affords even medium-long hitters the opportunity to go for it in two and secure a birdie or better to begin the round. The view from the first tee is breathtaking, with the Blue Ridge Mountains standing like age-old sentries in the distance.

The medium par-four #2 tees off up a hill with fairway bunkers on both sides, but it's the second shot here that's critical.

Caverns Country Club

HOLE NUMBER	Ra	Sl	1	2	3	4	5	6	7	8	9	OUT	10	11	12	13	14	15	16	17	18	IN	TOT
BLUE	71.2	117	509	385	350	155	527	376	152	380	372	3206	382	373	169	523	353	150	551	385	407	3293	6499
WHITE	69.8	115	86	370	334	150	517	366	148	370	362	3106	372	368	161	509	343	140	541	370	397	3201	6307
HANDICAP (m)			4	8	2	16	10	14	18	12	6		1	5	11	17	13	15	7	9	3		
PAR			5	4	4	3	5	4	3	4	4	36	4	4	3	5	4	3	5	4	4	36	72
RED	72.4	120	419	313	289	140	465	323	140	337	324	2750	325	334	151	448	302	118	420	302	349	2749	5499
HANDICAP (w)			8	12	10	16	2	14	18	4	6		1	5	9	11	7	15	13	17	3		

The view down the long par-five 1st hole at Caverns Country Club, with the Blue Ridge Mountains in the distance.

The long, narrow, two-tiered green is tucked back among pines and perched on a shelf carved out of a hill. It is nearly surrounded by a steep incline. An approach that fails to land squarely on the putting surface is likely to be propelled down the hill.

One of the most intriguing holes on the course is the short par-four #3, which is rated the second-most-difficult hole for men. From the tee the impression is of a benign dogleg right, but that's just the start of it. The blind tee shot plays over a hill to a landing area that's sloped severely to the right, and down near the irregularly shaped green the slope is inverted to the left, along with the green itself. Placement of your tee shot is critical. For women, it is only the number-ten handicap hole, partly because it's less than 290 yards from tee to green and the position of the forward markers straightens the dogleg considerably. It is the contoured topography of the hole that makes it a tough par.

The par-three #4 is a pretty little one-shot hole featuring a pond between tee and green. The water only comes into play if you boot your tee shot.

The 5th hole is rated the second toughest on the course for women. For a big-hitting man it's reachable in two if your drive gets some help where the fairway slopes downhill. You want to keep your drive slightly left of the marker flag. Past the marker, the fairway slopes down a steep grade that leads to a narrow ribbon of fairway, a trough with hills on both sides. Once on the slightly elevated green, this is a good birdie hole for men but a tough one for the ladies.

The front nine finishes with a pair of medium-length par fours that leads to the very solid, tough par-four #10, rated the

toughest hole on the course for both men and women. Elevated tees play downhill into a flat landing area. The approach to the elevated green is then back uphill. The green itself is tightly guarded by a cluster of pines. The closer your tee shot gets to the green, the more trouble there is, especially to the right side of the fairway.

The next four holes present a lovely and challenging trek among the hills, ponds, and trees that characterize Caverns Country Club. Not only does each hole require skilled shot making and steady putting, each is surrounded by a feast for the eye with panoramic views of the lovely Shenandoah Valley and Blue Ridge Mountains. The par-three #15 is deceptive. A bunker with vertical planking that could well have been the design of Tom Fazio or Pete Dye in a bad mood borders the front of the putting surface. While your eye may tell you that it's shorter than the card indicates, take plenty of club because it's far easier to chip back to the pin from behind the green or play from the rear bunkers than to try to extricate yourself from that monster in front.

The long par-four #18 is a wonderful finisher. The landing area on your tee shot is tight and requires precision to set up an unobstructed approach shot that avoids the trees. Another planked bunker, less severe than the one in front of the fifteenth hole, awaits a short or left approach to the final green. As with many of the holes on this course, it is the way the design skillfully blends with the mounds, rocks, trees, and natural contours of the land that sets it apart.

For women, it is a long but fair test (nearly 5,500 yards) that requires distance and accuracy from even single-digit handicappers. Several local women noted that it is possible for good or above-average women golfers to approach only a handful of the par-fours with irons. Most of the par-fours require two woods in order to chase birdies or pars. The 18th is "impossible!" grunted one female club member in the parking lot. Another added, "You need your career drive, your career second, dry ground, and a wind at your back." It's a hilly 349 yards from the red markers to the putting surface.

For some reason Caverns Country Club remains a largely undiscovered jewel in the Shenandoah Valley. While many golfers in the Virginias have heard of it, few seem to have played it, and for that reason starting times tend to be fairly easy to obtain, and play moves at a brisk pace. The golf course itself is a pleasure to play, and it is the kind of course that leaves you with a sense of satisfaction and a desire to return for another round.

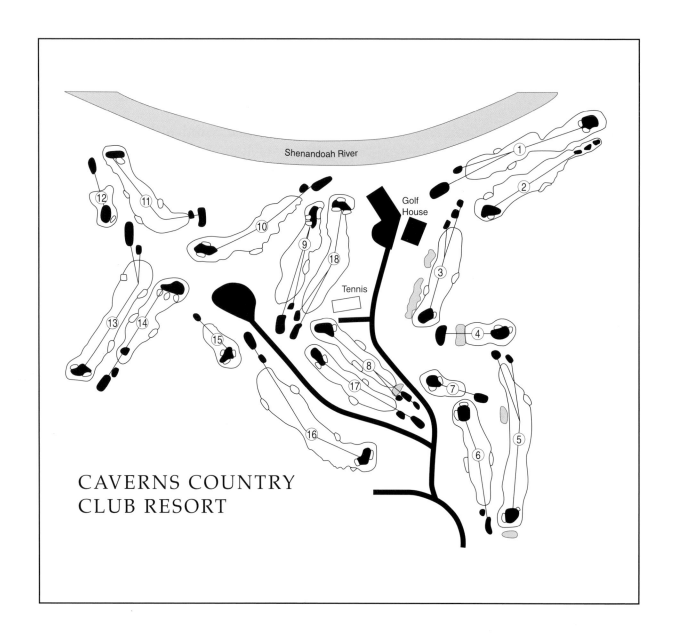

CAVERNS COUNTRY
CLUB RESORT

THE COLONIAL GOLF COURSE

Williamsburg, Virginia (From I-64 take exit 227; follow Route 30 & 168 south about 1½ miles to the stoplight at Route 60; follow Route 60 about 1½ miles to Forge Road, Route 610; turn right for about 3 miles to Diascund Road, Route 603; turn right for about 1 mile to golf-course entrance.)

Phone: (757) 566-1600   Fax: (757) 566-1664

Architect: Lester George   Year opened: 1995

Course rating/Slope rating for men:
Colonial - 73.1/132   Paces Paines - 70,5/127
Causey's Care - 68.4/116   Chaplain's Choyse - 65.8/111

Course rating/Slope rating for women:
Paces Paines - 76.3/141   Causey's Care - 74.1/135
Chaplain's Choyse - 70.6/121   Archers Hope - 66.3/109

The Colonial is the kind of golf course that is a pleasure to play over and over again. It lingers in the memory. It generates eager anticipation. It is a comfortable golf course, a friendly golf course, the kind of course you like the first time you play it and one that grows on you with each successive visit. The accolades for The Colonial started coming in shortly after it opened. *Golf Magazine* put it among the top-ten new courses in the United States, and *Golf Digest* ranked it among the top-ten public golf courses in Virginia.

"This is a golfer's course," said Ben Thompson, golf director. "It's designed to give everybody [high and low handicappers, men and women] a good test. Even from the forward tees you don't lose the integrity of the golf course." Too many new courses are so difficult or intimidating that they're not much fun, he suggested.

What architect Lester George did on the banks of the Chickahominy River was to caress and massage the landscape into yielding a golf course that looks as if it

has always been there and the trees simply grew up around it. Some golf courses have an artificial feel about them: the water, the contours, the hills, and the trees occasionally seem out of place or contrived. That is not the case with The Colonial, notwithstanding its youth. Even though a lot of earth was moved and shaped to create its final form, it bespeaks superior design and execution.

While The Colonial is a marvelous golf course for players of every stripe, it is an especially woman-friendly golf course. It features five sets of tees: the back four are rated and sloped for men, and the front four are rated and sloped for women. "We brought in the women's division of the USGA and the Virginia State Golf Association to consult about the women's tees: yardage, placement, the way they look at the golf course," said Francis Fenderson, owner and president of The Colonial. The result is a brilliantly fair and challenging design for female golfers, a design that respects their abilities and demands good shot

The demanding par-three 6th hole at Colonial requires players to carry a marshy wetland to a wide, thin green.

Colonial Golf Course

HOLE	Ra	Sl	1	2	3	4	5	6	7	8	9	OUT	10	11	12	13	14	15	16	17	18	IN	TOT
COL.	73.1	132	380	493	451	413	556	189	381	138	428	3429	523	345	175	412	151	418	402	461	493	3380	6809
PP	70.5 (m)/76.3 (w)	127 (m)/141 (w)	351	468	427	348	503	167	361	119	402	3146	491	313	152	387	130	374	384	438	467	3136	6282
CAU:	68.4 (m)/74.1 (w)	116 (m)/135 (w)	339	435	394	330	48	144	345	111	395	2982	469	268	143	346	106	353	373	390	441	2899	5881
CHA:	65.8 (m)/70.6 (w)	111 (m)/121 (w)	318	399	314	317	398	138	266	103	384	2637	448	255	125	323	93	377	334	355	415	2725	5362
HCP (m)			15	11	1	13	3	5	9	17	7		8	16	12	6	18	4	14	2	10		
PAR			4	5	4	4	5	3	4	3	4	36	5	4	3	4	3	4	4	4	5	72	
ARC:	66.3	109	310	363	280	288	373	93	203	82	292	2284	392	185	104	299	85	270	266	330	353	2284	4568
HCP (f)			11	1	9	7	3	13	15	17	5		2	14	16	10	18	12	8	6	4		

COLONIAL: COL   PACE PAINES: PP   CAUSEY'S CARE: CAU   CHAPLAIN'S CHOYSE: CHA   ARCHERS HOPE: ARC

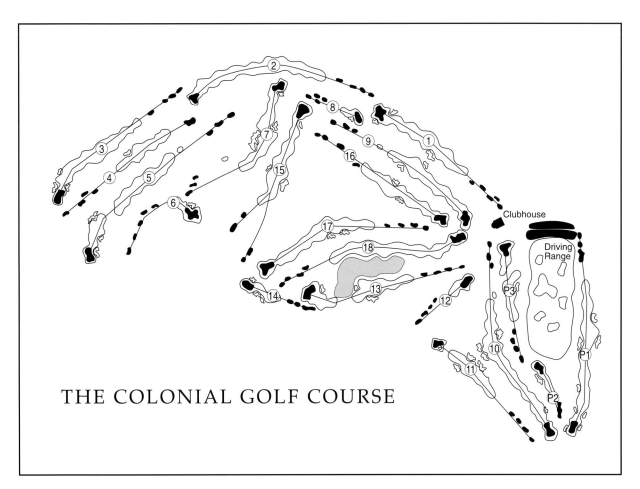

THE COLONIAL GOLF COURSE

making while eschewing any temptation to make it too easy or too short.

One look at the numbers shows that even the LPGA's best would have their hands full with the women's back tees rated 76.3 and sloped at a heart-stopping 141. The traditional red markers have been completely abandoned and replaced with green. "We try to match each player up with a set of tees to match his or her ability and give them a more pleasant experience," Fenderson said.

The tees themselves are named for people and places connected with Colonial Williamsburg. The tips are called Colonial, followed by Paces Paines, Causey's Care, Chaplain's Choyse, and Archers Hope, the shortest tees. Fenderson noted that the spellings are deliberate to reflect the English influence in Colonial times. Archers Hope was a plantation; the

antique spelling aside, Chaplain's Choyse is obvious.

The golf course, which plays to a par 72, offers a wonderful array of holes and demands a broad spectrum of golf shots. Good ball positioning, careful club selection, and a clear concept of how you intend to play each hole will yield good scores. The greens are subtle but fair. Louie Burns, a local member, counseled against reading too much into each putt. "Hit the ball hard enough to go two feet past the hole and you'll take most of the break out of the short ones," he said.

There are no bad holes on the course, and some are simply outstanding. A few of the notable ones include the most difficult hole on the course, the long, demanding par-four #3. The closer you get to the green, the more trouble there is. From about 150 yards out, a marshy ravine awaits any shot that drifts left, and the fairway slopes precariously in that direction. Do not be left of the green!

The solid par-five #5, a dogleg right with a blind tee shot, is the longest hole on the golf course. The second shot is paramount. It must avoid a nasty gorge along the left, which constricts the fairway against a marsh to the right. The elevated green has a tricky little bunker behind it to capture any approach that comes in too hot.

The next hole is a glorious, eye-appealing par three that plays across a swamp to a wide, shallow green. The putting surface is framed with laurels and dogwoods, which are simply breathtaking in the spring. At any time of year, club selection is the key to scoring well.

The 11th is a short par four. "One of the toughest challenges for the architect is to make a short par four a great hole," said Ben Thompson, golf director. "That's a fabulous little hole. It's open enough that with two good shots you're there. But with the hazard area in front [you have] a pretty demanding tee shot, and you can't be long." Think about hitting something other than a driver and even dropping down to a mid-iron in order to place your tee shot carefully. "Anybody can make a hole hard," Thompson added, "but to make a short one challenging is the deal."

The 15th, a moderate-length par-four dogleg left, is a wonderful exercise in design sophistication. The back tees require a long carry over an expanse of marshy wetland. The forward markers are spared the forced carry, but the price for that relief is an exacerbated dogleg and a tee shot that must avoid the towering forest to the left. In effect, depending on what markers you are playing, you have two entirely different looks at the hole that require two entirely different but equally demanding strategies for scoring.

The penultimate hole is one of the tightest and toughest on the golf course. It's a long par-four dogleg left. The fairway is a skinny mesa that's about as wide as a country road in the rural Tidewater, with unpleasant, ball-eating foliage on either side. A fairway bunker about 40 yards in front of the green looks like a greenside sand trap from the fairway and thus creates an optical illusion that the putting surface is closer than it really is.

The short par-five #18 provides a wonderful scoring opportunity at the close of your round. Your tee shot is over water. The question is how much. "It's a superior risk-reward hole," Thompson said. "You can eagle the hole." But he cautioned that if you bite off too much of the lake, it can drown your hopes and turn an eagle into a bogey or a double very easily.

In addition to the regulation eighteen holes, there are three regulation-length holes—a par three, par four, and par five—for practice and for use by The Colonial Golf Academy.

FORD'S COLONY

240 Ford's Colony Drive, Williamsburg, Virginia (Take I-64 to exit 234 and follow Route 199 south for about 1.7 miles to Route 60, Richmond Road; left onto Richmond Road for about 1.7 miles to Route 658, Old Town Road; right onto Old Town road for about 1½ miles to Longhill Road; right onto Longhill Road for about 1½ miles to Ford's Colony entrance on left.)
Phone: (757) 258-4130

Architect: Dan Maples   Year opened: 1985

White & Red course rating/Slope rating:
Blue 72.3/126   White 70.2/122
Red 72.3/124

Blue & Gold course rating/Slope rating:
Blue - 72.3/124   Red - 71.1/119
White - 70.6/120   Silver - 67.3/113

Ford's Colony is a thirty-six-hole golf complex that offers golfers two splendid, well-maintained, and interesting golf courses laid out among water and woods just a short putt west of Colonial Williamsburg. "It's one of the best-kept secrets in the state," said a golfing friend who has a passion for great golf courses and plays to scratch. "I liked it so much when I first played it that I almost joined. If it weren't so far from home, I would have." As it is, he drives from the Maryland suburbs of Washington, D.C., several times a year to play there.

The White & Red eighteen were the original track, opened in 1985; the Blue nine holes were completed in 1987 and the Gold nine opened in 1992. As we go to press, a second Blue nine and a second Gold nine are nearing completion and will be amalgamated within the existing structure to create a fifty-four-hole facility. As with the existing holes, the new ones will have a very similar feel and temperament, and visitors can be assured

of a challenge and an enjoyable golfing experience on all of them.

Local members seem divided as to which they pick as their favorites, as well as which they rate as the best, the toughest and the most needing improvement. The fact is that Dan Maples has designed lovely golf courses, all with his particular flair. Like Gary Player, he has a clever—if sometimes cruel—touch with sand. The bunkering is extremely well done and demands careful shot placement on almost every hole. Water, trees, natural hills, and machine-made mounds complete the arsenal of difficulties Maples arrays before the players who come to experience Ford's Colony.

The courses feature a wonderful variety of par fours. Maples has penchant for par fives that are solid three-shot holes for all but the longest of hitters, with little buttonhook greens that are difficult to approach. On virtually all of the par fives, the key to pars and birdies is the placement of your second shot. It must be

The big, undulating 3rd green at Ford's Colony's White & Red Course is typical of architect Dan Maples' use of water and sand.

White and Red Course

HOLE NUMBER	Ra.	SI	1	2	3	4	5	6	7	8	9	OUT	10	11	12	13	14	15	16	17	18	IN	TOT
BLUE	72.3	124	376	425	538	402	179	545	399	172	396	3432	359	569	398	333	332	176	475	149	515	3306	6738
WHITE	70.6	120	355	390	502	374	120	512	381	155	374	3163	333	546	369	297	312	157	452	125	483	3074	6237
HANDICAP (m)			13	5	11	1	17	7	3	15	9		12	2	6	10	14	16	4	18	8		
PAR			4	4	5	4	3	5	4	3	4	36	4	5	4	4	3	4	4	3	5	36	72
RED	71.1	119	342	345	451	352	102	463	334	144	327	2860	300	508	340	232	292	131	385	90	441	2719	5579
HANDICAP (w)			9	13	1	3	17	5	7	15	11		10	2	8	14	12	16	4	18	6		

guided to a point where the green is most accessible in order to score. Maples' par threes may be the most interesting element of an interesting agglomerate of golf holes. He uses water, natural topography, and a variety of tee boxes to present a series of challenging and aesthetically pleasing one-shot holes.

The Ford's Colony complex is a challenging test for most women. Most par fours tend to be 325 yards or longer, and two of the par fives are in excess of 500 yards from the red markers. As one local woman who plays there regularly observed: "We play them like par sixes."

White & Red Course

The opening holes on the White nine provide a relatively gentle introduction, but the character of the golf course becomes evident on the hilly, double-dogleg par-five #3. For women, it is the number-one handicap hole even though it measures only 451 yards from the forward markers. The reason for the degree of difficulty is the water that protects the green. While it's reachable in two shots for the longest-hitting male players, the best approach to the shallow little green is a high soft one. Anything that blazes in too hot is likely to skip right off the back.

The par-four #4 is rated the toughest on the card for men. It's a crescent-shaped dogleg left that features a little lake along its left length, with the long, extremely thin oval green jutting out into the water. An imprecise second shot can be very costly.

The 8th hole on the White nine is one of Maples's lovely little par threes. It features a series of tee boxes, all requiring a carry across a spit of water. Pin placement will govern club selection, because a ridge

intersects the 36-foot-deep green about two-thirds of the way back. It is imperative to be on the same level as the flag. This is a visually pleasing hole that can be an easy birdie or par; it can also be an easy double- or triple-bogey.

The Red nine is every bit as demanding as the White. The 11th hole, the toughest on the Red nine, is a brutal par five: 569 yards from the championship markers, 546 yards from the middle tees, and 508 yards for the women. A triangular lake intersects the fairway at the point it turns left. It's wide open on your tee shot, although an extremely long drive can catch the water. Your second and third shots play to an ever-narrowing landing zone.

One of the most intriguing holes at Ford's Colony is the short par-four #13, which the bravest and longest hitters can actually attempt to drive. It's quite a gamble, however, in that between tee and green—almost up to the collar of the green—is a little pond and wetland. If you opt to play an iron from the tee to the fairway in front of the green, you must successfully dodge five huge, hungry fairway bunkers. A mid-iron left of the bunkers leaves a short iron to the pin; a long iron amongst the sand traps can leave a wedge or sand wedge; if you try to drive the green and come up short, you're wet.

The finisher on the Red nine is a short par five that is reachable in two, although in his signature fashion, Maples has created a buttonhook of a hole, with the approach to the green the toughest shot you'll face. In this case, the green is guarded by three towering, ancient trees that overhang the apron to the right. If your approach is too low or too hot, you can bounce right off the long, thin green,

An aerial view of the Gold nine, with its lake and trees showing off their autumn colors. (Courtesy Ford's Colony)

and if you're off-line you can knock around in the timber or find the bunker that sits to the left front of the putting surface. It looks like a promising birdie hole on the card, but it's a testing finish for the White & Red Course.

Blue & Gold Course

If you harbor any fear of water, you might want to think about tackling another golf course. On the Blue & Gold Course at Ford's Colony, water comes into play on thirteen holes—granted that in some cases you have to hit a pretty wild shot to find it, but we are all capable of hitting the odd wild shot. In fact, on three of the holes water comes into play multiple times from tee to green. Add to that Dan Maples' penchant for bunkers, mounding, and trees and you have a sometimes-strenuous round ahead, although it must be noted that for all of the difficulties he presents, Maples has constructed a fair and playable golf course.

The greens are contoured but true, receptive, and not unreasonably fast. The tee placements generally present an interesting look at the hole. And in the best traditions of golf-course architecture, good shots are rewarded and errant shots are punished—but not to an unfair degree.

Maples lets you warm up a bit on the opening holes of the Blue nine. The course starts with a trio of medium-length par fours, with most of the trouble around the undulating greens. The opener sets the stage. It is a tight dogleg right that plays downhill from the tees and then back uphill to the green.

Enjoy the lovely, verdant Virginia countryside and then hold your breath on the long, tough, watery par-five #4,

rated the toughest hole on the card for men and women. One pond is in play off the tee, and a second comes into play about midway from tee to green. Unless you are long enough on your second shot to take the lake completely out of the picture, your shot must stay left of center or risk being drawn by gravity into the hazard. The par-five #7 offers a good scoring opportunity for men, save for the green that—in Maples' signature fashion—is hooked severely to the right among a stand of trees. For women, this is the second-hardest hole on the side, playing just under 400 yards and requiring a well-positioned second shot to set up a clear approach to the well-protected and difficult green.

The two par threes on the Blue nine both feature water and well-guarded greens. The 8th is the more difficult of the two, even though it is the shorter. The 5th offers a little bailout room to the right front; the 8th presents precious little room, and if you're short, you will still face the need for a high, soft approach over sand to the long, thin green.

The opening hole on the Gold nine is another stress-inducing par five. It's long and straight from the tee, and for most players their second shot will be a lay-up that must remain far enough right to open the green but avoid a strategically placed fairway bunker. Again, the green is hooked severely to the left on your approach. For women, this is a monster, more than 500 yards from tee to green and no bargains on the approach to the green. It's rated the second-toughest hole on the Blue & Gold Course—and justifiably.

The shortish #2—a splendid if deceptively difficult dogleg right playing to an elevated green—and #8—which presents a lovely vista of the golf course with its water and sand from elevated tees—are among Maples' best par fours. They both feature strategically placed and devilishly difficult water and sand, coupled with the element of visual intimidation on every shot. Your drive on the Gold nine's #8 is from a hillside, going across water to a fairway that is tightened like a noose about 100 yards in front of the green by a pair of ponds on either side.

I anticipate that by the time this book is in your hands, the Blue nine will be part of a new Blue Course and the Gold nine will be part of a new Gold Course—all the work of Dan Maples and all in keeping with the character of the facility since its opening.

Blue & Gold Course

HOLE NUMBER	Ra.	Sl	1	2	3	4	5	6	7	8	9	OUT	10	11	12	13	14	15	16	17	18	IN	TOT
BLUE			409	408	394	535	195	383	528	192	378	3422	583	393	183	418	408	379	182	386	415	3347	6769
WHITE			360	378	342	510	151	359	451	173	327	3051	539	376	143	396	368	368	158	377	382	3107	6158
HANDICAP (m)			3	7	5	1	17	11	9	15	13		2	4	16	12	10	14	18	6	8		
PAR			4	4	4	5	3	4	5	3	4	36	5	4	3	4	4	4	3	4	4	35	71
RED			325	325	322	437	127	331	398	125	292	2682	509	325	114	306	333	309	128	334	358	2716	5398
SILVER	67.3	113	325	291	260	437	127	293	398	100	292	2523	467	284	106	264	240	276	118	257	280	2292	4815
HANDICAP (w)			5	9	11	1	17	7	3	15	13		2	10	18	12	8	14	16	6	4		

THE GAUNTLET AT CURTIS PARK

58 Jesse Curtis Lane, Hartwood, Virginia (Take I-95 to exit 133B, Route 17 north toward Warrenton; go about 5 miles to Route 612; stay on Route 612 about 2 miles; turn right into Curtis Memorial Park.)

Phone: (540) 752-0963

Architect: P. B. Dye   Year opened: 1995

Course rating/Slope rating:
Gold - 72.8/126   Black - 69.9/117
White - 68.1/113   Red - 69.6/113

The Gauntlet is carved from a dense forest of hardwood trees and towering pines, built around a lake, and crisscrossed by a series of streams. There are a wide variety of holes, most punctuated with abundant fairway and greenside sand traps. The greens tend to be large and tricky, and while occasional risk taking can reap dividends, skilled course management will tame The Gauntlet to a far greater degree than naked aggression. It is a serpentine track that features ten dogleg holes. The first five holes will leave you gasping for air.

The opener is a short par-four dogleg left that plays downhill. Your tee shot must stay left of center. A drive that's too long or too far right will slide through the fairway into inhospitable territory. The hill becomes progressively steeper and narrower as you approach the undulating green, which sits in a little valley, nestled tightly against a ridge and a stand of trees.

The second hole is a short par five, another dogleg left, that's reachable in two. But there is trouble galore for the unwary or the overly brave. Your tee shot is blind and plays from the side of one hill over another. The women's tee shot is straight uphill and must reach the crest or

you face a very long lay-up to the marsh. On your second shot the fairway slopes downhill and right to left. If your drive is long enough, your second shot then plays across a small inlet of water and a marshy area. You must decide how much of the hazard to try to carry. The green is a peninsula jutting into the lake, and a pair of snarling bunkers guards the right as you approach. However anything too long will catch a steep slope beyond the bunkers and can be directed into the hazard on the other side. A huge grass pot bunker sits to the right front of the big oval-shaped domed green.

The moderate-length par-three #3 requires pinpoint accuracy from the tee. All of the difficulty with this hole is on and around the green, which is a long, gigantic multilevel shelf, 46 yards from front to back.

The short par-four #4 is a signature hole of The Gauntlet, and it's a monster despite its limited yardage. It proves the time-worn axiom that length is not the only yardstick by which the difficulty of a golf hole should be measured. It is not rated the toughest hole on the course, but an argument could be made that it should be. It plays from elevated tees to a tiny landing area that's protected by a moonscape

The ribbon of fairway leading to The Gauntlet's 4th green is guarded on the left by a marsh and a lake and on the right by a minefield of sand.

of bunkers, mounds, trees, and marsh on all sides. Think about using something less than a driver for your tee shot. Placement is everything. The hole makes a sharp left turn, almost 90 degrees, and leaves an approach shot that plays up a thread of fairway guarded by marsh on the left and a series of bunkers on the right to a long, hilly, kidney-shaped green. This hole is a shot maker's delight; but anyone unable put a medium to short iron on the sprinkler head of their choice is in trouble.

There's no time to catch your breath. The next hole, #5, is a very solid S-shaped par five that's bisected by water and wetland. Your tee shot plays straight away. Left-center is ideal placement. The hole then turns sharply to the left and starts up a substantial hill. About 70 yards in front of the huge, well-bunkered elevated green in the shape of an inverted pear, the hole turns back to the right.

The next two holes provide a little relief before you face the long, tight, straight-away par-four #8. It's rated the toughest hole on the golf course because of both its length and the trouble that can punish an errant shot. The blind tee shot is over a hill that cascades down toward the point at which the fairway is intersected by a marshy creek. The elevated green features a series of ridges; the front third slopes sharply back down toward the fairway, while the back left slopes sharply away from the approaching players.

The splendid front nine, a lovely example of some of Dye's most innovative work, finishes with a fine, medium-length par four, straight and tight to an extremely long, narrow green. There's a bunker to the right front that creates an optical illusion on the approach. The bunker is not greenside, though it looks as if it is. It's about 20 yards from the putting surface. A small pond to the left will catch a shot that drifts over that way.

The short par-five #10 offers a good scoring opportunity to begin the inward nine, but it's back to the challenge immediately thereafter. The 11th hole is rated the second toughest on The Gauntlet and features a mammoth dogleg right. The dogleg is straightened considerably for the ladies, whose tee box is more than 100 yards forward of the men's markers. How far you hit your drive will determine how much of the dogleg and its trouble you'll have to negotiate on your second. The multicontoured green can be devilish if your approach is not on target.

The 13th and 14th—a long, straight par five with strategically placed bunkers across the fairway about driving distance, and a very solid par four also with

trouble for a tee shot that doesn't find the short grass—lead you to the long par-three #15 and the tough little L-shaped #16 (par four). Men and women may want to consider hitting something other than a driver from the tee to set up their approach to the wide, shallow, and tricky green.

If there is a controversial hole on The Gauntlet, it is the par-four #17. No one who has played it comes away feeling neutral about it. Some players declare it a breathtaking challenge. Others dismiss it as too hokey and artificially tricked up to be taken seriously. One friend who played on the PGA Tour for a short while excoriated the design, saying, "The only things missing were a trapeze and a tightrope."

The hole plays from a set of elevated tees to a very small landing area. The fairway is intersected by a marshy area and a creek about 100 yards from the elevated, multitiered green. You want your tee shot about as close to the marsh and cart path as you can get it and still stay in the fairway. The approach to the elevated hourglass green is blind and almost vertically up a hill with nasty rough and trees to the left and a dense forest and rocks to the right. The green has more tiers and terraces than Madison Square Garden, with the front shelf canted dangerously and precariously back down the hill. Perhaps the greatest drawback of the hole is that short of going up the hill to see where the pin is placed, gauging the distance on your approach is nearly impossible. In a big tournament, players obviously would make the trek and take a look, but if everybody on this busy course climbed the hill before playing the shot, things would grind to a halt. Unfortunately, failure to get your approach close to the pin is a recipe for bogeys, doubles, or worse.

The finishing hole looks tame by comparison, but it is a very solid par-four dogleg right that plays over one hill, down into a little vale, and back up to a huge, undulating green that's 45 yards deep and difficult to read. In typical Dye fashion, the approach is bunkered within an inch of its life, with only a little bailout room to the right front on your second shot.

The Gauntlet at Curtis Park is not without its critics, however, even leaving the contentious #17 aside. My wife and many other good women players say Dye underestimated their playing ability and made the course too easy for them, the difficult greens notwithstanding. They point out that two of the four par threes are less than 100 yards from tee to green for women, and all but two of the par fours are less than 300 yards. Overall, the red markers are some 1,900 yards shorter than the championship tees.

Nonetheless, it is a well-run, well-maintained golf course that is well worth playing, even if only to join in the debate.

The Gauntlet

HOLE NUMBER	Ra	Sl	1	2	3	4	5	6	7	8	9	OUT	10	11	12	13	14	15	16	17	18	IN	TOT
GOLD	72.8	126	369	493	178	375	558	178	355	470	390	3366	480	459	142	563	408	244	386	377	432	3491	6857
BLACK	69.9	117	325	458	155	374	518	161	313	423	377	3104	434	412	122	528	382	215	343	339	376	3151	6255
WHITE	68.1	113	315	433	137	362	495	136	278	406	341	2903	417	398	99	502	335	202	325	322	325	2925	5828
PAR			4	5	3	4	5	3	4	4	4	36	5	4	3	5	4	3	4	4	4	36	72
HANDICAP			13	5	15	7	3	17	11	1	9		12	2	18	4	6	16	10	14	8		
RED	69.6	119	277	389	109	262	407	93	230	352	305	2424	376	298	86	460	295	181	281	270	284	2531	4955

GLADE SPRINGS RESORT

3000 Lake Drive, Daniels, West Virginia (about 6 miles south of Beckley
from I-64 off Route 19)
Phone: (800) 634-5233

Architect: George W. Cobb   Year opened: 1974

Men's course rating/Slope rating:
Blue - 73.5/135   White - 70.1/129

Women's course rating/Slope rating:
Yellow - 71.4/130   Red - 67.6/118

George W. Cobb is a highly significant figure in the development of golf-course architecture. Cobb laid much of the groundwork for the transition from the classical architects, such as Donald Ross, A. C. Tillinghast and Harry Colt, to the modern designers, including Jack Nicklaus, Pete and P. B. Dye, and Tom Fazio. A great deal of the machinery used in the construction of modern golf courses did not exist or was not in common use before World War II; the eventual creation of this machinery gave architects such as George Cobb new tools with which to expand their horizons and turn their visions into reality.

The golf course at the Glade Springs Resort is a splendid example of Cobb's later work and demonstrates why his designs have merited enduring praise and acclaim.

The resort was the brainchild of Austin Caperton Jr., who in 1967 visited Hilton Head Island, South Carolina, and played two of Cobb's courses. The designs so impressed Caperton that two years later he oversaw the purchase of an old tract of farmland and retained Cobb to plan the design of the golf course.

What is now the back nine opened first, with the second nine being completed the following year. It was a monumental task of construction, with more than a million cubic yards of dirt and rocks pushed, prodded, and coerced into the contours and lines of the golf course. Ponds and lakes come into play on eight holes.

The course features enormous, well-bunkered greens with vast amounts of subtle—and not so subtle—breaks and rolls. This is a course that can improve your "greens in regulation" statistics, but it is very hard to score on and routine two-putts can be nerve-wracking. Getting on George Cobb's greens is much easier than getting close. Almost every hole is lined with mature forests, and tight fairways are the rule.

The course is a fine test for women and features two sets of tees that are rated and sloped for women (along with the back two sets of tee markers that are rated and sloped for men). Men whose handicaps are low teens or lower might think about playing the tips and giving themselves a real challenge with nearly 700 yards of additional length. Women whose handicaps are in the teens and below would

The signature hole at Glade Springs, the long par-four #16, tees off over the water and then requires a forced carry over a second lake to the well-bunkered and elevated green.

enjoy the loftier challenge of the yellow markers. While it is not a monster in terms of overall yardage, it is a superior test of the game that demands good shot making and course management.

The opening two holes set the stage. A moderate-length par-four dogleg right with an elevated and sloped green is followed by a par five that's reachable in two, with a long, thin green hooked to the right and compressed by two gaping bunkers to the right and a third sand trap to the left.

It's a course of deliberate, sometimes subtle, sometimes overt contrasts for men and women. For example, the par-five #5 is a good scoring opportunity for men but a very difficult test for women. On the other hand, the par-four #6 is the toughest hole on the card for men and the number-seventeen handicap hole for women.

The 5th is a dogleg right. Just beyond the bend in the dogleg, a pond sits between two hills, and a drive that is too bold risks careening down the hill into the water. Women are confronted with either hitting a massive drive and then carrying the water on their second shot or laying up to the crest of the hill, crossing the pond, and then trying to get a chip up and down. For women and men, once you've negotiated the difficulties on the way to the green, the enormous putting surface presents myriad contours and breaks along with several distinct levels.

The par-four #6 is a long, tight hole for men that demands a drive from a set of hilltop tees to a hilltop fairway across a no man's land of deep grass. The red markers, however, play less than 250 yards, and with the open, relatively unprotected green, this is a wonderful scoring hole for women. Everybody needs to be aware of the extremely tight out-of-bounds on the right side.

The par-four #9 provides a wonderful view of the distant mountains, but it's tough. There is a precariously tight out-of-bounds down the left, and the shallow green is guarded by a gaping, deep-faced bunker in front.

Two short par fours on the back nine are among the most interesting of George Cobb's layout. A lake intrudes nearly all the way across the 11th fairway, isolating the green behind a pair of bunkers. All players must guard against hitting too boldly from their tees lest they find the water. The 15th is a fascinating little hole with a 90-degree dogleg right. The height of the trees in the dense, ancient forest along the right length of the hole precludes even the biggest hitters from going for the green, so everybody hits a mid- to long iron to guard against going through the fairway and into the trees on the other side.

The three finishers on Glade Springs are simply terrific.

The 16th hole is a spectacular and visually intimidating par four, the signature hole on the golf course. Water is in play from tee to green. Everybody must carry water on his or her tee shot to a landing area that is sandwiched between lakes. A player whose tee shot fails to get midway between the two lakes will be faced with a long carry to the green. The elevated green is tucked behind a second water hazard. There is bailout room to the right, but it's about as wide as a thread. The green, less than fifteen yards wide behind the deep-faced front bunker, demands a high, soft approach; a low, hot shot that doesn't catch the sand may well skitter off the back. Many golfers reportedly say they enjoy this hole much more when recalling it over a post-round drink than when they are actually playing it.

The 17th is a long, difficult uphill par three that plays across a lake. For women, the lake is only marginally in play, but women must carry a high shot over a steep-faced bunker. The serpentine green has three separate levels, and being safely on the putting surface in one is no guarantee of an easy par.

The closing hole is a long, tight, dogleg-right par five that plays uphill, with the fairway canted sharply from left to right. A rocky creek intersects the fairway just beyond driving distance for most players. The uphill approach to the green tightens as you get closer to the putting surface, and your shot to the flag must clear huge bunkers right and left.

The Glade Springs course is immensely popular in the region and hosts a wide variety of local tournaments. It is consistently rated by the local and national press as among the best golf courses in West Virginia.

Glade Springs

HOLE NUMBER	Ra	S1	1	2	3	4	5	6	7	8	9	OUT	10	11	12	13	14	15	16	17	18	IN	TOT
BLUE	73.5	135	412	520	204	361	510	427	211	390	418	3453	406	376	503	209	381	363	419	197	534	3388	6841
WHITE	70.1	129	367	482	173	323	469	395	171	361	381	3122	365	337	459	176	323	326	393	176	499	3054	6176
HANDICAP (m)			5	7	11	17	15	1	9	13	3		6	14	10	12	16	18	2	4	8		
PAR			4	5	3	4	5	4	3	4	4	36	4	4	5	3	4	4	4	3	5	36	72
GOLD	71.4	130	316	456	146	289	432	360	152	318	360	2829	335	294	423	155	293	262	303	148	424	2637	5466
RED	67.6	118	285	426	132	250	397	244	121	284	323	2462	306	253	392	124	268	255	290	116	420	2422	4884
HANDICAP (w)			11	5	13	15	3	17	9	7	1		4	12	8	14	16	18	2	6	10		

GOLDEN HORSESHOE

401 South England St., Williamsburg, Virginia (Take exit 242A from I-64 and follow Route 199 West; turn right at Henry St. for about 1½ miles; turn right onto Newport Ave. about a ¼-mile; the Gold Course is directly across the street from the Williamsburg Inn; the Green Course and clubhouse are about a mile away and well marked.)
Phone: (757) 220-7696

Gold Course Architect: Robert Trent Jones Sr.   Year opened: 1963
Green Course Architect: Rees Jones   Year opened: 1991

Gold Course rating/Slope rating:
Blue - 72.4/135   Gold - 73.6/138
White - 70.7/129   Red - 70.6/127

Green Course rating/Slope rating:
Green - 73.4/134   White - 70.1/122
Blue - 72.5/130   Green - 69.3/109

The Golden Horseshoe is one of the country's premier golf complexes, featuring the world-class Gold Course, the delightful and challenging Green Course, and the surprising and delightful executive course named for Gov. Alexander Spotswood, one of the Old Dominion's first chief executives. In fact, the Golden Horseshoe is associated with a daring and dangerous expedition Spotswood led to the Shenandoah Mountains in 1716 to explore the westernmost reaches of the Colony of Virginia. On his return, Spotswood presented the members of the expedition with golden horseshoes as a tribute for their bravery and valor.

The venerable and much-written-about Gold Course can bring a high handicapper to his or her knees and leave low handicappers weeping or brokenhearted. The Green Course, on the other hand, is less severe and less punishing, though thoroughly challenging. In comparison with the relentlessly tight and unforgiving Gold Course, the Green Course will render you a bit breathless, but you'll still be able to enjoy it. This effect was a deliberate decision at the time Rees Jones was commissioned to design the Green Course. Frankly, neither golf course is suitable for a raw beginner, but the Green Course is by far the more golfer-friendly of the two layouts. On the other hand, virtually everybody—from scratch players to thirty-plus handicappers—will enjoy the Spotswood Course.

Gold Course

From May 1997 to the summer of 1998, the Golden Horseshoe's fabled Gold Course underwent a multimillion-dollar face-lift—not that there was very much wrong with the Gold Course. It had long been regarded as one of the classic championship golf courses of the East Coast, a track whose very name was uttered in hushed whispers and that inspired awe in the hearts of many who trekked to the famed Robert Trent Jones Sr. monument to try to tame it. Time simply caused enough subtle changes that the decision was made to renovate the course, and the project was launched under the keen eye of Rees Jones, son of the man responsible for the original design.

"Rees Jones may well be the best golf course renovator in the world," observed Ben Thompson, golf director at the nearby Colonial Golf Course. "He does about as good a job at renovating a course as there is."

The goal was to modernize the Gold Course and trim it up a bit, but not to change its character or personality in any way. It was a face-lift, not a lobotomy. A few of the trees that had grown too big over the years and overly constricted certain holes were pared back or removed. In a few places, fairways that had become too domed or sloped with time were made more playable. And some of the greens were leveled a bit. "When Robert Trent Jones Sr. built the course in '63, a lot of the break in the putts was determined by the amount of slope," explained Howie Barrow, the Golden Horseshoe's golf director. "But as grasses got better and equipment got better, some of the slope on these greens was far too severe." That is not to suggest that the greens have been rendered flat or easy. Far from it!

In addition, several of the tees were leveled and raised, and a few bunkers were

Robert Trent Jones Sr. broke new ground by being among the first architects to create an island green, doing so here on the Gold Course at The Golden Horseshoe. This is a view of the par-three #16 from the championship tees, with the par-four #17 stretching up the hill behind it.

added or removed. But the bulk of Robert Trent Jones's magnificent design was kept just as he made it, with only subtle changes to improve playability and drainage.

The Gold Course may be one of the tightest, most claustrophobic, and most treacherous golf courses in the world. PGA star Lee Trevino was once reportedly asked how he liked the course. "It's great!" he replied. "But it was a little lonely out there. It's so tight we had to walk single file most of the way."

It is a short golf course and plays to a par 71. But do not be misled by the yardage. This is a brutal and rigorous test. It is among the narrowest in the land, with small, well-guarded greens and abundant trees and water to send you scurrying for the aspirin. The course is simply unrelenting. The shot-making challenges are arduous at best and terrifying at worst.

The par threes are among the best anywhere, both for their extraordinary beauty and the standard of golf they demand. In

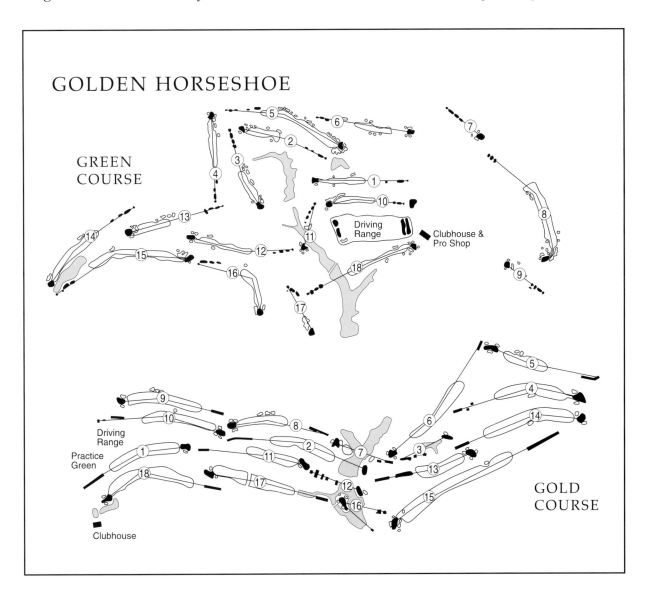

GOLDEN HORSESHOE

GREEN COURSE

GOLD COURSE

fact, when people in the golf business talk about the Gold Course, they invariably talk about the par threes, and most—even the Golden Horseshoe's competitors—agree that the four par threes are the finest collection on one golf course in the region and possibly in the country.

The par fours cover a broad range, with special attention paid to the shorter holes. Robert Trent Jones Sr. did not believe that length was the only critical factor in creating a challenging golf course. In fact, many of the par fours invite something other than a driver from most players. Fairway woods and long irons are highly recommended.

Certain holes leave you gasping. The short par-five #2 is a risk-reward hole that features a blind uphill tee shot and leads the unsuspecting or unwary player to believe that it is reachable in two. It is. But the attendant risks may not be worth it. This hole has generated as much controversy as any in the Virginias since it was first revealed to the golfing public. Only when you crest the hill and gaze down the other side do you realize what it is Jones hath wrought. The small green is perched on a platform sculpted from the hillside and across a lake. "It's driver, eight iron, eight iron," grumbled one local assistant pro. "Or you try to put it on in two, put it in the water, take your penalty, and hope for a six."

That lake, which first makes its presence felt on #2, is the watery soul, the aquatic essence of the Gold Course. Robert Trent Jones Sr. made that modest body of water such an integral part of the design that it is impossible to imagine the golf course without its character infusing it. Three greens are caressed by it; four holes traverse it.

Once you have experienced #2, you face the first of the four magnificent par threes. The 3rd is a long carry across another lovely pond to a tiny oval green that's only 13 yards deep and is set among the towering trees. The target looks very small and very far away as you gaze down on it from the tees.

The long, arduous, tight par-four #4 simply demands all of your shot-making skills; the short par-four #5 is rated the second-easiest hole on the course, but it's tight and potentially treacherous. The second of the incredible quartet of par threes, the long, tough #7, plays from elevated tees, across that all-important lake, to a triangular hillside green. Unlike the par threes on most golf courses, which invariably rank among the easiest holes, this is rated the number-five handicap hole, and with good reason. It's 206 yards from the back tees; women face only 92 yards from a small island that is the forward tee box, but the shot is all uphill, and while women can see the flag, they cannot see the putting surface.

The gorgeous par-three #12 plays from an elevated set of tees back across the critical lake to a tiny green—only 16 yards

Gold Course

HOLE NUMBER	Ra	SI	1	2	3	4	5	6	7	8	9	OUT	10	11	12	13	14	15	16	17	18	IN	TOT
GOLD	73.6	138	402	498	201	421	348	485	206	337	372	3270	466	403	188	363	445	634	169	435	444	3547	6817
BLUE	72.4	135	383	476	174	403	337	471	186	323	360	3113	450	386	169	350	429	613	159	422	431	3409	6522
WHITE	70.7	129	369	470	145	394	328	463	165	313	355	3002	392	362	149	340	420	600	150	412	421	3246	6248
PAR			4	5	3	4	4	5	3	4	4	36	4	4	3	4	4	5	3	4	4	35	71
HANDICAP			11	3	9	1	15	5	7	17	13		8	14	12	18	2	10	16	4	6		
RED	70.6	127	316	416	126	325	293	415	92	274	333	2590	350	264	93	330	358	468	97	308	310	2578	5168

The beautiful par-three #11 on the Green Course at The Golden Horseshoe is a shot-making challenge.

deep. As a matter of design philosophy, Robert Trent Jones Sr. does not believe in giving golfers much room to bail out on his one-shot holes. In this case, the water laps up almost to the collar of the green and wraps around it to the right as well.

If the par threes are the jewels in the crown of the Gold Course, the par fours are the foundation. While many are short, they are all difficult, and Jones serves notice that inaccuracy will be dealt with severely. The long par fours are unyielding and can be devastating. The short par-four #13 and the long par-four #14 form a devilish pair of steely-eyed monsters. There's a punitive little vale in front of the 13th green that will suck in a drive that's too long; an overabundance of caution on the dogleg-right #14 will render the green unreachable, blocked out by the towering trees to the right.

On almost every golf course designed by Robert Trent Jones Sr. there is one extremely long par five. On the Gold Course #15 is it. It is tight, straight, and loooong. From the back tees the green looks to be in another area code, 634 yards away. In fact, all of the men's markers are 600 yards or more. Women get a bit of a break with a redesigned tee box but still must traverse 468 yards from tee to green.

The picturesque #16, the last of the marvelous par threes, is an island hole with five bunkers surrounding the putting surface. "It was an island hole long before the seventeenth at [the TPC Course at] Sawgrass got all the attention on television," said Jim Bradley, the public-relations manager for the Golden Horseshoe. "We believe this is where the idea was born." It plays from a hillside set of tees and looks far scarier than it really is. The green is actually larger than many others on the Gold Course, and like most of the greens, it is receptive to a high, soft approach. While the sand is a less-than-ideal place to land, it does prevent many stray shots from rolling into the water, and the size of the green will allow a sand save if that becomes necessary.

The Gold Course finishes with a pair of long and demanding par fours that will etch forever into your golfing psyche that this is a tough golf course for serious golfers. The uphill #17 will leave you breathless; the dogleg-left #18, with its extremely well-protected green, will leave you gasping.

Jack Nicklaus owns the course record of 67, scored in 1967. It still stands.

Green Course

In the late 1980s the managers of the Golden Horseshoe determined that more was needed than one fabled golf course to compete successfully in the expanding market of resort golf. Williamsburg, long a popular tourist stop for its history and other amusements, was on its way to becoming one of the country's top golfing venues. Therefore, Rees Jones was commissioned to build the Green Course. The desire was to create a golf course that was not quite as difficult as his father's Gold Course but would attract golfers of all levels and leave them fully satisfied.

What Rees Jones designed is an exceptional test of the game that is especially good for women. In fact, the magazine *Golf for Women* named the Green Course as one of the most women-friendly golf courses in the country. That is not to suggest it is a pushover. Its undulating fairways with 115 sculpted bunkers and abundant mounds and hills make it a narrow, demanding golf course, especially if you venture too far from the short grass.

The tiny 8th green on the Spotswood Course is perched on a hillside shelf and requires pinpoint accuracy.

Green Course

HOLE NUMBER	Ra	Sl	1	2	3	4	5	6	7	8	9	OUT	10	11	12	13	14	15	16	17	18	IN	TOT
GREEN	73.4	134	429	404	360	380	558	450	188	538	196	3503	352	195	444	396	466	616	397	220	531	3617	7120
BLUE	72.5	130	407	383	335	357	537	427	163	520	176	3305	332	173	426	373	441	575	379	206	512	3417	6722
WHITE	70.1	122	382	334	305	328	502	402	134	503	153	3043	307	153	399	345	412	553	345	199	488	3201	6244
PAR			4	4	4	4	5	4	3	5	3	36	4	3	4	4	4	5	4	3	5	36	72
HANDICAP			5	7	15	13	9	1	17	3	11		18	12	4	14	2	8	16	6	10			
GREEN	66.2	120	316	416	118	346	293	404	95	274	333	2595	350	248	83	309	321	523	97	322	311	2564	5159

In general, Rees Jones' architectural philosophy is similar to that of his father: build a very straightforward course that is fair and playable. What you see is what you get. No tricks. No gimmicks. Not much hidden trouble. Just a very solid, very enjoyable golfing experience that requires thought and strategy on every hole and tends to jump up and bite you when mental lapses occur.

The receptive greens are filled with undulations and subtleties that make putting on them a real test. Nonetheless, "Virtually every green has a bump-and-run entry," observed Jim Bradley, the Golden Horseshoe's public-relations manager, so that if you don't want to fly your ball to the pin, you can at least safely reach the putting surface. Few are so elevated that such a shot becomes an exercise in pure luck rather than skill.

A quartet of par fours opens the Green Course. The 1st and 2nd holes are both fairly straight and heavily bunkered and mounded along their right and left sides, creating the effect of a trough for the fairway. The 2nd green is tricky, with lots of contours. The 3rd hole is a short par four that plays down into a slight valley and then back up to a gently elevated green. The 4th, the last of the opening par fours, is medium length, but any shot that drifts right has an odds-on chance of finding one of the eight sand traps that form a minefield along the right side of the fairway from about 165 yards out all the way to the right rear apron of the green.

The solid three-shot par-five #5 presents you with thirteen bunkers from about driving distance down the left side of the fairway to the green. The green itself is irregularly shaped and presents you with a sharp drop to the right and front into an enormous bunker that's shaped like a bird when viewed from above and lurks like a buzzard waiting for your ball to die into it.

Rated the most difficult hole on the course, #6 is a long, straight par four. Your tee shot should be played down the right-center of the fairway, but the fairway stops about 100 yards from the front of the green, replaced with a grassy gully filled with unforgiving moguls and humps. A shot that feeds into the gully often continues to the right into an even deeper ravine littered with rocks, gnarly scrub, deep rough, and trees.

Rees Jones is nearly as skilled with par threes as his father was. The lovely one-shot #7 and the visually appealing #11 are reminiscent of the four brilliant par threes on the neighboring Gold Course. The 7th plays from an elevated series of tees across a stretch of marshy wetland to a good-sized green that's about level with the middle tees. The locals say play about one club longer than you think you need. On #11, you tee off from above the putting surface and down to a green that's fronted by a pond. Arching around the green on the hill behind it are four artfully sculpted bunkers.

A trio of long, difficult par fours follows. The 12th presents you with one of the narrowest fairways on the Green Course, only about 30 yards across in places. The 13th green is well protected with abundant breaks and bends. And big hitters should be aware that on the dog-leg-left #14, the lake that hugs the left side of the fairway from about 170 yards out to the green can come into play off the tee.

Rees Jones's #15 is a huge par five, 616 yards long from the back tees, reminiscent of the long par fives his father favored. The dogleg right requires a powerful tee shot that stays left of center in order to get a second-shot lay-up into scoring position.

The 18th is a glorious, tight, and demanding par-five finisher for men. It plays across a pond for the men and requires a long carry to the landing area. Women get the privilege of teeing off from across the water, and the hole poses a wonderful scoring opportunity for long hitters, who can get on in two and finish with an eagle or birdie. As you cross the bridge over the pond, look to the right. The old brown boathouse visible at water's edge used to belong to John D. Rockefeller, one of the prime movers behind the restoration of Colonial Williamsburg.

Spotswood Course

This is a par-31 executive course featuring six par threes, two par fours, and a par-five, and it is the only such course included in this book. It obviously would not make it standing alone, but grouped with its siblings and given its rich history, it's worth both a few words here and a few minutes of your time to play while you're in Williamsburg.

As you might expect from a Robert Trent Jones Sr. golf course of any length, it is tough, with plenty of character. It was part of the original golf course on that location that was built in the late 1940s. The greens range from small to minuscule. The first hole, for example, plays less than 100 yards to a green that's on a shelf on the side of a hill overhung by leafy old trees. Miss it right or short and your next shot will leave the putting surface (the size of a card table) and possibly the flag invisible.

The 8th hole is quintessential Robert Trent Jones Sr. It's a par three with no bailout room or margin for error. The hole plays only about 100 yards over a ravine to a green that's about as big as a king-sized bed, carved out of the side of a hill with a sheer drop into a creek in front for shots that are too short, and a nasty bunker behind the green to leave a terrifying shot back to the pin for those who play it too safe. "You'll see as many sixes as deuces," said a man strolling on the road behind the tee.

So-called "executive courses" usually elicit sneers from serious golfers. Sneer not at this little gem unless you're among the ranks of the rare few who shoot it in par 62 or less.

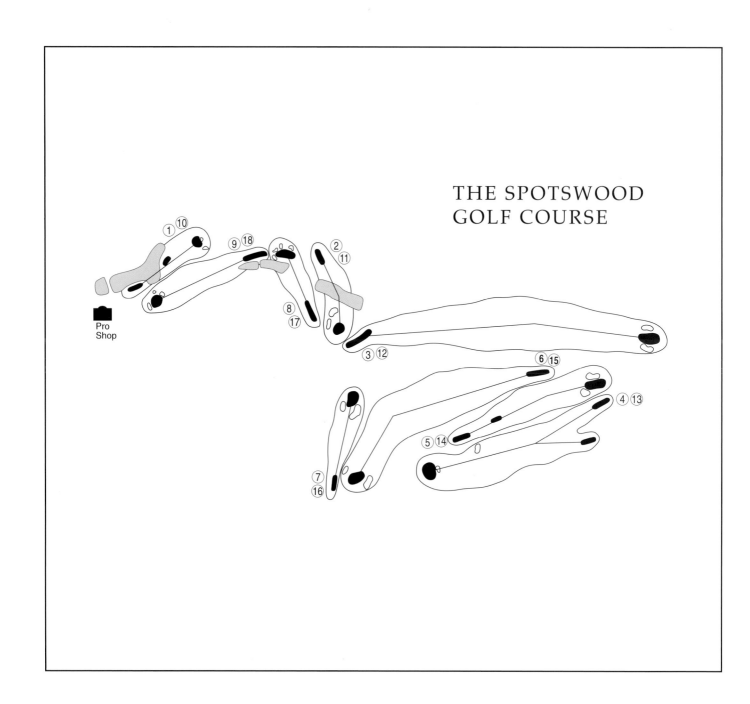

THE SPOTSWOOD
GOLF COURSE

Spotswood Course*

HOLE	1	2	3	4	5	6	7	8	9	TOT
WHITE	90	100	470	260	215	325	120	100	185	1865
GREEN	145	110	480	285	155	305	135	90	175	1880
PAR	3	3	5	4	3	4	3	3	3	31

*The nine-hole course is played twice from two different sets of markers, for an eighteen-hole total yardage of 3745 and a par of 62.

THE GREENBRIER

300 West Main St., White Sulphur Springs, West Virginia (From I-64
take the White Sulphur Springs exit and go north about a mile through town.)
Phone: (800) 624-6070 or (304) 536-1110

Old White Course Architects: C. B. Macdonald and S. J. Raynor Year opened: 1913
Greenbrier Course Architect: Jack Nicklaus Year opened: 1924/1978
Lakeside Course Architect: Dick Wilson Year opened: 1963

Old White Course rating/Slope rating:
Blue - 72.1/130   Men's Gold - 69.2/124
White - 70.6/127   Women's Gold - 74.5/129
Red - 69.9/119

Greenbrier Course rating/Slope rating:
Blue - 73.1/135   Women's White - 76.3/139
Men's White - 71.2/132   Red - 70.1/119

Lakeside Course rating/Slope rating:
Blue - 69.8/122   Women's White - 74.6/127
Men's White - 68.5/119   Red - 68.3/113

Golf came to the already well-established Greenbrier spa and hotel in 1910, when a little nine-hole track was opened. It didn't amount to much by today's standards, but golf in America in those days was more an oddity and a light diversion than a serious sport. Little of that original course exists anymore. A bit of it lives on as a part of today's Lakeside Course, the easiest, gentlest, and newest of the resort's three beautiful golf courses. Part of where the original golf course once resided is now the practice range. Unlike those old days when riding, hunting, shooting, and taking the mineral waters were the main attractions of The Greenbrier, today, golf is one of the principal reasons tourists flock there from all over the world. Of course, they also come for the service, ambiance, food, and other highly regarded resort amenities.

The golf, however, is akin to a spiritual mission at The Greenbrier. To walk onto any of the three golf courses is to venture into pristine territory. There are few golf courses as well maintained anywhere in the world as those at The Greenbrier. You half expect to see workers with tweezers and scissors manicuring the greens. The flawless fairways are more barbered than mown. The rough is tended better than most suburban yards. And the floral plantings around tees, greens, shelters, refreshment stands, and cart paths are extraordinary. The physical impression is one of opulence and serenity.

A good measure of the golfing excellence that is a tradition at The Greenbrier must be credited to Sam Snead, the facility's revered golf pro emeritus. In 1936 the resort hired the youthful Snead from the neighboring resort, The Homestead, just across the state line and a couple of mountains away in Virginia. It was Snead—even before he earned the moniker "Slammin' Sammy"—who transformed golf at The Greenbrier into another dimension and set the stage for the golfing mecca the resort was to become.

During World War II the hotel was sold and turned into a military hospital, but Snead remained. He called on the top pro golfers of the day—giants such as Jimmy Demaret and Byron Nelson—to play for the benefit of the recovering soldiers and help them with their golf swings as part of their therapy. In the mid-1950s Dwight Eisenhower was a regular, along with Bob Hope, Bing Crosby, Patricia Kennedy (JFK's sister), and countless other luminaries.

Old White Course

Only a few design modifications have been made in the Old White Course since it opened in 1913. What you play today has very much the feel and character of an early twentieth-century golf-course design: narrow fairways, lots of trees and natural hazards, and relatively small greens. It was considered a premier course in its early days, and it has stood the test of time.

The Old White Course demands good, fundamental golf. Hit your tee shots in the fairway and put your approaches on the green and you will score. Deviate from that formula and your troubles will compound exponentially. It is a very subtle, very beautiful, very well-maintained golf course. There is nothing tricky or artificial about it. As with most golf courses constructed before the machines of man could redesign what nature put there, there is very little that does not meet the

eye almost immediately and present itself too you. It has the feel of a nineteenth-century parkland golf course in England or Ireland.

The par-four #1 is one of the most spectacular opening holes anywhere. A platform has been constructed next to the clubhouse almost overhanging the stream thats splashes below and well above the level of the fairway. The Allegheny Mountains look like a movie set in the distance. "It's the number-three handicap hole," said the veteran starter as he sized up the latest group of visitors to climb the steps to the tee. "But Sam Snead says it's the hardest hole on the course." He's said it a thousand times, but it's news to the visitors. The hole is a slight dogleg right from the back tees. The forward markers poised across the stream play relatively straight. If women are denied the panoramic view on their drives, they are forgiven nearly 100 yards and presented with a far better scoring opportunity than from the platform by the clubhouse.

The Old White Course is a par 70 with only two par fives, both on the back nine. As a result, the bedrock that underlies the course is its par fours, a splendid amalgam of holes that forces players to use a wide variety of shots. The long #2 requires players to avoid a menacing fairway bunker just about driving distance down the right side. The short #4 demands precision from the tee and then to the green. Many players use something other than a driver here. Your tee shot must split a pair of fairway bunkers, and then your approach must carry to a well-protected green shaped like an inverted pear, with big sand traps right front and left front.

The 6th hole is rated the toughest on the course. It's a long, demanding par four with a highly contoured fairway and a green hooked slightly to the right as you

The difficult par-three #15 on The Greenbrier's Old White Course plays across the stream that meanders through the golf course to a green pinched in front by a pair of big bunkers.

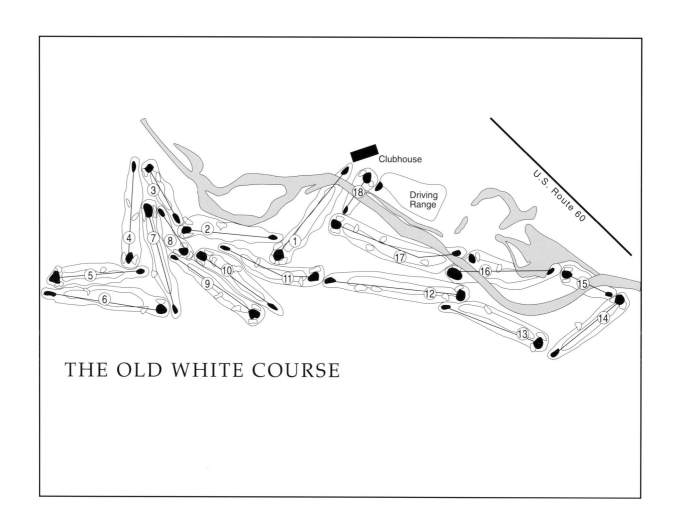

Clubhouse

Driving Range

U.S. Route 60

THE OLD WHITE COURSE

Old White Course

HOLE	Ra	SI	1	2	3	4	5	6	7	8	9	OUT	10	11	12	13	14	15	16	17	18	IN	TOT
BLUE	72.1	130	437	405	228	386	340	444	390	187	412	3229	369	419	549	396	365	220	417	514	162	3411	6640
WHITE	70.6	127	425	385	180	372	332	435	379	178	399	3085	354	409	535	380	354	197	394	505	140	3268	6353
GOLD	69.2 (m)/74.5 (w)	124 (m)/129 (w)	418	368	163	359	332	377	368	169	385	2939	337	399	525	344	348	171	377	486	118	3105	6044
PAR	4	4	3	4	4	4	4	3	4	34	4	4	5	4	4	3	4	5	3	36	70		
HCP			3	7	17	9	13	1	11	15	5		12	8	2	10	16	14	4	6	18		
RED	69.9	119	342	306	163	291	321	324	313	128	316	2504	296	337	462	308	313	130	326	460	80	2712	5216

approach behind a large fairway bunker about 50 yards in front of the putting surface, which appears to be greenside as you look at it from the fairway.

The par-three #8 is a longer, more difficult, and subtler hole than it appears from the tees. The green is uphill, and there is a precipitous drop-off to the left. The green itself is a wide, thin oval tucked behind a gaping bunker with a very steep face.

A long par four finishes the outward side. The hole gets tighter and tighter as you approach the green. A bunker about 60 yards in front and slightly right of the green compresses the fairway to the width of a handkerchief.

The back nine on the Old White Course features two par fives, two par threes and five par fours. The two par fours that start the side set the stage for the par-five #12, justifiably rated the second-toughest hole on the course. It's a dogleg right with a blind tee shot. A creek meanders into play about 150 yards from the green down the right rough. The hole plays around the corner, down the hill, and then back up to a slightly elevated green.

The par-four #16 may be the most interesting hole on the golf course both from a design perspective and from its visual impact. The hole can play to one of two widely separated greens. For either, the tee shot requires a long carry over a lake to a thin little fairway. The left green is across a wide stream, well protected by water, trees, and bunkers. The other green is well to the right of the landing area hidden by mounds, trees, and bunkers; in fact, you might not even know it's there. It is a treacherous hole if your tee shot strays.

The brilliant little par-three #18 plays across a stream. The clubhouse is perched on the hill overlooking the putting surface.

The green is uphill from the tees and requires a substantial carry across the water—the same stream that meanders through the golf course, the same stream across which the men tee off on the adjacent 1st hole. The highly contoured green demands precision putting, and the people enjoying a drink in Slammin' Sammy's bar far above see a lot more bogeys than birdies.

Greenbrier Course

This landmark of golf opened after two years of construction and development in 1924, becoming the second eighteen-hole golf course at The Greenbrier. The original designer was George O'Neil. Back then, as now, The Greenbrier was a playground retreat for the rich and famous. Big-name celebrities have long been lured to the place for seclusion and pampering. Some of the greatest names in golf were eager to sample the golf courses. The legendary Bobby Jones was among the first to play the new Greenbrier Course when it opened. Walter Hagen and Gene Sarazen staged matches there for the entertainment of the resort guests.

On May 16, 1959, resident pro Sam Snead shot a blistering 59 on the Greenbrier Course to set a pro record that stood until Notah Begay III matched it on May 15, 1998—almost thirty-nine years to the day later—at a Nike Tour event at the Dominion Club near Richmond, Virginia. When Snead registered his 59, Notah Begay III wasn't born, the Nike Tour didn't exist, and the Dominion Club was not built. David Duvall matched the 59 mark on the PGA Tour in early 1999.

In 1978 the venerable old Greenbrier Course underwent a major face-lift. Jack Nicklaus redesigned it for the 1979 Ryder

The view from the par-three #17 green, with the par-four #2 across the lake in the background on the Greenbrier Course, the site of the 1979 Ryder Cup.

Cup, in which the American team—led by such superstars as Lee Trevino, Lee Elder, Tom Watson, and Hale Irwin—defeated a British/European team that included such luminaries as Nick Faldo, Seve Ballesteros, Peter Oosterhuis, and Sandy Lyle. That series of matches brought the newly redesigned Greenbrier Course to the attention of the Senior PGA, which staged an annual event there from 1985 to 1987. In 1994 it was the site of the Solheim Cup, which featured top LPGA pros against their European counterparts.

While Jack Nicklaus golf courses tend to have certain distinct characteristics that are his trademark—including a construction process that often requires movement of millions of cubic feet of earth and the creation of copious man-made lakes—those are largely absent from Nicklaus's work at the Greenbrier Course. What Nicklaus lovingly and painstakingly created is a marvelous, old-fashioned-style golf course with the feel of a track designed by one of the classical architects such as Donald Ross, Alister MacKenzie, or A. C. Tillinghast.

The front side of the par-72 golf course is unique, featuring three par threes, three par fours, and three par fives. A pair of par fours set the stage. The lovely straight opener has a huge old tree to the left that

76

will block out any drive that fails to hug the right side of the fairway. The second is a pretty dogleg left with a lake that can come into play for tee shots that drift too far to the right. The lake then curls up to protect the right front of the long, narrow green.

Two of the three par fives on the front are reachable in two shots, but they are risk-reward holes and can also render par impossible in return for errant play. The short #8 is deceptively difficult. Your tee shot must clear a long, strategically placed fairway bunker along the right side of the hole. Your next shot must either clear or stay short of the L-shaped bunker that juts out into the fairway, almost intersecting it, about 50 yards from the putting surface.

All three par threes are tough. The 4th hole has a difficult two-tiered green. The 7th is in the neighborhood of 200 yards from the blue and white markers; the red tees face a 168-yard carry to the putting surface.

The long, bruising par-four #6—a dog-leg left that plays to a long, narrow green angled to the left and hooked behind an enormous bunker—is rated the toughest hole on the course. It is an extremely thin hole that requires your drive to hug the right side of the fairway in order to set up a successful approach.

The back nine begins with a beautiful golf hole, a short par four. A wide creek intersects the fairway about 50 yards in front of the pear-shaped, contoured green. The par fours are the strength of the back nine, a handful of unique, well-conceived golf holes that will challenge the skill of every player. The 14th, for example, is a fascinating little hole. While the bravest of the long-ball hitters might think about

trying to drive the green, unless you're going for it in one, something less than a driver is called for. Men must negotiate a gnarled old tree on their tee shot, and everybody must avoid the 100-plus-yard-long bunker in play down the left side of the fairway and wraps around the left side of the green. A second big bunker at front right closes and offsets the entrance to the green to the point that a high, soft approach will be required of almost everybody.

The short #14 is followed by a pair of anxiety-producing par fours. The 15th is long, with many of contours in the fairway and a huge green that features a tier in front and a tier in back divided by a little vale in the middle. The 16th is narrow off the tee and gets progressively narrower toward the green. A bunker to the left and a tongue of water to the right constrict the entrance to the highly contoured green.

The Greenbrier Course finishes with a long par five that plays uphill to an enormous undulating putting surface that is half of a double green shared with #18 on the Lakeside Course. It is a beautiful finishing hole that readily yields pars to players who keep their shots under control; it yields bogeys and worse to those who stray from the fairway or fail to get their approach shots close to the flag.

Some of the European players on the 1979 Ryder Cup team complained bitterly about the golf course, accusing Nicklaus of making it too difficult. Some visitors to the resort have similar complaints, but the majority of golfers—at least those in a highly unscientific sampling over drinks in the bar after my round—conclude that it is a superior golf course, possibly the best that Jack Nicklaus has ever designed.

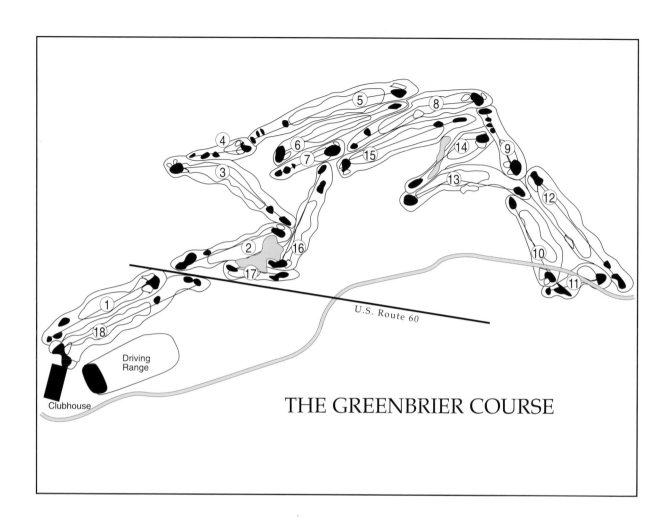

THE GREENBRIER COURSE

Greenbrier Course

HOLE	Ra	Sl	1	2	3	4	5	6	7	8	9	OUT	10	11	12	13	14	15	16	17	18	IN	TOT
BLUE	73.1	135	423	403	475	177	551	456	211	490	197	3383	339	176	510	404	305	438	406	160	560	3298	6681
WHITE	71.2 (m)/	76.3 (w)	368	388	462	166	527	441	194	474	158	3178	326	135	491	384	293	426	397	114	537	3133	6311
PAR			4	4	5	3	5	4	3	5	3	36	4	3	5	4	4	4	4	3	5	36	72
HCP			11	5	9	13	3	1	15	7	17		12	16	8	10	14	2	4	18	6		
RED	70.1	119	273	312	437	120	419	377	168	401	137	2644	292	102	408	323	211	302	303	123	442	2506	5150

Lakeside Course

The Greenbrier is home to a pair of world-class golf courses, but not every player who visits the resort is up to a steady diet of such arduous golf. In fact, one of the assistants noted that many guests—especially some of the older ones—find the other two courses a little too strenuous. For them, the Lakeside Course is perfect.

The original golf course at The Greenbrier opened in 1910, a short nine-hole layout that was incorporated, in part, into this lovely, if toned-down, golf course in a 1962 expansion and redesign. This course is not a grueling test of the sport, but it's a satisfying ego booster for good players, with plenty of birdie opportunities. It is a lovely course for the vacation golfer, the player who only picks up a club a few times a year, the high handicapper, or the senior player who doesn't necessarily want to leave the track panting and puffing.

While Lakeside is visually interesting, with abundant lakes and forests and the surrounding mountains, it presents few really menacing hazards or nuances of difficulty that distinguish the more difficult golf courses. The Lakeside Course is a mature, sedate, old-fashioned golf course with some design features reminiscent of Cherry Hills Country Club in Englewood, Colorado (another course President Dwight Eisenhower used to visit frequently). The greens on the Lakeside Course are relatively flat and

While the Lakeside Course is less daunting than the other two Greenbrier courses, the par-four #11, seen here, is no pushover.

open; the fairways are generous in most places; and even the trouble that presents itself, such as trees and hills, is scaled back.

The course plays to a par of 70, with only one par five on the outgoing side and three challenging par threes. The back side has two par fives and two par threes. The stream that meanders through the Old White Course is also an integral part of the Lakeside Course, although with a few exceptions it poses less severe challenges there. For example, the stream flows down the right side of the opening hole, a short par four, but it is so far to the right that it takes a really stray shot to find it.

Not so on the par-three #2, one of the tougher holes. The water is directly in front of the green, although there is ample bailout room to the right front. The water remains in play on the par-four #3, a medium-length dogleg left.

The 4th hole is the longest par five on the track, a double dogleg that is constricted by a big old tree at the point where the dogleg bends right. The hole opens generously, however, as it curves back to the left up near the green. It is rated the toughest hole on the course, a position it has earned.

The remaining two par threes on the front—the long #5 and the slightly shorter #7—are good tests of the game. In fact, at 172 yards from the red markers, #5 may play like a short par four for many women, although there is ample room to come up short and still have a makable up and down. One of the most interesting and demanding holes on the outgoing side is #8, a moderate-length par-four dogleg left. The fairway tightens on both sides at the bend in the dogleg and then plays uphill to the green. Your tee shot must stay well left of the right-side fairway bunker in order to open the elevated green for your approach.

The back side opens with a short par five that offers a good scoring opportunity. The hole plays slightly uphill to an elevated green. It's followed by a pair of pretty par fours. The long 11th is one of the tougher and tighter holes on the golf course. The green sits behind an indentation in the fairway and is well bunkered, especially to the front and right. The 12th is a sharp dogleg left with a blind tee shot. Your drive must avoid the bunker to the left. The green plays downhill from the landing area.

The 16th is a visually intimidating par four with as much real trouble as any hole on the course. Everybody tees off across water that arcs around the right side of the fairway and comes back into play on the right and left about 60 yards from the green. While there is a little neck of fairway over the stream, a bump-and-run shot is perilous. The far better shot is to fly the ball, high and soft, to the putting surface.

The 18th is a solid par-four finisher and one of the best holes on the golf course. Your tee shot is flat and straight, but it must stay to the right of the strategically placed fairway bunker. Your second shot is straight uphill to a huge, well-guarded green, half of the enormous double green that's a Siamese twin of the 18th green on the adjacent Greenbrier Course. The huge bunker to the left-front of the green is one of the biggest on the course and can provide an unpleasant finish for a pleasant round if you are unlucky enough to hit into it.

LAKESIDE COURSE

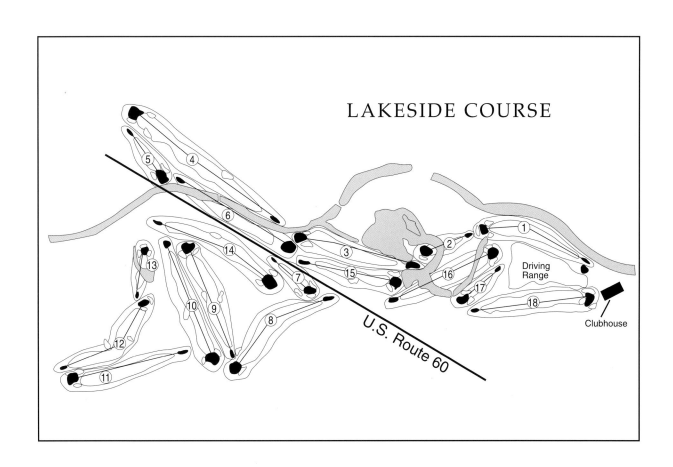

Lakeside Course

HOLE	Ra	Sl	1	2	3	4	5	6	7	8	9	OUT	10	11	12	13	14	15	16	17	18	IN	TOT
BLUE	69.8	122	353	188	394	579	198	430	173	387	389	3091	471	409	377	179	537	352	368	163	389	3245	6336
WHITE	68.5 (m)/74.6 (w)	119 (m)/127 (w)	332	174	378	569	187	416	160	376	383	2975	465	394	366	158	496	333	356	152	373	3093	6068
PAR			4	3	4	5	3	4	3	4	4	34	5	4	4	3	5	4	4	3	4	36	70
HCP			11	13	7	1	15	3	17	5	9		12	4	10	16	2	14	8	18	6		
RED	68.3	113	266	146	327	442	172	296	145	303	313	2410	423	319	292	128	437	322	263	133	293	2610	5020

Hanging Rock's treacherous 18th hole plays as a par three for most golfers, but it's a par four from the back markers. Either way, pars and birdies are rare.

HANGING ROCK GOLF CLUB

1500 Red Lane, Salem, Virginia (Take exit 140 from I-81; turn left onto Route 311 north
to the first left onto Mountain Heights Drive; first left onto Edgebrook Road.)
Phone: (800) 227-7497 or (703) 389-7275

Architect: Russell Breeden   Year opened: 1991

Course rating/Slope rating:
Black - 72.3/125   Gold - 69.0/115
White - 69.5/120   Red - 62.6/106

This golf course is an extremely popular with players from the Roanoke area and lures golfers from all over southwestern Virginia as well. Hanging Rock is a mountain course with panoramic views and an abundance of up- and downhill shots to test your skill. It's like a large number of courses in the Rockies on which a little local knowledge is extremely useful, especially with regard to the greens. "Everything breaks away from Fort Lewis Mountain," head pro Billy McBride cautioned. It is a good idea before you tee off to check with the pro shop or the starter to determine exactly which lofty peak is Fort Lewis Mountain.

Par on the course is either a 72 or 73 depending on whether you play the back markers—in which case #18 is a par four—or the forward markers—in which case it's a par three. For women it is a short course from the red markers, only 4,463 yards, but it's interesting and fair. Women whose handicaps are twenty or lower should consider playing the gold markers. The course won't leave the low-handicap men panting for breath, but from the back markers it is a fine test at more than 6,800 yards.

The design features three par fives on the front for a par of 37 on the outgoing side. And it should be noted that the par fives are all superior golf holes. The opener, for example, looks like a snap on the card until you realize that your tee shot is all carry across a lake, and then the hole plays severely uphill. To reach the green you must hit over a steep ridge that intersects the fairway.

"This is my favorite hole," said one-time NFL Tampa Bay punter Rob Collie, who has played Hanging Rock regularly since his days as a football star at nearby Virginia Tech. "I play here all the time, and I probably par this one as often as I par any of them. It's not that hard if you hit it long." Long is not a problem for him.

The short par-four #2, with a two-level green, demands pinpoint accuracy on your approach. "It makes all the difference in how you score," said Collie. "That green slopes back so steeply that if you're on in two and above the flag, I guarantee you'll bogey it."

The second par five on the front side, the 4th hole is a very solid dogleg left that plays downhill from elevated tees. A deep, grassy chasm intrudes into the fairway from about 150 yards away from the green, and while playing out of it is possible, it is not optimal and leaves a blind shot to the steeply uphill green.

Hanging Rock's signature hole, perhaps the most fascinating hole on the golf course, is the par-four 5th. I've played golf courses that have two greens on one hole—Hawthorne Valley (in West Virginia), the Old White Course at The Greenbrier, Ballybunion (in Ireland)—but I've not played one on which there's a pin on each putting surface and the player gets to chose the green. In this case the short hole tees off steeply downhill to a moderately cramped landing area with a lake that hugs the right side of the fairway and gobbles up a huge number of golf balls that drift left to right. On your second shot you must decide which green to play to—the one straight up the hill or the tiny one that's sharply to the right on a shelf out in the lake. That very thin green is only about ten yards wide at its narrowest point. "The easiest one is straight ahead and up the hill," said pro Billy McBride. "But you've got the option."

The 9th is the third par five on the side and the first of a pair of par fives. Nine is a double-dogleg, going right and then left, but it offers a good opportunity for low numbers in that it's easily reachable in two shots, even from the red markers if a woman hits two solid shots. The biggest difficulty is the well-protected green at the end of the second dogleg. The 10th is tight, a dogleg right. You drive from an elevated set of tee boxes. A creek intersects the fairway in front of the tees and then meanders down the entire left length of the hole. A steep hillside cants the fairway to the left and runs much of the length of the right side of the hole, constricting it both in perception and reality.

The 12th is a long par three over a depression in the terrain to a well-protected green. Thirteen is the easiest hole on the card, a cute little short par four that's slightly uphill and has enough perils to trip you up if you take it for granted.

One of the most interesting holes on the back nine is the par-four #14, a dogleg right. You drive downhill into a valley, a shot that simply must stay on the short grass. Your second shot is back uphill to an undulating, multilevel green. Placing your drive in the fairway is critical but not easy. The landing area is between a steep drop into a grassy gully to the left and a well-treed rocky hill to the right. The approach invariably requires a longer shot than it appears.

Hanging Rock is blessed with a large number of memorable holes, and #18 is among the most memorable. It is a very demanding par four from the back markers and is no pushover as a par three from the forward markers. The approach to the green is over a cliff and across a creek. The green is guarded by a towering, multitrunked pine tree that has a proclivity for reaching out and knocking down golf balls. Pro Billy McBride said the hole was redesigned as a par three for most players: "We had to do that because it's just too difficult for the average player" as a par-four. It is a lovely, if devilish, finisher.

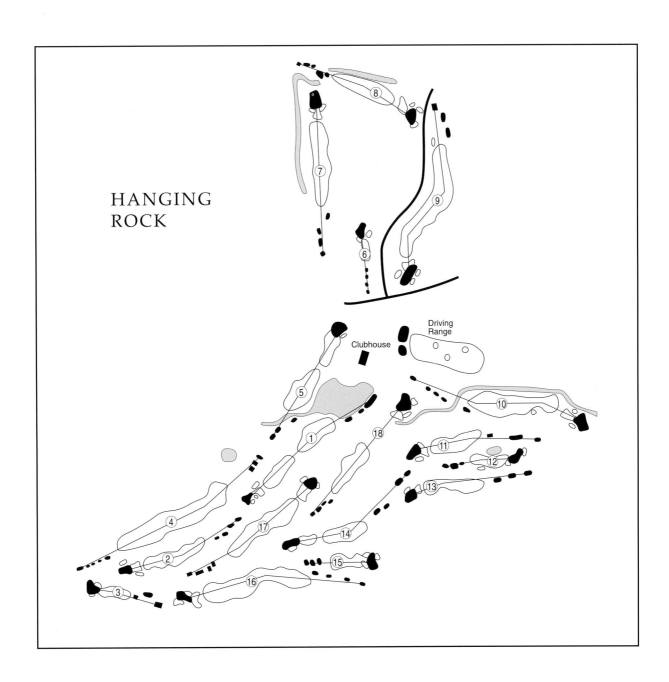

Hanging Rock

HOLE	Ra	Sl	1	2	3	4	5	6	7	8	9	OUT	10	11	12	13	14	15	16	17	18	IN	TOT
BLACK	72.3	125	500	367	195	551	392	166	434	318	521	3444	515	358	197	343	413	190	512	435	421	3384	6828
WHITE	69.5	120	464	339	160	517	369	147	400	291	466	3153	456	327	173	262	397	171	488	401	394/179	3069/2854	6222/6007
GOLD	69.0	115	436	311	148	495	295	128	363	238	425	2839	426	295	152	245	374	151	436	344	153	2576	5415
PAR (b)			5	4	3	5	4	3	4	4	5	37	5	4	3	4	4	3	5	4	4	36	73
PAR (f)			5	4	3	5	4	3	4	4	5	37	5	4	3	4	4	3	5	4	3	35	72
HCP (m)			9	11	7	13	3	17	1	15	5		14	16	8	18	2	10	12	4	6		
RED	62.6	106	373	272	120	434	228	98	304	208	333	2370	354	225	105	182	280	129	388	330	100	2093	4463
HCP (w)			1	7	13	3	11	17	9	15	5		10	16	14	18	6	12	4	8	2		

The par-three 3rd hole, with a vertical drop of about 75 feet from tee to green, typifies the way architect Gary Player has used the natural topography to enhance the character of Hawthorne Valley Golf Course.

HAWTHORNE VALLEY GOLF COURSE

Snowshoe Mountain, West Virginia (Take Route 219 south from Elkins for about 35 miles, turn left at sign to Snowshoe Ski Resort, and go about 1½ miles to the golf club entrance.)
Phone: (304) 572-1000

Architect: Gary Player   Year opened: 1994

Course rating/Slope rating:
Black - 74.9/139   White (men) - 69.6/124
Blue - 71.4/131   White (women) - 74.7/132
Red - 65.4/113

In the winter this is a popular ski area, but from the time that the spring thaw melts the snow and replaces the winter white with wildflowers, lush forests, and verdant fairways, this is home to a wonderful mountain golf course. In fact, the Hawthorne Valley Golf Course is one of the most visually spectacular courses in the country, as well as being a world-class golf venue. This is a must stop on the itinerary of any golfer who travels within a hundred miles of it. In fact, it is so good, so challenging, and such a fine experience that after you've played it once, you'll find excuses to return to the mountains of north-central West Virginia.

There really isn't a weak hole on the track; the greens are superb; and the design verges on brilliance, although Gary Player had considerable help from Mother Nature, who provided the basics for this layout. It can be argued that this is some of Mother Nature's finest work, and it certainly ranks among the best of Gary Player's creations as a golf-course architect.

From the first hole you are swept into a mountain milieu that is unparalleled outside of Colorado, Wyoming, or Montana. In fact, the ambiance is strikingly similar to what Vail was three decades ago, when Vail Village consisted of a few condos, a few restaurants, some mighty fine skiing, and only one tough golf course, which played out and back alongside Eagle Creek.

While the playing difficulty of Hawthorne Valley is unquestionable, Gary Player has designed a fair course that is a challenge for golfers of all levels (excluding the rankest beginners). There is a fine line between hard and traumatic; Player has masterfully stayed on the golfer's side of that line. The course features three sets of men's tees and two sets of markers for women, although at a rating and slope of 74.7/132, the white markers present a daunting test for female golfers. At the risk of contradicting the golfing world's powers that be, the rating and slope for the red markers are deceptive. For almost all women, the golf course is tough, even though it's about 2,600 yards shorter from the red tees than from the championship black markers. Women of all playing levels will find it

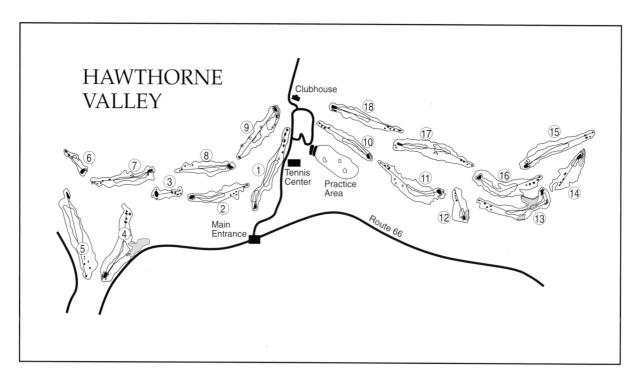

challenging and enjoyable, even though it can be physically and visually intimidating at times.

The fact is that very few players play from the black markers at all. "It's pristine back here," said Rob Mahan, a ski instructor during the winters at the Snowshoe Ski Resort and a champion amateur golfer. "There's not a single divot on this tee." He gestured around the championship tee box on the 1st hole. "And when you play from way back here, you find you're playing the holes from places nobody else has seen."

What Gary Player has done as an architect is to design a golf course he would enjoy as a player. The par fives are long and tight; the par fours are varied and require a large number of different shots to score; and the par threes are unique and fascinating holes. The test begins before you hit your first drive, staring down the long, narrow par-five 1st hole. Once off the tee, your second shot must either clear or stop just short of a split in the fairway. The fairway is intersected by a creek and an expanse of rocks and deep rough that also provides a drop in elevation to the second stretch of short grass, which is angled slightly right and plays to a small green caressed by a stand of trees.

The par-three #3 is a breathtaking hole that captures your eye and your imagination when you walk down to the tees. The tee boxes are shelved on the side of a cliff that looks down on tall trees, rocks, and a creek. You realize that your tee shot will launch your golf ball into the great beyond, a vertical drop of some 75 feet to a wide, thin, two-level green that is edged in front by a natural rock wall. It's a short iron for everybody, and success is entirely determined by club selection. Your shot must be long enough to clear the unforgiving wilderness that lies between the tees and the putting surface. At the same time, a shot that's too long risks being jailed on the steep incline behind the green among the towering trees, providing almost no way to recover.

If you thought you faced a launch into space on that hole, hold onto your hat on the next one. The tees on the par-four #4 are carved out of the side of a mountain. Your tee shot will face a vertical drop of some 200 feet before finding solid ground beside the creek bed that plays down the left side of the hole and at the foot of the hills to the right. Seven bunkers protect the green.

The 5th is the second-toughest hole on the course, a long par five made even longer by the fact that it plays uphill. The two-tiered green is hooked even more severely uphill to the right, and the base of the plateau on which the green sits is guarded by a creek and deep rough and the trees that constrict the entrance to the putting surface.

A trio of par fours wraps up the front side, with two monstrous holes sandwiching a short one. The 7th is a long hole, uphill from the tees and downhill to the green. It bends slightly to the left, with the well-protected green hooked even more severely left. Keep your tee shot right of center. The approach to this depressed green, which is slightly lower than the level of the fairway, is tricky. A rock retaining wall guards the right side of the green and, behind the right front greenside bunker, a huge old pine tree sits in a deep gulch.

The 9th is a spectacular short par four that tees off from a hillside. From the tees you are not hallucinating: you are indeed seeing two separate and distinct greens. One green is straight away; the other is hooked to the left beside the creek and above the front green. A sand trap separates the two putting surfaces, and if you land on the wrong one, it's a free drop. Golf champion Rob Mahan described Gary Player standing where the tee boxes are now during his design work and saying, "I see two greens out there." And so it came to pass. Your tee shot is a long carry over the creek to a generous landing area—generous at least by Player's demanding standard on Hawthorne.

There's not much of a breather between nines. The 10th hole, a solid par four, plays from elevated tee boxes to a fairway that descends on three separate terraces down to an awesomely bunkered green. Gary Player, who is one of the best sand players ever, decided to fill the hill that arcs around the left and rear of the green with eighteen separate sand traps. Still other bunkers wait below the green to the right. This is an extremely intimidating green to approach.

The 11th is the hardest hole on the golf course. It's a long par-four dogleg left that requires a long carry across a moonscape of mounds, moguls, rocks, and knee-deep grass to a highly contoured fairway that drops off to the left along most of its length. There's trouble right as well, including hills and mounds. A creek guards the front of the two-tiered green.

The 13th is one of the most interesting holes, among an abundance of interesting holes, on the back side. It's a par-five double dogleg that is reachable in two, with a well-placed tee shot to set it up. The fairway is constricted and divided by a lake at the extreme end of the landing area. To set up a shot to the green you need a long drive that stays right of center. If you go for it, it's all carry over the length of the lake, threading a needle between dense forest to the left and a stand of pines to the right. It's a risky shot through an extremely narrow entrance. If you can't reach the green in two, your lay-up second shot must be far enough to let you see the green behind the stand of pines.

The 14th is a long par three with water right and bunkers on three sides. Short is the only bailout area. From the red markers, however, it's only 82 yards and affords women an excellent scoring opportunity.

A pair of fine par fours and the shortest of the par fives on the golf course lead to the exceptional finisher. The 18th presents an intimidating tee shot across what the locals generously describe as a "natural area"—more like a wilderness—to a narrow landing zone lined with mounds on both sides. A little island has been built in the "natural area" for the red tee markers. The intimidation continues on your approach to the long, thin green, which is guarded by sand to the left and a sheer rock wall as tall as a building to the right. Whew!

Throughout the round, Gary Player's design will test your courage and ability, requiring you to employ every bit of your stamina, endurance, and creativity. And when you're finished, you'll be pondering what you'll do differently the next time you play it.

Hawthorne Valley

HOLE	Ra	Sl	1	2	3	4	5	6	7	8	9	OUT	10	11	12	13	14	15	16	17	18	IN	TOT
BLACK	74.9	139	557	399	127	433	611	163	420	363	359/329	3432/3402	396	445	200	548	202	453	417	516	436	3613	7045/7015
BLUE	71	4 131	524	371	113	420	515	127	399	341	297/257	3107/3067	367	400	176	497	181	392	400	482	395	3290	6397/6357
WHITE	69.6 (m)/74.7 (w)	124 (m)/132 (w)	484	312	100	418	511	105	385	333	239/199	2887/2847	342	370	161	474	162	388	370	450	372	3089	5976/5936
PAR			5	4	3	4	5	3	4	4	4	36	4	4	3	5	3	4	4	5	4	36	72
HCP			6	10	18	8	2	14	4	16	12		13	1	15	9	17	5	7	3	11		
RED	65.4	113	355	268	53	286	423	93	296	261	150/110	2185/2145	212	236	130	342	82	284	281	328	283		4363/4323

THE HOMESTEAD

Hot Springs, Virginia (Take Route 220 to the center of Hot Springs andlook for the landmark tower; The Old Course is right at the hotel; Cascades is about 3 miles south off 220; Lower Cascades is about 7 miles west off Route 615.)
Phone: (800) 838-1766 or (540) 834-7740

The Old Course architect: Donald Ross   Year opened: 1892
Cascades architect: William Flynn   Year opened: 1923
Lower Cascades architect: Robert Trent Jones Sr.   Year opened: 1963

The Old Course rating/Slope rating:
Blue - 69.7/120   White - 67.9/115
Red - 67.7/116

Cascades rating/Slope rating:
Blue - 72.9/136   White - 71.6/134
Red - 70.3/124

Lower Cascades rating/Slope rating:
Blue - 72.2/127   White - 70.4/124
Red - 66.2/110

The history of golf in America and the history of The Homestead merged as the nineteenth century was about to yield to the twentieth. The first six-hole golf course at the hotel was unveiled for the amusement of hotel guests in 1892, the same year that the spa and the first tennis court were opened.

The original Homestead was built a decade before the American Revolution, in 1766, and underwent a series of peaks and valleys through the War of 1812, the Civil War, and into the late 1800s. In 1891 major stockholders of the Chesapeake and Ohio Railway Company bought the hotel and its land and, not surprisingly, a year later the C&O began passenger service into Hot Springs, Virginia, opening the town and the resort to the outside world as never before.

The golf courses of The Homestead have been touted around the world since the Roaring Twenties, when the sport enjoyed fad status among the wealthy elite and those who aspired to be like them. The 1928 U.S. Women's Amateur Championship was played at the Cascades. Sixty years later the nearby Lower Cascades was a qualifying course for the U.S. Men's Amateur Championship.

In 1998 the resort changed the names of two of its golf courses. Lower Cascades remains just that, but the course that for three and a half decades was known as Upper Cascades is now back to its original name: Cascades. The venerable Donald Ross masterpiece, long officially called The Homestead Course, is now just The Old Course. "That's what everybody called it anyway," said Paula Hank, the resort's publicist.

The view from the green back down the par-five 3rd hole, with the par-three #16 in the background, on Donald Ross's magnificent Old Course at the Homestead.

The Old Course

When you play a Donald Ross golf course, you will invariably encounter little bits and pieces of Royal Dornoch, the course at the northern reaches of Scotland on which Ross grew up, learned the game, and served as pro and groundskeeper. Even though Ross left his native land, that golf course was as much a part of him as his burr or his beard and, as such, he made its characteristics his trademarks. You see it at Pinehurst No. 2, the Detroit Country Club, and St. Augustine's Ponce de Leon Resort Course; you feel it at every course designed by the venerable Scot. You experience the plateau or turtleback greens, the tiered putting surfaces, the uneven fairways, and the rough-covered hills.

The Homestead's Old Course was one of Donald Ross's first major American projects. He was commissioned in 1913 to convert the six-hole golf course at the Hot Springs, Virginia, hotel to a regulation eighteen. He did it with a crew of men and an earthmover pulled by horses. In what turned out to be a gesture of historic proportions, he kept the original first tee, as did Rees Jones, who was brought in to update the Old Course and modernize it. That tee, which was first used in 1892, is the oldest tee box in continuous use in the United States.

Rees Jones, who has earned the reputation as one of the country's premier golf-course renovators, left most of Donald Ross's features intact, including his tiny, often-elevated greens and the open, old-fashioned feel of the place. Jones added a few bunkers, reshaped a couple of greens, and moved the 18th hole. The par-72 track's design is unusual in that it features an equal number of par threes, par fours, and par fives—a half-dozen of each. One

thing Rees Jones did not change was the visual image of Royal Dornoch's plateau greens. While there are a lot of sand traps, not every green is tightly bunkered; nonetheless, the notion of a pitch-and-run or bump-and-run approach is less rewarded here than soft, high chips that land on the putting surface and hold. These greens favor a good, precise short game.

It is the easiest of The Homestead's three golf courses, and low-handicap men will want to consider playing the back tees. But what it lacks in length and difficulty, it more than compensates for with charm.

The round begins, as noted, from the oldest tee in continuous use in America, where the first golf ball was struck in 1892. Every drive takes its place as a little piece of U.S. golf history. There is nothing tricky about the hole. What you see is what you get: a straight, long, and tight par-five with an uphill green. The tree-lined fairway and the distant mountains make for a lovely setting from which to commence play. The opener is rated the toughest hole on the card.

The second par five of the side, the short #3, plays into a little valley and then back uphill to the green. This one is reachable in two even for medium-length hitters. The 4th completes the par fives on the outgoing side; it's the second of back-to-back par fives and is an interesting golf hole. It's reachable in two, but that may not be the smart play. A drive that's too long can find itself on the downslope of a severe drop that divides the fairway. Put your tee shot at the target pole, lay up inside 100 yards from the green, and then face a short, uphill chip that you can land softly. That seems to be the formula for birdies here.

The 5th hole, the second par three of the

side, plays to a tiny, inverted pear-shaped green squeezed in front by a pair of bunkers, the right one being especially nasty.

A trio of short par fours follows. The 6th tees off down a hill, leaving a touchy approach that's steeply uphill to a well-protected, nearly domed green that sits on a hillside and that is hooked behind a cluster of deep bunkers. The 8th fairway is highly contoured and provides one of the bigger greens on the course. Like the natural terrain of the hilly fairway, the green is one of the most contoured on The Old Course, clearly an echo of Royal Dornoch.

A short par three finishes the side and sets the stage for the gentle beginning of the back nine. But get ready for a test on #12 and #13. Walk away with two pars on these two back-to-back par fives and you've played well. The long #12 is a dog-leg right downhill from the tee and then back uphill from about the turn of the dogleg to the green. Thirteen is the longest par five on the card, it's a three-shot hole for everybody but maybe Ernie Els or Vijay Singh. Your severely downhill tee shot has to be kept left of the big, leafy old tree that guards the right side of the fairway and marks the bend in the slight dogleg.

The three finishing holes are delightful. The pleasant par-three #16 is longer than its yardage would indicate because it is an uphill shot. The short par-four #17 is a severe dogleg right that tees off over a grassy gulch. Think about something other than a driver here. Even a long iron will leave most players with a wedge or nine iron to the flag. The green is hooked behind a big bunker and against a stand of trees. The final hole is the newest one on the course and is also among the prettiest. It's a downhill par three that can yield birdies and give you a fine finish.

The Old Course at The Homestead is a far cry from the sandy, windswept linksland of northern Scotland. The ocean is hundreds of miles away, and gorse and heather are nowhere to be found. But when you play it you still, somehow, seem to hear the distant skirl of bagpipes and the smell of peat smoke that are vestiges of Royal Dornoch and the man who carried that special place with him from the Old World to the New.

THE OLD COURSE

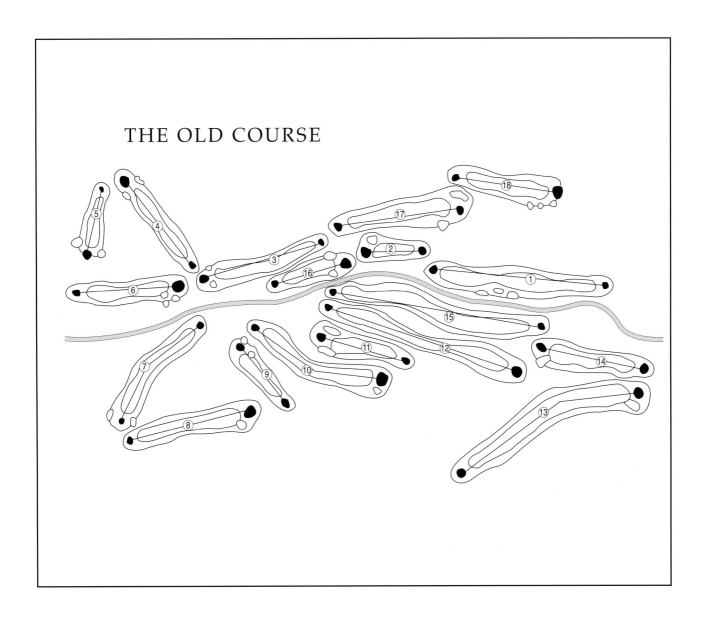

The Old Course

HOLE NUMBER	Ra	Sl	1	2	3	4	5	6	7	8	9	OUT	10	11	12	13	14	15	16	17	18	IN	TOT
BLUE	69.7	120	519	153	465	473	163	383	329	323	147	2955	381	199	544	581	355	502	169	354	171	3256	6211
WHITE	67.9	115	506	142	419	458	148	366	313	289	131	2772	352	172	512	555	333	478	152	316	154	3024	5796
PAR			5	3	5	5	3	4	4	4	3	36	4	3	5	5	4	5	3	4	3	36	72
HANDICAP			1	15	5	3	13	7	9	11	17		8	14	4	2	10	6	18	12	16		
RED	67.7	116	414	127	400	404	137	314	275	259	100	2430	329	154	411	432	215	365	97	290	129	2422	4852

The approach to the brilliant par-five #17 at Cascades must avoid Cascades Creek, which winds its way throughout and imparts character to one of the world's finest golf courses.

Cascades

HOLE	Ra	Sl	1	2	3	4	5	6	7	8	9	OUT	10	11	12	13	14	15	16	17	18	IN	TOT
BLUE	72.9	136	394	430	283	208	576	369	425	151	450	3286	375	191	476	438	427	222	525	515	204	3373	6659
WHITE	71.6	134	381	403	278	190	550	362	416	136	425	3141	366	172	434	408	396	213	488	480	178	3135	6276
PAR (m)			4	4	4	3	5	4	4	3	4	35	4	3	4	4	4	3	5	5	3	35	70
HCP (m)			9	3	13	15	1	11	7	17	5		12	16	4	10	8	14	2	6	18		
RED	70.3	124	286	296	272	166	469	309	330	114	275	2517	279	147	367	358	317	132	409	358	157	2524	5041
PAR (w)			4	4	4	3	5	4	5	3	4	36	4	3	4	4	4	3	5	4	3	34	70
HCP (w)			5	3	15	7	1	9	11	17	13		12	18	6	8	10	14	2	4	16		

Cascades

This legendary and much-chronicled golf course far surpasses its press clippings. Everybody ranks it in their listing of the best golf courses, including *Golf Magazine* and *Golf Digest,* to name but a pair of major publications. The fact is that it is nearly impossible to name a better golf course anywhere, and that includes such golfing supernovas as Augusta, Pebble Beach, and St. Andrews. It is the kind of golf course that you will remember as long as you play the game. It defies superlatives because every element of it is so outstanding and fundamentally sound, from its setting to its design to its underlying fairness to the demands it imposes on every player of every playing level. But even that doesn't cover it.

Major golf tournaments have been held at The Cascades from the 1920s on. The Cascades hosted the U.S. Women's Amateur in 1928, the U.S. Men's Amateur in 1988, and the Merrill Lynch Senior PGA Shoot-Out in 1995. Lanny Wadkins, the resort's PGA touring pro, won the 1970 Virginia State Golf Association Championship at The Cascades. And that's just a fraction of the story.

What William Flynn created in 1923 is a masterpiece of the game of golf. It has earned him a place among the greatest architects the game has known, designers such as Dr. Alister MacKenzie, A. C. Tillinghast, Harry Colt, and Donald Ross. On one hand, it is a difficult and demanding challenge that requires skilled shot making, intense concentration, and course management to shoot to your handicap; but on the other hand, it is brilliantly designed, rewards skilled execution, and is extremely fair and playable for all golfers beyond the ranks of the merest beginners.

For women, it is an extraordinary golf course: exquisitely designed, tough and challenging, but fair. While some holes have a little different look from the forward markers, there is not a single instance in which women receive anything less than William Flynn's full consideration and respect. This in itself is highly unusual, because in the 1920s many courses did not even allow women to play. Women were a designer's afterthought, with the red markers often plunked down anywhere there was a bit of flat ground a few yards ahead of the men's tee box. On Cascades every tee is a work of art, every nuance has been considered, and for every player, male and female, each shot is critical and can make the difference between reward or rejection.

As a player, it is a rare treat to have such a complete and fulfilling golf experience. From the lovely opening par four to the long, pretty par-three finisher, this is golf at its very best, offering a rare degree of maturity and depth.

Lee Peery, starter and caddymaster, grew up on Cascades. His uncle was the pro for forty-three years; his father was the caddymaster before him. "This is not a tricky course. It's just sort of there. You just have to hit good shots," he said. "You hit a good drive, good second, knock it on the green, and you'll be looking at birdie. Looking at the card, it doesn't look hard. It's not all that long. Only par 70. We got five par threes and only three par fives. But it's great golf holes with lots of variety." He speaks of the golf course like it's a favored member of the family. "There's not a boring hole on the course. You've got to start thinking when you tee it up, and you don't let up until you walk off #18. It's got a shot for every club, and there's some you probably don't have a club for."

Lee Peery has seen thousands of golfers come and go, including some of the biggest names in the game. He walked around with some of the pros during the 1995 Senior PGA Shoot-Out. "Bob Murphy told me that these are the best greens he's ever putted on anywhere," he said. Murphy also could have noted that the fairways are superb, the rough is long but playable, the sand is uniform and well maintained, and the tees are in wonderful condition.

This magnificent golf course opens with a trio of par fours. The 2nd is incredibly tight, with the fairway sloped severely left to right. The tiny par-four #3, less than 290 yards from the back tees, is a dogleg right that plays uphill. Almost nobody hits a driver. The fairway ends about 90 yards in front of the green and dips into a grassy ravine. The putting surface is guarded by trees to the left and a big bunker to the right, with virtually no bailout room. The best option is to leave yourself about a 100-yard shot to the pin.

The 4th is a long, stunning par three with a severe elevation change. The tees are on a hill above the green. Club selection is critical. Men and women have the same look at the hole. That's followed by the brilliantly designed long par-five #5, a three-shot hole for virtually everybody, except maybe Tiger Woods or Laura Davies. It's rated the toughest hole on the course. Your drive is across a creek, uphill to the point at which the fairway divides and turns right; across the division is another hilltop, and then your approach is to a green that sits at the base of the second hill.

A pair of lovely par fours—the short #6, on which a long iron or fairway wood will put you at about the 100-yard marker, and the long #7, which plays downhill and then back up to a green perched on a shelf on a hillside—sets the stage for the short par-three #8, ominously named "Cemetery Ridge." It's a downhill tee shot to a green that is strangled by two big bunkers in the front. The outgoing #9 finishes with a long par four that tees off across a brushy waste area loaded with trees and bushes and rocks and inhospitable stuff. The green is fairly open and receptive in front either to a high, soft approach or one that runs up to the flag.

The back side opens with a short par-four dogleg. It's a blind tee shot presenting the distinct possibility of hitting through the fairway. The fairway drops away to one plateau between 150 and 100 yards out and then plays down to yet a second plateau, where the domed putting surface surrounded by bunkers sits. Three more fabulous par fours follow the long par-three #11. On #12, three big bunkers intersect the fairway about 100 yards from the green. A creek plays along the left length of #13, with bunkers dividing the fairway diagonally to create the left dogleg.

The four finishers are simply magnificent. Two par threes bracket a pair of back-to-back par fives. The one-shot #15 is very long—more than 200 yards for everybody—and tees off from a chute of pine trees. "We take bets on who's going to make it and who isn't," said a maintenance worker pruning bushes nearby. "More miss it short than not."

The 16th is an awesome double-dogleg par five, with the landing area for your tee shot guarded by a cluster of fairway bunkers and the green hooked to the left into a stand of trees and behind a pond created from a dammed-up bit of the stream. The 17th features a blind tee shot to a dogleg left with trees tight left and a stream to the right. The green is tucked behind a series of pools to the right and guarded by a bunker at left. A series of cascades splash from pool to pool, and while it's visually glorious, the number of golf balls that look back from the clear water testifies to the number of shots that stray into the hazard.

Cascades finishes with a lovely but long par three. You drive across a pond from hillside tees to hillside green.

Little can be added in mere words to one of the great golfing experiences in the world. The entire golf course transcends being merely memorable. To pick one hole, one feature, is simply impossible. If golf were religion, The Cascades would be a sacred experience. If it were a theater, it would be The Old Vic. It is akin to having heard the Beatles or Elvis in person, having been present at the fall of the Berlin Wall. It is a golf course you will find yourself thinking about long after you have played it for the first time. If you are fortunate to play it more than once, it will become a part of you, a part of your golfing psyche. You'll compare other courses to it, and like an old friend, you will find yourself contemplating when you will see it again, experience it again.

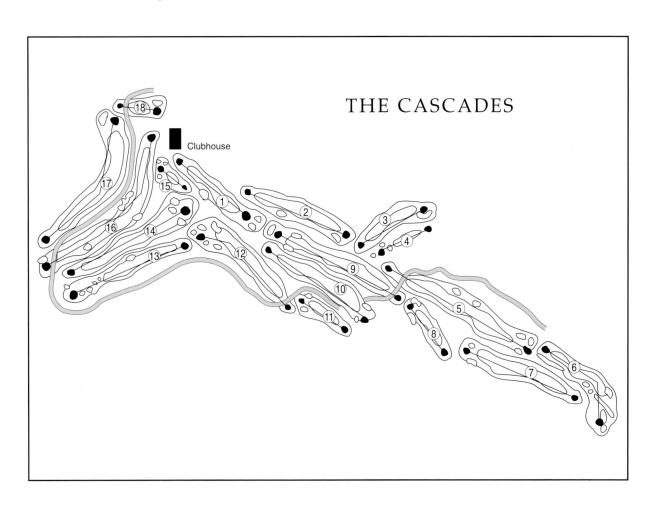

THE CASCADES

Clubhouse

The 18th green on The Homestead's Lower Cascades is pinched at its entrance by towering ancient trees.

Lower Cascades

Since he wasn't around to ask, there's no way to verify the claim, but one of the local members declared with an air of certainty, "This is Sam Snead's favorite course. He plays here all the time." Snead, who has maintained his family farm only a few miles from Hot Springs all his life, was the pro at The Homestead in the 1930s before being hired away by The Greenbrier only a few miles away at White Sulphur Springs, West Virginia. Always with his signature straw hat, Snead is still a frequent guest at the tavern in Hot Springs that bears his name.

While the Lower Cascades does not quite rise to the sublime level of its more chronicled and famous sibling, it is a fine golf course that is often and unfortunately overlooked because of its proximity to Cascades, about ten miles away. Cascades Stream meanders throughout the course. It has typical Robert Trent Jones Sr. greens—moderate in size and fraught with subtle and not-so-subtle breaks, bends, and contours. The four par-three holes form a very good test demanding a smorgasbord of shots; the par fives generally play tougher for women than for men, but there are those who suggest that Robert Trent Jones Sr. did not have much use for women on golf courses at all and thus did not go very far out of his way to make his layouts very easy for them. The par threes range in length from moderate to long.

Lower Cascades opens with a short par four. There's a steep elevation change from the tees to the landing area, and the ideal tee shot is just to the left of the big fairway bunkers that mark the bend in the dogleg. The short par-five #2 is the toughest hole on the course for women.

It's a dogleg right that then plays back to a green that's hooked behind two bunkers to the left and guarded by two more to the right. The toughest hole for men, the solid par-four #4 with a dogleg to the right, plays down into a little valley and then back up to an elevated green. The green itself is tucked behind a steep indentation that wedges in front of the putting surface from about 65 yards out and mandates a high, soft approach to hold the wide, thin green.

A pair of splendid par fours follows the long par-three #4. The short #5 presents a blind tee shot for men—women can see the flag—to a very tight fairway for everybody. The hole narrows the closer you get to the green. The long par-four #6 is a slight dogleg left with a blind tee shot. Two fairway bunkers form a bottleneck and tighten the fairway, which then remains ribbon-thin all the way to the putting surface.

The 7th, a short par five that doglegs around a pond, is reachable in two, although unless you hit your drive far enough to open the green, you have to carry a big, deep bunker that sits between the putting surface and the water. The 8th is a splendid par three that tees off across the creek and plays uphill to a well-bunkered green. That leads to the closing hole of the side, a par four with a tee shot that plays uphill. The fairway is intersected diagonally by a grassy ridge that presents you with a steep change in elevation on your approach to the green and sets up a visually spectacular, if distracting, panoramic view of the distant mountains.

The second nine opens with a short par-four with the unique feature of two separate greens: one is fairly straight, the other is tucked behind it, hooked up a hill and into a stand of trees to the left. Your tee shot is critical for the approach and must stay to the right of the marker post in the middle of the fairway. The lower green is two-tiered, with the left tier much higher than the right; the second green is a postage stamp that is extremely hard to hit.

On #12, elevated tees reveal the landing area on this double-dogleg par five. A ridge divides the fairway about 150 yards from the green. Your tee shot needs to stay clear of the fairway bunkers on the right, and your second needs to hug the left side of the fairway in order to open up the green. The 14th is a lovely par three that plays across Cascades Stream to a long, undulating green that is pinched at the front by a pair of gaping bunkers.

Robert Trent Jones Sr. likes to put at least one very long par five on virtually every one of his golf courses. The 15th is it on Lower Cascades, 544 yards from the tips, 524 yards from the white tees, and 413 yards from the reds. Your tee shot must thread its way between fairway bunkers to a contoured fairway. Your second shot must come up short of the creek that lurks in front of the green. The penultimate hole is a tough par three that plays uphill. It's deceptive in that it plays longer than it looks and requires your tee shot to carry the bunker that sits directly in front of the green.

Lower Cascades finishes with a lovely par-four dogleg left, with men getting the better view from their hilltop tee box. Women tee off down the hill. The stream is in play down the left side of the fairway and then intersects the fairway at the dogleg. It is very tight as you near the elevated green, which is nestled back among trees and protected by a pair of bunkers. Your tee shot must be just about dead center looking straight in at the flag or you'll find yourself blocked by trees to the right or by one gnarled, leafy old tree that canopies over the left front of the putting surface.

Robert Trent Jones Sr.'s golf courses can usually be defined in varying degrees of goodness. In fact, there are few of his designs that don't rise to that level and many that are superior. Lower Cascades is a very pleasant, very challenging, and picturesque golf course worthy of a return trip even if it were not part of The Homestead's family of exceptional golf courses.

THE LOWER CASCADES

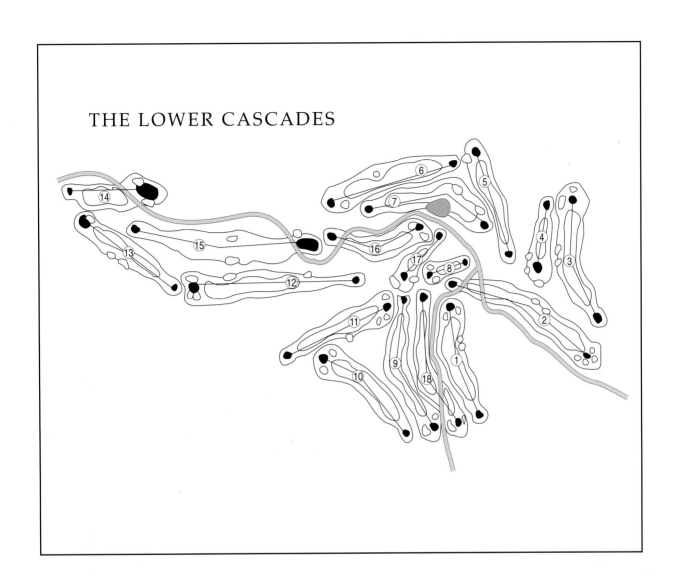

Lower Cascades

HOLE NUMBER	Ra	Sl	1	2	3	4	5	6	7	8	9	OUT	10	11	12	13	14	15	16	17	18	IN	TOT
BLUE	72.2	127	348	527	450	202	351	415	493	161	413	3360	317	358	533	386	172	544	357	173	379	3219	6579
WHITE	70.4	124	332	479	388	172	344	405	480	153	400	3153	299	352	484	375	157	524	332	161	363	3047	6200
PAR (m)			4	5	4	3	4	4	5	3	4	36	4	4	5	4	3	5	4	3	4	36	72
HANDICAP (m)			13	3	1	15	11	7	5	17	9		12	14	4	8	18	2	10	16	6		
RED	66.2	110	223	404	261	116	235	304	367	146	322	2378	191	311	364	253	92	413	313	102	269	2308	4686
PAR (w)			4	5	4	3	4	4	4	3	4	35	4	4	4	4	3	5	4	3	4	35	70
HANDICAP (w)			13	1	9	17	11	7	3	15	5		14	6	4	12	18	2	8	16	10		

The view from Kiln Creek's 7th green at the long, tough par-four #8, which plays around the lake to a well-protected green.

KILN CREEK GOLF AND COUNTRY CLUB

1003 Brick Kiln Blvd., Newport News, Virginia (From I-64, take exit 61B, Jefferson Avenue, east to the first traffic light; turn right onto Brick Kiln Blvd.)
Phone: (804) 874-0526

Architect: Tom Clark   Year opened: 1990

Course rating/Slope rating:
Gold - 73.4/130   White - 68.8/121
Blue - 70.4/125   Red - 69.5/119

Once upon a time, the tract of land on which Kiln Creek is built was scarcely fit for anything. It was a scrubby, swampy piece of real estate about a driver and a three wood from I-64 and about two par fives and a long par four from Newport News Airport. But an inhospitable piece of land in the hands of a superior golf-course architect such as Tom Clark can be transformed, almost magically, into a lovely and challenging golf course. That's what happened in the case of Kiln Creek.

Naturally, the magic is performed by earthmoving machinery and is completed only with backbreaking effort. Construction of Kiln Creek was an exercise in reshaping the landscape. Clark used skill, know-how, and imagination to replace much of what nature put there with eighteen holes of championship golf and another mostly unused nine holes for good measure. Transforming the flat wetland, Clark created most of the visual contours by moving more than three million cubic yards of dirt, trucking in more than twelve thousand tons of sand, and shaping, sculpting, and molding thirteen lakes at strategic points. Kiln Creek looks and plays like a maturer golf course than its years would suggest.

The course presents an aesthetically pleasing yet sporting experience for players of every caliber. It is an especially fine test for women, with the forward tee placement carefully considered for both fairness and playability. It's a very solid track measuring just over 5,300 yards from the red markers and will provide great satisfaction for women who play it to their handicaps. Two of the par fives are in the 450-yard range, which is long for women; the par fours offer a good variety both in terms of shot selection and course management; and the par-threes are all fair and challenging.

In general, the greens are moderate in size and relatively flat, though many contain subtle breaks and contours. Clark is not a proponent of bump-and-run approaches to greens, and almost all of his greens are encumbered in front by bunkers, mounds, and water, requiring a skilled short game for successful scoring. The fairways are narrow. The rough is kept fairly short. And bring plenty of golf balls—there's water in play to one degree or another on seven holes.

If there is a single standout architectural characteristic of Kiln Creek that lingers in the memory long after you've finished

KILN CREEK GOLF & COUNTRY CLUB

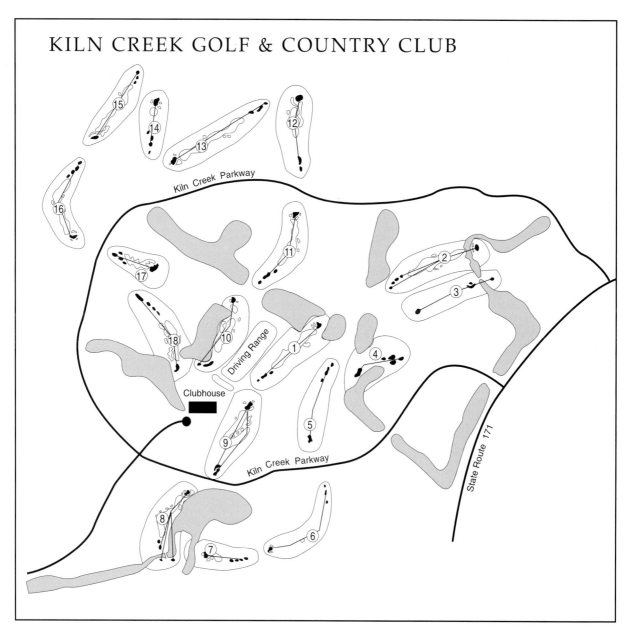

playing the golf course, it is Tom Clark's innovative use of gigantic bunkers. It is the type of bunkering one sees in the southwestern desert on courses around Phoenix, Palm Springs, or San Antonio. While Southwestern-style bunkers are something of an oxymoron in Virginia's tidewater, they are a refreshing surprise at the heart of this golf course. On the 6th hole, for example, Clark has created a Saharan monster that measures about 150 yards

long; on the 12th hole he has placed a Y-shaped bunker that is both a fairway and greenside sand trap, in play from 150 yards out and arching around the front half of the green; on the 15th hole he has constructed a sand trap that runs across the fairway; on the par-three 17th your entire tee shot is a carry over sand.

The par threes on Kiln Creek are all moderate in length, with the exception of #14, which plays 223 yards from the back markers. Unlike some designers who have no sympathy for golfers playing the one-shot holes, Clark provides at least a modicum of bailout room on all four par-three holes, even #4, which requires a substantial carry over water to get close to the pin.

The par fives are an interesting mix. Two are reachable in two for long hitters. The second requires a drive to the crest of a hill, with the serious decision making on your second shot. If you lay it up, you must come to rest short of the lake in front of the green; if you decide to gamble and go for it and come up short, you're wet. The 6th is a long, tough piece of work. An enormous bunker measuring 150 yards in length guards the right side of the fairway and sets up both a physical barrier and an element of optical intimidation. How much of that bunker you opt to carry on your drive depends on your physical ability and your mental confidence. Almost everybody except the shortest hitters (who will bail out to the left) will carry at least some of it. The short par five offers a good scoring opportunity for men and women who can hit long and straight. It's a good risk-reward hole, with abundant sand traps scattered all over to catch stray golf balls.

The strength of Kiln Creek rests on the par fours and their rich variation, both in length and in what they require of the golfer's course-management skills. The opening hole is moderately long and straight, playing to a slightly elevated, well-protected green. The 3rd hole, the toughest on the course for women, is a relentlessly uphill test. Unseen from the tee boxes is a deep indentation that bites into the left side of the fairway about 150 yards from the green. An approach shot that lands short or left a can leave you

with a difficult, blind uphill recovery shot and render par nearly impossible. The moderate-length, dogleg-left #5 is a tight hole that demands a long, precise tee shot. It must primarily avoid the enormous bunker to the left, which measures more than 80 yards from nose to tail. At the same time, your drive must also stay clear of the series of lofty hills to the right that leave you little stance and less of a shot if your ball hangs up in the long grass.

The front side finishes with a pair of splendid par fours, especially the 8th hole. This long and challenging dogleg right is the number-one handicap hole for men. The lake across which you drive from the back tees is dangerously in play down the right length of the hole. The hole features two of Tom Clark's signature big bunkers along the right as well—one adjacent to where your drive should land, the other wrapping around the right side of the green. Near the green the fairway is pinched by a pair of sand traps from about 100 yards out. The 9th is an interesting short hole with a series of bunkers splitting the fairway. The decision is whether to tee off with a five wood or four iron to the right or to try to position a longer tee shot along the ribbon of fairway to the left.

The back side opens with a trio of very solid, demanding par fours. The 12th is fraught with trouble the closer to the green you get. It features another of Tom Clark's giant sand traps—this one a Y-shaped critter that lurks to the right of the fairway and then extends all the way around the turtleback green. It is justifiably rated the second-toughest hole for women. The 16th, a long dogleg right, is considered the second-toughest hole on the course for men. Big hitters can think of cutting the dogleg, over a small stand of trees and the first two fairway bunkers to the left, but the perils are severe if the shot is less than perfect. Most players will want to position their tee shot between the right and left bunkers visible from the tee boxes. The approach plays to a slightly elevated green.

Kiln Creek finishes on a spectacular note. The 18th, the last of Tom Clark's well-designed par fours, is a dogleg right that is tightly constricted by sand and water from the landing area to the green. There's water to the left and water to the right. An 80-yard-long bunker guards the right from about 160 yards out, and five greenside sand traps are waiting to catch shots that don't find the small, irregularly shaped green.

This is a fine and satisfying golf course, superbly designed and well maintained. It is well worth a detour if you're in the Williamsburg or Virginia Beach area. While they are only irregularly in use, Kiln Creek has an additional nine holes with many of the same characteristics as Clark's other eighteen.

Kiln Creek

HOLE NUMBER	Ra	Sl	1	2	3	4	5	6	7	8	9	OUT	10	11	12	13	14	15	16	17	18	IN	TOT
GOLD	73.4	130	414	513	452	178	391	552	194	416	322	3432	359	413	369	536	223	469	459	159	469	3456	6888
BLUE	70.4	125	384	473	344	151	362	518	158	418	308	3116	345	370	360	500	202	457	426	150	431	3241	6357
WHITE	68.8	121	368	430	328	147	349	502	140	354	303	2921	326	345	335	484	173	432	388	137	356	2976	5897
HANDICAP (m)			7	9	11	13	5	3	15	1	17		14	10	12	6	8	16	2	18	4		
PAR			4	5	4	3	4	5	3	4	4	36	4	4	4	5	3	5	4	3	4	36	72
RED	69.5	119	338	365	317	117	298	467	108	314	292	2616	303	306	321	445	133	385	352	119	336	2700	5316
HANDICAP (w)			7	9	1	11	13	5	17	3	15		8	10	2	12	16	14	4	18	6		

KINGSMILL RESORT

1010 Kingsmill Road, Williamsburg, Virginia (From I-64, take exit 242A; follow Route 199 for about 2 miles; turn left at the first traffic light, the entrance to the Kingsmill complex.)
Phone: (757) 253-3906

River Course architect: Pete Dye   Year opened: 1975
Plantation Course architect: Arnold Palmer   Year opened: 1986
Woods Course architect: Tom Clark   Year opened: 1995

River Course rating/Slope rating:
Gold - 73.3/137   White - 65.3/120
Blue - 69.7/129   Red - 67.5/116

Plantation Course rating/Slope rating:
Gold - 71.3/119   White - 66.1/107
Blue - 68.9/114   Red - 67.9/116

Woods Course rating/Slope rating:
Gold - 72.7/131   White - 69.0/121
Blue - 70.9/126   Red - 68.7/120

In 1736 an English colonist named Richard Kingsmill built a plantation on approximately three thousand acres along the banks of the James River, only about three miles from the bustling city of Williamsburg. That active James River landing also served as a port for the colonial capital and the surrounding area. It was a strategic outpost during the Revolutionary War and again for the Confederacy during the Civil War. With golf in those days largely the pastime of highland shepherds back in the British Isles, it's doubtful Richard Kingsmill could have envisioned what his place would become.

What it has become is one of the country's finest, foremost golf facilities, a complex with something for absolutely every golfer of every level and even for those family members who might be along for the ride but who don't play golf. For golfers in the Williamsburg or Virginia Tidewater area, it's a *must*.

The River Course was the first eighteen holes of Kingsmill to open. Designed from the beginning to be a championship golf course, it has been wildly successful in achieving that goal. Since 1975, golf lovers worldwide have become familiar with it and have watched it grow to be one of Pete Dye's most famous courses. It's home to the PGA Tour's Michelob Championship, but it's also accessible to the average player wanting to imagine what it must be like to play before a cheering gallery for hundreds of thousands of dollars—in a place where it actually happens. Arnold Palmer's pleasant but comparatively easy Plantation Course is the most golfer-friendly of any at Kingsmill, but it's hardly a pushover. Golfers expect brilliance from Arnie, and the Plantation does not disappoint, with undulating greens and no shortage of demanding shots. The newest of

A cannon on the site of a Revolutionary War and Civil War fortress sits above the 16th green at Kingsmill's River Course, home of the Michelob Championship.

Kingsmill's three golf courses, Tom Clark's brilliant and challenging Woods Course, is a favorite among members and visitors alike. The Woods is worth playing even if for some reason you can't get on the fabled River Course.

River Course

In 1975, in the days before his name was a star in the firmament of golf-course designers, Pete Dye was commissioned to take a quintessential and historic piece of Virginia real estate and turn it into a championship golf course. His success is revealed each year when the River Course plays host to the Michelob Championship at Kingsmill. It is a popular tournament among both players and spectators. Its winners have included David Duvall, Fuzzy Zoeller, Mark McCumber, Calvin Peete, and Lanny Wadkins. Its television

110

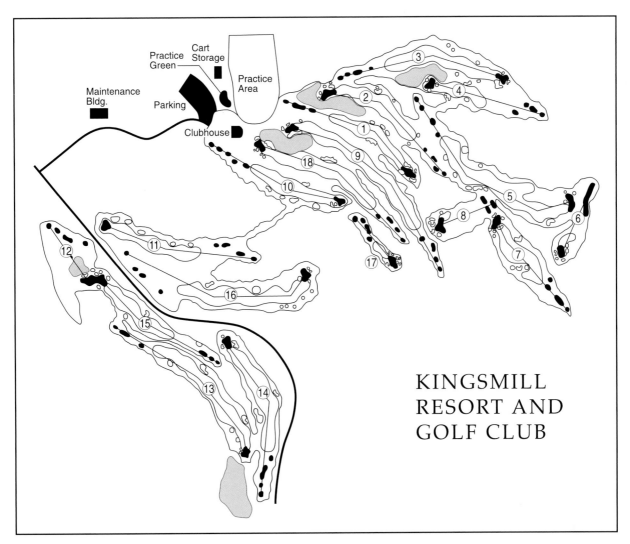

KINGSMILL
RESORT AND
GOLF CLUB

viewers number in the millions, and with each passing year the River Course establishes itself more firmly among great golf courses.

The course plays to a challenging 6,837 yards from the championship markers, with a par of 71. And while many visiting amateurs want to try their hand at what they see on TV, only the most proficient find much success from way back there where the big boys play. Rated 73.3 and sloped 137, it is simply loaded with trouble. Even low handicappers will find the blue tees quite enough of a challenge, thank you, with a slope of a mere 129.

The men's white markers and the women's red tees offer an interesting look at this championship golf course, but with substantially less stress and, some women complain, with less interest as well. The women's tees, for example, are nearly 2,200 yards shorter than the gold tees from which the pros play, and some low-handicap women contend that it's not as much of a challenge as some expected after seeing the layout on TV.

While almost every golf fan knows the three finishing holes, what precedes them is also well worth attention. The River Course opens with a short but demanding par four. A big bunker in the middle of the landing area splits the fairway. The optimal shot is to the left, which opens the green. A patch of fairway below the bunker to the right presents a forced carry over a cluster of sand traps. The great wide green features two plateaus at either side, with an indentation between them in the middle of the putting surface.

The modest par-three #2 is followed by a tough par five. Your drive on #3 is blind. The treacherous green sits on a hill behind a trough. There are steep drops from all sides of the rolling, breaking, and tricky putting surface. It is rated the most difficult hole on the men's card. The medium-length, par-four dogleg-left #4 is straightened considerably from the forward—white and red—markers. If you're thinking about hitting a right-to-left tee shot, beware that the hole slopes that way and that anything left of the first cut of rough stands a good chance of running all the way into the forest. The one-shot #5 features a creek diagonally intersecting the fairway from the tee boxes to the right side of the green. Don't miss this green right.

The short par-four #6 plays mostly uphill to an elevated green, and the tough, very tight par-five #7 hides severe trouble from view and sneaks up on the unwary from 175 yards in front of the green. The fairway dives into a deep depression, leaving a severely uphill, blind shot to the pin. The pretty par-four #8 plays across a series of hilltops, with the two-tiered green on a hillside ledge well above the fairway. It's rated the number-one handicap hole for women. The outgoing side finishes with a straight par four and lets you catch your breath before you tackle the back nine.

The back side opens with a long, fairly straight par four. The green is button-hooked behind two big bunkers and protected by pine trees. The 11th is a short par four for everybody but those playing the championship markers. It's 428 yards from back there, nearly 100 yards longer than from the next set of tees. It's a dogleg left that narrows precipitously the closer you get to the green. The left rough is about 3 feet lower than the fairway, and a planked retaining wall runs the length of the hole. The domed green is guarded by two bunkers. In signature Pete Dye fashion, the little potlike bunker in front has a planked face against the apron of the green. Behind the diminutive putting surface there's a grassy collection area to harvest hot or overly bold approaches.

The 12th hole is a medium-length par-four that doglegs left down a well-treed fairway. Thirteen is an attractive par three with a green perched on the side of a hill. Anything short or right will cascade into no man's land. The tee is adjacent to the remnants of Johnston's Mill, which used

River Course

HOLE NUMBER	Ra	Sl	1	2	3	4	5	6	7	8	9	OUT	10	11	12	13	14	15	16	17	18	IN	TOT
GOLD	73.3	137	360	204	538	437	183	365	516	413	460	3476	431	428	395	179	383	506	427	177	435	3361	6837
BLUE	69.7	129	339	161	486	385	151	341	467	371	385	3086	412	330	361	148	362	447	413	138	384	2995	6081
WHITE	65.3	120	234	145	415	321	113	321	437	307	316	2609	315	274	300	107	292	363	346	113	282	2392	5001
HANDICAP (m)			7	15	1	5	11	17	9	3	13		4	14	8	18	12	2	10	16	6		
PAR			4	3	5	4	3	4	5	4	4	36	4	4	4	3	4	5	4	3	4	35	71
RED	67.5	116	229	141	410	255	108	251	359	302	279	2334	304	270	294	95	275	356	336	110	272	2312	4646
HANDICAP (w)			9	15	5	13	17	11	3	1	7		6	10	4	18	14		8	2	16	12	

to process grain for the Kingsmill Plantation. Fourteen is a straight par-four, with a blind tee shot from the side of one hill to the top of another. And the 15th hole is a long, tight par five.

But everything on the back nine of the River Course is a prelude to the three spectacular finishers. It begins with the long, fascinating #16. This architecturally brilliant par four starts with a blind tee shot to a landing area about at the bend of the dogleg. Many of the long-hitting pros will use something other than a driver here. Most amateurs can use everything they've got in the bag. What your eye does not tell you on the tee is that just beyond the bend in the dogleg, a man-made cliff intersects the fairway. A planked retaining wall drops as much as a dozen feet to the mounded, bunkered approach to the elevated green, which is sculpted out of the side of the hill below what was once a military fortification. There's a cannon on the hill overlooking the putting surface, and the James River is visible behind it, both on the approach and from the green itself. On the hilltop adjacent to the cannon are the remains of a Revolutionary War fort built in 1775 that was rebuilt by the Confederacy during the Civil War. The fortification was to protect Col. Lewis Burwell's Landing, the pier into the river that served as the port of Williamsburg.

With the sound of the James River lapping at the shore below, the 17th hole—where the resident PGA touring pro Curtis Strange's *Strange Navy* moors itself during the Michelob Championship—plays across a deep ravine and a corner of the remains of Burwell's Landing to a long, thin elevated green with the river along the right length of the hole. The green itself is full of contours and breaks,

leaving no doubt why so many of the tournaments are won or lost on that lovely one-shot hole.

The splendid finishing hole is a long par-four dogleg left across a lake to an undulating fairway. The forward markers—white and red—are more than 150 yards shorter than the two back sets of tees and present a fairly straight 18th hole. Everybody, however, must approach that famous huge multitiered green up on the hillside on which so many great moments in golf have occurred. The lake extends along most of the left length of the hole. The finishing green is large enough to be fairly easily hit, but it's a snap to three- or even four-putt on it.

Playing the River Course is a pleasure, and your enjoyment of watching the Michelob Championship will be enhanced by having experienced the golf course that is its home.

Plantation Course

This is not the most difficult or demanding golf course ever designed by Arnold Palmer. It is certainly the easiest of the three tracks at Kingsmill. But, as might be expected from a remarkable champion with a deep and profound love of the game, even a friendly and serene golf course can be made interesting and challenging. The Plantation Course is deliberately designed to accommodate golfers of every skill level. Players who will find the River Course and the Woods Course simply too difficult will enjoy the Plantation.

But don't let yourself be lulled into a false sense of security. Even if you are a single-digit handicapper looking for a little ego boost, be ready to use your skills if you expect to score. This is a golf

The par-three #9 on the Plantation Course at Kingsmill was designed by Arnold Palmer.

Plantation Course

HOLE NUMBER	Ra	Sl	1	2	3	4	5	6	7	8	9	OUT	10	11	12	13	14	15	16	17	18	IN	TOT
GOLD	71.3	119	396	503	379	401	181	374	345	485	123	3187	419	436	481	379	151	566	348	174	402	3356	6543
BLUE	68.4	114	352	484	351	373	149	355	333	462	102	2961	386	414	444	357	141	547	331	161	350	3131	6092
WHITE	66.1	107	255	364	336	356	126	332	306	421	88	2584	365	383	425	333	123	512	313	147	318	2919	5503
HANDICAP (m)			11	3	9	1	15	7	13	5	17		6	4	8	10	14	2	16	12	18		
PAR			4	5	4	4	3	4	4	5	3	35	4	4	5	4	3	5	4	3	4	36	72
RED	67.9	116	251	337	293	314	116	279	279	361	86	2316	329	332	332	305	107	465	275	132	287	2564	4880
HANDICAP (w)			11	13	3	1	15	5	7	9	17		2	4	10	6	18	8	12	16	14		

course of contrasts. What Arnie has offered by way of generous fairways, ample landing areas, and playable rough, he has taken away with fiercely undulating and breaking greens. The greens on the Plantation Course are perilous at best and fearsome at their harshest. "It breaks at the windmill, and then you shoot for the clown's nose," said one frustrated Californian on a brilliant spring day while sizing up his third putt on one particularly uncompromising green

While the greens are true and not as lightning quick as those on the River Course—especially as tournament time approaches—they are tough to read. In addition, unlike some designers who make the majority of their greens all one size, Palmer varies the size and shape of his greens to fit the hole and the terrain. His greens range from gigantic all the way down to puny and churlish.

The course tends to favor players who can work the ball left to right, and since the majority of right-handed players tend to slice, this is good news. It's a visually pleasing golf course and will forgive more wayward shots than either of Kingsmill's other two eighteens.

For low-handicap women, it is a short golf course, nearly 1,800 yards shorter than the men's championship markers, and in many cases women do not face the same challenges as men from their tee box. The reality is that this is an upscale resort and, as one of the veteran starters pointed out, "We just don't get that many low-handicap women out here." Nonetheless, everybody must putt on Arnie's greens, and that alone makes the Plantation Course worth it.

The opening hole is a gentle beginning to the Palmer design, but #2 will get the attention of even low handicappers. It's a very solid par five, with the drive for men across a creek. Women get a huge break in length and get to tee off from across the hazard. In an effort to humble those who overestimate their own ability, there's a sprinkler head at about 245 yards from the green on which you might expect to find the yardage. It's inscribed with the words: "Just hit it!" The approach to the slightly elevated green, which is surrounded by five greenside sand traps, is plenty tough. And Palmer has placed one bunker about 40 yards in front of the green to create an optical illusion from the fairway that it's actually much closer to the putting surface than it is. The hole doglegs past old Richard Kingsmill's plantation house.

The 3rd hole, a short par-four dogleg right, is followed by the number-one handicap hole, a long, demanding par-four dogleg left, with water caressing the left side of the fairway from about 160 yards out to the left front of the long, narrow, undulating green.

A pair of par fours—one moderately long, the other short—and a short par five that's a good scoring hole are sandwiched between a pair of interesting one-shotters. The pleasant par-three #5, with a smallish, irregularly shaped green, requires proper club selection and accuracy. The green, slightly below the level of the tee boxes, is surrounded by deep bunkers and steep mounds. A ridge intersects the putting surface and makes getting your ball close from long distance highly problematic and complicates chipping and putting enormously. The 9th is a short hole, but the green is devilish, with three separate terraces along with assorted other ridges and mounds. It's a great birdie hole if you can put it close; it's likely to yield a bogey or worse if you don't.

The back side opens with a long, gentle par-four dogleg right. There's a lake along the right side from about midway from the tees to the green, and the fairway is split by a grassy hill of rough in front of the green. The green is tough to approach, with the crowned putting surface poised to reject shots that drift to the right into the water and those that stray to the left into a trio of greenside bunkers.

The 12th is another par-five that long hitters can reach in two, but the fairway is intersected in front of the green by a creek bed. If you lay up, make sure you're short of it. The par-four #13, a dogleg right, features water in play to the left front of the green. Be aware that the water hazard remains hidden from view until you're almost on top of it.

The middle of the back side includes the short par-three #14, with a diabolically tough green, the long, tough par-five #15, and the short par-four #16, which plays across a little valley. The approach to the difficult 16th green is tricky because Palmer has surrounded it with a minefield of sand.

The Plantation Course concludes with two interesting holes. First, the picturesque, lovely #17 is a testing par three that plays across a deep hazard to a green carved out of the side of a hill. This is again a hole on which club selection plays the key role. It is imperative to take enough stick. The severe dogleg-right #18 requires a strategic decision on your tee shot. Many players may want to hit something other than a driver, because a drive that's too long can slide through the fairway. Cutting the corner is dicey because of the dense stand of trees guarding the bend in the dogleg.

Woods Course

Architect Tom Clark's fine Kiln Creek golf course, in nearby Newport News, was five years old when the Woods Course at Kingsmill opened, so many local golfers were already familiar with his work. Nonetheless, the Woods Course achieved instant and understandable popularity with both local members and visitors. It's a little tougher test than the Plantation Course, although not quite as difficult as the River Course. But then it's not geared to PGA tournament play the way the River Course is. One of the reasons it is so popular with members and visitors alike is that it's a fair test that allows them to score well if they play well.

Clark joined forces with PGA champion Curtis Strange—who calls Kingsmill home and who has long been the facility's resident touring pro—to create this gem at Kingsmill. Unlike his other area course, Clark had better real estate to work with than he did at Kiln Creek. The Woods Course is laid out among the ancient trees, rolling hills, and creeks that form the fabric of the landscape of what was once the nether reaches of Richard Kingsmill's colonial plantation. Although a long and challenging course, it is fair for all levels of play and is an especially good test for women.

Clark has demonstrated a lovely touch with the idiosyncrasies of local topography that he has confronted throughout his career. In some cases he has been forced to move a lot of dirt to create what he seeks in a golf course; in other cases, such as this one, he simply caressed and molded what Mother Nature put there in

Looking back across the 18th green from the clubhouse at Kingsmill's Woods Course.

the first place. Clark is not a predictable designer, and that is his strength. Curtis Strange's personal affection for the area is reflected in his collaboration with Clark on this project.

Clark and Strange decided to feature three long par fives and one that's reachable in two for the big hitters. The 5th is rated the toughest hole on the course for men and women. It is a double dogleg left with a green protected by a cavernous indentation in the terrain filled with nasty, inhospitable plant life that comes into play from about 100 yards away right up to the apron of the green. The long dogleg-left #9 is a tough way to finish the side, with the green hugged on the left by a lake. The 13th is reachable in two for long-hitting men, but for women it's the toughest hole on the back nine. The small, undulating green has a steep drop-off to the right front of the putting surface, and an especially errant approach can find a lake that's part of the nearby Busch Gardens.

The par-threes are all different in length—ranging from long to very short—and will require a different club on each. Even short hitters will have to put away their woods on at least one and possibly three of the one-shot holes. The 12th is the most interesting of the par threes. Your tee shot is to a two-level double green, with a bunker in the middle of the steep incline delineating the two halves of the putting surface that's shared with the par-four 15th hole.

But in the final analysis, it is the amalgam of par fours on the Woods Course that stands out as especially noteworthy, both for its variety and for its shot-making demands. Mental lapses will be punished, as will imprecise shots. Tee-shot placement is important on virtually every

par four and can make the difference between scoring well and scoring poorly. Men and women of every handicap level will be required not only to use every club in the bag but also to use them to the best of their ability. There are holes that demand less than a driver to set up the proper approach and those that leave you a long iron or fairway wood to the green no matter how massively you crunch your tee shot.

Both the 1st and 2nd holes feature blind tee shots and tiered greens. The 2nd green is protected front and left by a lake that plays down the left side of the fairway from about 150 yards out. The planked retaining wall that separates water from land comes up almost to the left collar of the wickedly tiered green. The short, straight #4 has a multilevel green—two elevated wings with a trough between them, all canted back toward the fairway—with water to the right. Clark took pleasure in placing his greens on many of the holes on this course behind valleys, gullies, and canyons. On #7, make sure your tee shot stops no closer than 100 yards to the green or you're in a deep chasm.

On the back nine the variation continues. The 10th is a long, gentle dogleg left that plays downhill, with another of Clark's depressing depressions in front of the green. The drive on #11 is blind. It's rated the second-toughest hole on the men's card. The landing zone is breathlessly narrow to set up an approach to the green that's slightly below the level of the fairway and nestled back into a stand of trees. The 14th is long and tight, playing from hilltop tees over a valley to a hilltop landing area. Ideal placement is to carry the bunker to the left. The approach is downhill to a generous green.

The finisher is a lovely golf hole that begins with a blind tee shot. It's a dogleg left, with water in play for about the last third of its length. The optimal landing area is adjacent to the right-side fairway bunker. Beware of the lake on your approach. If you're short or right, you're wet.

Looking back over the panorama of the Woods Course from above the 18th green or from the clubhouse balcony is to reflect on a fine and fair golf course. With its stately trees, sun-dappled ponds and gentle hills, it is the kind of design, the kind of course, that one can play again and again with great satisfaction and eager anticipation.

Woods Course

HOLE NUMBER	Ra	Sl	1	2	3	4	5	6	7	8	9	OUT	10	11	12	13	14	15	16	17	18	IN	TOT
GOLD	72.7	131	389	395	462	320	542	196	284	146	582	3316	404	423	195	493	433	388	516	154	462	3468	6784
BLUE	70.9	126	364	375	442	301	517	181	267	134	557	3138	377	398	170	472	408	375	483	143	429	3255	6393
WHITE	69.0	121	356	347	415	292	510	169	261	127	550	3027	347	342	146	461	375	365	463	109	395	3003	6030
HANDICAP (m)			9	7	3	13	1	11	17	15	5		10	2	16	12	6	14	8	18	4		
PAR			4	4	4	4	5	3	4	3	5	36	4	4	3	5	4	4	5	3	4	36	72
RED	68.7	120	315	307	333	245	488	139	195	121	485	2588	284	307	97	411	332	316	393	79	333	2552	5140
HANDICAP (w)			11	7	5	13	1	15	17	9	3		12	14	16	2	8	10	4	18	6		

One of the only downhill holes on the outgoing nine, the par-five #5 on the Lakeview Course provides a spectacular view from the tees.

LAKEVIEW RESORT

Morgantown, West Virginia (Take I-68 west from Morgantown to the exit sign for the
Lakeview Resort.)
Phone: (800) 624-8300 or (304) 594-2011

Lakeview Course architect: Jim Robinson   Year opened: 1953
Mountainview Course architect: Brian Ault   Year opened: 1984

Lakeview Course rating/Slope rating:
Blue - 73.1/132   White - 71.3/129
Red - 71.8/118

Mountainview Course rating/Slope rating:
Blue - 70.7/119   White - 69.4/116
Red - 70.4/122

This is a popular resort, especially for business and social groups that want to incorporate golf into their annual sales meetings, conferences, or retreats. Organizations from Ohio, Pennsylvania, West Virginia, and Virginia make their plans a year or more in advance, and many that go there once return over and over. The facility features thirty-six arduous holes of mountain golf that will often leave you gasping and more than occasionally leave you frustrated. Weekend golfers or those who dust off their clubs only for social outings quickly learn that the golf courses of the Lakeview Resort are serious and will not submit gently to erratic play. After losing at least a dozen balls on the front nine of the Lakeview Course and after playing far more among the trees than in the fairway, one gas-equipment executive from Pennsylvania stormed off the course, declaring himself headed to the bar for solace.

Play both golf courses to your handicap and you have earned a spell by the pool or the lake with your feet up and a cool drink in your hand. If you've not played there before, know that both courses are loaded with holes that can simply destroy your round before you know what's happened to you.

Lakeview Course

This course originally opened in 1953 as a nine-holer and was lengthened to eighteen two years later. It is characteristic of many golf courses constructed in the decade after World War II in that it was built before designers learned just how much earth they could move and how much they could disrupt, disfigure, and deface what nature put there in their quest to improve the land's golfability. The machinery available was, of course, a far cry from an ox pulling an earth grader, but this was a transition period in golf-course design. The Lakeview Course benefited. Today, it is a lovely, scenic, mature golf course, classical in its design and a testament to architect Jim Robinson's skill. The course is well maintained and expertly managed.

But make no mistake: this is a tough,

LAKEVIEW COURSE

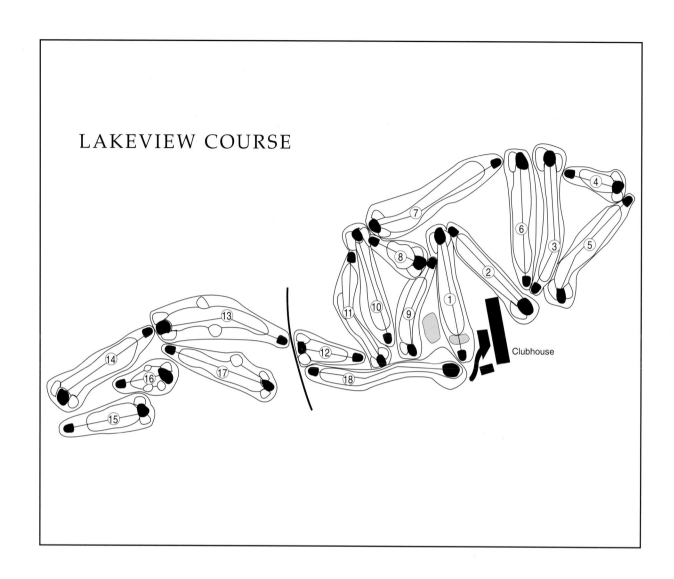

Clubhouse

Lakeview Course

HOLE NUMBER	Ra	Sl	1	2	3	4	5	6	7	8	9	OUT	10	11	12	13	14	15	16	17	18	IN	TOT
BLUE	73.1	132	317	367	392	194	492	429	564	189	319	3263	396	346	199	399	560	427	171	379	620	3497	6760
WHITE	71.3	129	305	348	376	177	474	400	541	153	307	3081	370	321	176	378	532	406	151	340	602	3276	6357
HANDICAP (m)			13	7	3	11	9	1	5	17	15		8	12	16	6	10	4	18	14	2		
PAR			4	4	4	3	5	4	5	3	4	36	4	4	3	4	5	4	3	4	5	36	72
RED	71.8	118	211	262	283	173	376	305	517	129	298	2554	327	312	165	367	495	313	106	327	466	2878	5432
HANDICAP (w)			15	13	5	7	9	3	1	17	11		8	10	16	6	4	12	18	14	2		

demanding mountain golf course. The front nine is a monster; take a deep breath and get ready for a real test—both of golf and of stamina—on the outgoing nine. There are only three downhill holes on the entire front side. Everything else plays partially or entirely uphill, and often steeply uphill, which makes the 3,263 yards from the back markers, 3,081 from the middle tees, and 2,554 from the women's tees seem like a marathon. Short shots stay short. The tight, mountainous terrain waits at every turn to jail your golf ball in the forest, cascade your shot into the rocks and knee-deep rough, or send you scrambling into one of the deep, difficult bunkers. The greens are subtle and generally kept very fast, requiring focus and concentration to score, but they are not the greatest obstacle to pars and birdies. The most daunting perils are on the way to the putting surfaces.

This is a superior golf course, consistently and justifiably ranked among the best golf courses in West Virginia. The course record, 67, was set in 1959 by Sam Snead in the West Virginia Open and later tied by Jack Nicklaus. "If you keep it straight here—you don't have to be particularly long—and you're a good putter, you're going to be OK," said head pro Charles Wiedebusch.

Water is not a concern. There is only one water hazard on the entire course, a little man-made pond in front of the first tee, a short par four with a blind tee shot to the crest of a hill. The green is hooked slightly to the left behind a sand trap, with another bunker and a bushy tree guarding the right. This is the flattest hole on the side. Now get ready to start an arduous series of uphill holes. The par-four #2 is a tough hole for women in that while they get about a 100-yard distance break over the back tees, they also face a more acute uphill tee shot than do men. The subtly contoured green is perched on the side of a hill, with any shot to the right destined for a gloomy fate.

The dogleg-left par-four #3 looks moderate in length on the card but plays long because of the uphill gradation. The 4th is a brilliant par three, long and uphill to an elevated green. Club selection here is the premium. For women, it's an extremely difficult one-shot hole that plays 173 yards straight up the hill. The shot is blind; you can see the flag but not the putting surface.

Finally a downhill hole. The par-five 5th is a dogleg left that's reachable in two shots if you keep it straight. The closer you get to the green, the more the fairway narrows, with trouble invisible from the fairway behind the green. The out-of-bounds is extremely close to the back of the green, and any shot that's too hot or too long will be rejected into the land of penalties and double bogeys. And so it's back to the ascent. The long par-four #6 is rated the toughest hole on the golf course for men. Long, accurate shots will be rewarded, but a giant deciduous tree stands strategically about 20 yards to the right front of the green. Any shot that's too far right, even in the fairway, will have an obstructed approach.

The 7th is a long, glorious par five that plays downhill and features a lovely view. It's the number-one handicap hole for women, mostly because it stretches 517 yards from tee to green. The green is protected by a mound out of which a steep-faced bunker has been carved. The front side finishes with an uphill par three to one of the smallest greens on the side, followed by a short, downhill dogleg-left par four. Few players should think about hitting a driver here.

There's a snack bar by the 10th tee, and after that front side, some refreshment may well be needed.

The back nine features some very fine holes, but it is the easier of the two sides and actually provides five relatively flat holes after the arduous up-and-down trek of the front side. The par-four 10th is the first of the flat holes and is really the first chance to catch your breath. It's followed by the short par-four #11 and the long par-three #12. That green is guarded by big, difficult bunkers right and left that pinch in the entrance to the putting surface and render any kind of run-up shot very hard.

The 14th is the first of two long par fives on the back. The drive is from the side of a hill with a steep drop to a tight fairway. The 15th is a long, extremely tight par four with out-of-bounds precariously close to the right side of the fairway. The owners of the beautiful homes that line the hole probably never have to buy a golf ball because of the number of stray shots that land in their yards. Length is an advantage here. The farther you hit the ball, the more the hole opens up. Sixteen is a lovely uphill par three with a green terraced on the side of a hill overlooking the 15th green. Trees and bunkers combine to make the entrance to the putting surface tricky to approach.

The finisher is one of the premier holes on the golf course, an enormous, tight, long par five, 620 yards from the back tees. In fact, it is one of the longest golf holes in West Virginia. "It's never been reached in two," said pro Charles Wiedebusch. "Tiger Woods or John Daley might make it, but a lot of others have tried and failed." The hole is relatively flat, but the well-protected green is uphill from the fairway.

The Lakeview Course is a fine test of the game, and the front nine is an especially good example of classical mountain-golf-course design.

Mountainview Course

If the older and more famous sibling of this course is classical and mature, this is a fine example of modern, aggressive mountain golf-course design. It's uphill, downhill, sidehill, with few flat lies and lots of blind tee shots. People who play it either love it and seek to play it more than once or hate it and never want to see it again. There is very little middle ground and very few players who are neutral. Better players are more prone to like it, while poorer players or shorter hitters will be critical of its difficulty. Some say it verges on the unfair, but the modern designers argue that with all the modern, high-tech equipment—clubs, shoes, balls—golfers should hit fewer errant shots. That debate will hardly be resolved in these pages.

Much less has been written about the Mountainview Course because it sits in the shadow of its more glamorous and admired relative a few miles away, but if you like mountain golf, relish the challenge of keeping your shots under control, and put a premium on shot placement and control, this is a worthy test. The greens are not quite as fast as those on the Lakeview Golf Course, but what they lack in speed they make up for with breaks, bumps, ridges, mounds, and contours.

The course is rated and sloped as if it's a walk in the park. The park is more like

The 10th green on the Mountainview Course is perched on a hillside above a ball-gobbling pond.

Yellowstone than the village green, and a case can be made that the rating and slope are not an accurate reflection of the difficulty of this golf course. The first hole offers a taste of what's to come. It's a par four with a blind tee shot that plays uphill and then back down with deep and unforgiving trouble all along its right length. The par-five #3 is long, straight, and rated the toughest hole on the course. Get ready for an uphill journey that does-n't let up until you're on the putting surface. The 6th is a pretty little par three that tees off across a cattail-filled marsh and downhill to a small green. A pair of par fours—the short #7 to an elevated green and #8 with its steeply canted fairway that directs all shots to the left—blazes the trail for the brilliant and treacherous turning holes.

The turning holes—#9, #10, #11, and #12—are as difficult as they are spectacular.

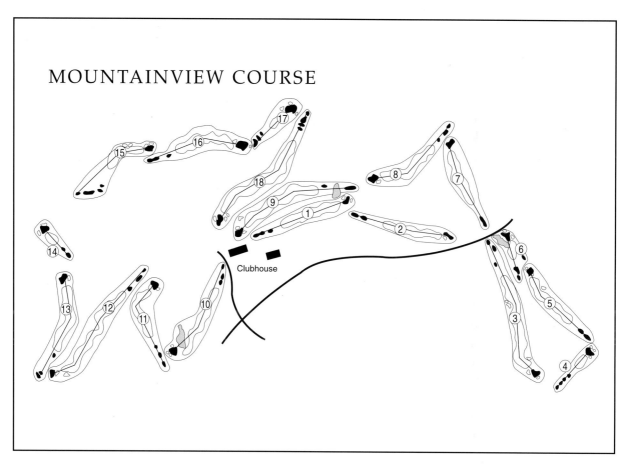

MOUNTAINVIEW COURSE

They demand some of the best shot making anywhere in order to score, and if you walk away from these four with a quartet of pars, you've played some seriously good golf.

The par-five #9 is simply devilish, a fine shot-making test. It looks reachable in two on the card, but its severe contours and sinews make that a risk that might not be worth the gamble. Your drive is across a deep, marshy gully, uphill to a tiny landing zone. A mighty drive will make the crest of the hill; most shots won't reach it, and the golfer is left with a blind second to a ribbon of fairway, a left-sloping ledge about as wide as a footpath on a hillside. Locals say golf ball after golf ball is rejected there into the deep rough and grueling mounds to the left. The green itself sits at the base of a little ridge.

From about 100 yards away the approach is like hitting off a cliff.

The 10th hole is an aesthetically beautiful but difficult par four on which a driver may not be the best club selection. It's a downhill drive to a ridge overlooking a little lake in front of the green. If your shot crests the ridge, the slope is precariously downward to the water. The hole presents two course-management problems: a really big drive will reach the water, and the closer to the water you get, the more severe the downhill lie you will have for an uphill shot to the putting surface. This hole is very difficult for women, in that if they want a relatively flat stance, they are left with about a 150-yard carry; if they want a shorter carry, they have a difficult downhill, sidehill stance.

The short #11 is a par-four dogleg right

that's as beautiful as it is dangerous. Your tee shot plays into a deep, mounded valley. Your approach plays back uphill to a green perched on a hillside ledge. The temptation is to cut a lot off the dogleg, but Ault has used the terrain to create an optical illusion, making it seem the green is closer than it really is. Your tee shot needs to be long enough or left enough to be able to see the flag; if you are too far into the valley to the right, your second is completely blind.

The 12th is another extremely demanding hole that plays around a hill to the right. The par five tees off from an elevated set of tees, but the trouble is hidden from view on the tee shot. The lay-up second and the approach to the green are perilous. The elevated green is hooked to the right, sitting on a shelf with a chasm guarding the left front and left side and a steep hill to the right and rear. The entrance to the green is about as wide as your belt. The only way to approach this is with a high, soft, and accurate chip that will probably be struck from a stance that is anything but flat.

You can begin to catch your breath a little on the medium-length par-four #13. Your drive is blind to the point where the dogleg bends to the left. But there's a generous landing area, and while the green is then steeply uphill, it's a fairly open approach. That's followed by a little downhill par three, a short par four with a well-guarded green, and a long par-four dogleg right with a blind tee shot. The 17th is a long, lovely par three that plays from the side of a hill down to a well-bunkered green.

Then it's back to the long and fearsome for the finish. The tough, twisting par-five #18 mirrors the brutal #9, only it's slightly easier. That still renders it a very arduous golf hole. Your drive is uphill to a fairway that slopes sharply left. Your second shot must negotiate a treacherously narrow downhill fairway with trees right and a rocky, grassy dungeon left. From about 150 yards away the downhill slope becomes severe and, as with #9, there's an almost vertical drop about 80 yards short of the putting surface.

The Mountainview Course is not going to be ranked as one of the greatest courses in the region, but it's a tremendous amount of fun. And regarding the debate about its merits, you can't join in unless you've played it. On the other hand, if you tend to hit big slices, wild hooks, or are just plain inaccurate, you might well be advised not to be tempted.

Mountainview Course

HOLE NUMBER	Ra	Sl	1	2	3	4	5	6	7	8	9	OUT	10	11	12	13	14	15	16	17	18	IN	TOT
BLUE	70.7	119	387	380	514	183	332	161	328	367	505	3157	387	310	529	391	149	369	406	200	549	3290	6447
WHITE	69.4	116	367	374	488	159	324	131	314	354	487	2998	378	296	493	389	141	344	386	186	538	3154	6152
PAR			4	4	5	3	4	3	4	4	5	36	4	4	5	4	3	4	4	3	5	36	72
HANDICAP			3	9	1	15	11	17	13	7	5		8	16	2	12	18	10	6	14	4		
RED (L)	70.4	122	322	344	416	135	297	97	300	305	392	2608	323	266	443	289	112	328	335	166	515	2777	5385
RED (S)	69.4	122	322	344	416	107	297	97	300	305	392	2580	323	234	443	289	112	309	335	146	471	2662	5254

One key to success on the par-four #17 at Lansdowne is to avoid the huge bunkers that guard the fairway just about driving distance from all four tee boxes.

LANSDOWNE GOLF CLUB

44050 Woodbridge Parkway, Lansdowne, Virginia (From the Capital Beltway take Route 7, Leesburg Pike, west about 18 miles; turn right onto Lansdowne Blvd., and right onto Woodbridge Pkwy.)
Phone: (703) 729-8400

Architect: Robert Trent Jones Jr.   Year opened: 1992

Course rating/Slope rating:
Tournament - 74.0/130   Regular - 69.0/121
Championship - 71.5/126   Forward - 75.0/134

Renowned golf-course architect Robert Trent Jones Jr. is responsible for the design of a lovely golf course. To build it he transformed a splendid tract of Virginia land a stone's throw from the Potomac River, a wilderness of dense forests, bubbling streams and rocky outcrops, and a patchwork of farm fields into a fair but demanding test of the game of golf. In essence, Jones worked with land featuring two different temperaments and personalities, yielding a delightful, if somewhat schizophrenic, result. The golf course can only be diagnosed as having a split personality. The outgoing nine looks fairly flat and benign, playing among gentle hills and forests to the south of the resort complex; the second nine is an oval around some brutally gnarled terrain that includes devilish streambeds, rocks, forests, and steep hills. Do not be fooled into thinking the front nine is a snap. It merely gets you psychologically ready for the ordeal you face on the more demanding back.

In general, if you can hit the ball fairly straight and long, you will do very well on Lansdowne. If you are given to errant shots or tend to stray from the fairway, you will be faced with some painful results. In his introduction to the stroke-saver book,

Jones warns players that the ability to judge the effects of elevation—uphill and downhill—are the keys to success. Add to that the fact that keeping the ball in the fairway is of at least equal import.

For women, the course rating and slope would lead one to believe that it is a monster. My wife, who has played it several times, suggests that the course is a better and fairer test from the forward tees than the numbers would indicate. She points out that the majority of the par fours hover in the 300-yard range, which for most women sets up a realistic opportunity to hit almost all of them in regulation.

For men and women, Jones has created four splendidly varied par threes and four challenging but fair par fives.

The opening three holes, all relatively short par fours, are visually deceptive. They require finesse and course management to avoid suddenly finding yourself in debt and wondering what's next. The second is a sharp dogleg right, guarded by water in front and featuring a wide, shallow, undulating green. A rock-infested pond guards the entire left side of the third hole and the two-tiered green is hooked at almost a right angle behind the water and rocks. The scorecard rates it as easy for men and women; in fact, the

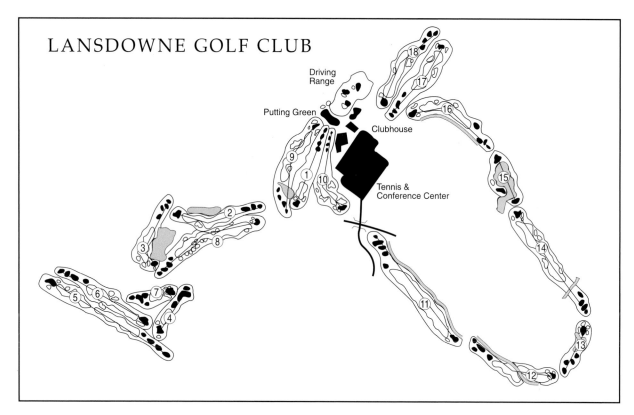

LANSDOWNE GOLF CLUB

slightest mishit will yield a bogey or worse in a heartbeat.

The long par-three #4 sets the stage for three monstrous holes, including the par-five #5 that measures more than 600 yards from the tournament tees and approaches 500 yards for the ladies. It's rated the hardest hole on Lansdowne for women. The long, tight par-four #6, which plays to an undulating kidney-shaped green, is the number-one handicap hole for men. Both will reward long, accurate shot making.

On the other hand, the par-five #8, which plays downhill and often downwind, is reachable in two big hits, but Jones—who was clearly in a bad mood on the day he designed this one—placed fourteen bunkers in strategic places from tee to green. The medium par-four #9 features a blind tee shot to a well-bunkered green that is the highest point on the golf course and offers a splendid panorama of Virginia horse country. The

ideal tee shot carries the big fairway bunker on the right.

The 10th launches you onto the roller-coaster inward nine. The short, downhill par-four dogleg left requires a precise tee shot that avoids the gaping bunker lying in wait just through the fairway. Many players opt for something less than a driver here unless they have the skill to cut the dogleg, take the bunkers out of play, and land in an area that's about as wide as a compact car.

A nasty and inhospitable rock-strewn streambed runs the left length of the par-five #11 and intersects the par-four #12. It is visually intimidating, and while it must be avoided, care must also be taken not to go so far to the right that the trees and deep rough prevent you from scoring. The 11th is rated the second-toughest hole on the course for women, mostly as a result of its demanding 426-yard length from the red markers.

The par-three #13 and par-three #15 are aesthetically pleasing and demanding holes. Both feature water. The 13th plays downhill across a small rocky stream to a big, hilly green. The 15th has a bailout zone to the left, but beware the hourglass-shaped bunker on the left front of the putting surface.

Lansdowne's three finishers are among the best in the Virginias. The 16th is a par-four, dogleg left with a stream running tightly along the left side from tee to green. The hole is all the longer for the fact that it plays uphill. Two devilish fairway bunkers serve to constrict the fairway. The extremely long, thin green is perched about 50 feet above the point between the bunkers where most drives will come to rest, and it is protected on the left front by an enormous deep bunker and on the right front by another stretch of sandy unpleasantness. The huge green is loaded with breaks, both subtle and obvious, and even landing safely on the putting surface in regulation is no guarantee of a birdie or par.

The serpentine par-four #17 plays downhill from tee to green, and even the green is canted away from the approaching golf ball. Your tee shot must navigate between three fairway bunkers—two to the right and a Saharan monster to the left—that tighten the fairway, which meanders some 100 feet below the tee boxes. An approach that's too hot to the tricky green, which is shaped like an inverted pear, has a tremendous potential of skipping right off the back and into a collection area.

That 100-foot drop on #17 is reversed on the brilliant and treacherous finishing hole at Lansdowne. The green sits high above the tees on this short but tricky little par four. The elevation makes it play substantially longer than the 337 yards it measures from the white tees. The dogleg left demands a tee shot that avoids the fairway bunkers to the left but that also stops short of the bunker lurking just through the fairway. As with the 9th green, the view of the Potomac River Valley from the 18th is a lovely way to catch your breath after you've holed out.

These eighteen holes are a superior and fair test of the game for men and of almost all levels of ability, although it's simply too much for a raw beginner. While the front nine is a very solid track, the back nine is simply tremendous. At Lansdowne, Robert Trent Jones Jr., has taken the natural terrain and caressed a golf course around it; the finished product is both a pleasure to play and a pleasure to witness. And while some people might disagree, I would have to rate the back nine at Lansdowne among the overall best—from a standard of playability, design, aesthetic brilliance, and sheer golfing enjoyment—in Virginia and West Virginia.

Lansdowne

HOLE NUMBER	Ra	SI	1	2	3	4	5	6	7	8	9	OUT	10	11	12	13	14	15	16	17	18	IN	TOT
TOURN	74.0	130	368	397	353	225	610	442	177	504	424	3500	379	580	441	210	533	203	417	393	401	3557	7057
CHAMP	71.5	125	334	380	346	196	571	400	153	495	385	3260	345	550	398	183	498	190	388	367	373	3292	6552
REG	69.0	121	303	339	319	160	525	363	128	461	348	2946	319	513	377	167	456	140	358	341	337	3008	5954
HANDICAP (m)			17	7	15	11	5	1	13	9	3		18	6	8	12	10	14	2	16	4		
PAR			4	4	4	3	5	4	3	5	4	36	4	5	4	3	5	3	4	4	4	36	72
FOR	75.0	134	277	296	273	148	493	335	102	440	290	2654	297	426	334	139	366	103	292	294	308	2559	5213
HANDICAP (w)			11	7	13	15	1	5	17	3	9		10	2	6	16	4	18	14	12	8		

The tees on the par-three 14th hole at Lee's Hill Golfers' Club—a long carry over a lake and a marsh—sit below the site of Gen. Robert E. Lee's winter headquarters of 1862.

LEE'S HILL GOLFERS' CLUB

10200 Old Dominion Parkway, Fredericksburg, Virginia (Take I-95 to exit 126; go south on U.S. 1 for about ½-mile, then turn left onto U.S. 17 for about 1⅓ miles to Old Dominion Parkway; turn left to the clubhouse.)
Phone: (540) 891-0111 or (800) 930-3636

Architect: Bill Love   Year opened: 1993

Course rating/Slope rating:
Cannon - 72.4/128   Saber - 68.2/117
Rifle - 69.7/120   Pistol - 69.2/115

It was in the winter of 1862, not long after the cannons fell silent and the sounds of war diminished in the aftermath of the Battle of Fredericksburg, that Gen. Robert E. Lee determined to bivouac his Confederate troops in the Massaponax Creek basin. After months of brutal warfare against aggressive Union soldiers, Lee's tired Army of Northern Virginia dug in to fight the elements as best they could in trenches amid the trees and brush. Lee chose a point of high ground for his command center that became known by local residents as Lee's Hill.

The landmarks remain and are commemorated by plaques alongside the eighteen lovely, picturesque golf holes that now unfold among the hills, forests and marshes through which Massaponax Creek still flows. Particularly notable are the hill next to the 14th tee, from which Lee commanded his forces, and the remains of the trenches where his troops hunkered down for the winter adjacent to the 18th fairway.

Bill Love, a principal with the golf-course design firm of Ed Ault and Associates, is responsible for the layout of the championship course. As with most Ault-style golf courses, Love favors big, rolling greens with a lot of character and challenge to them. Two man-made lakes were incorporated into the design, along with an interesting amalgam of bunkers, mounds, and plantings. With the notable exception of the 15th hole, the one piece of general advice on Lee's Hill Golfers' Club is to aim at the 150-yard-marker stake on the par fours. Most members will also tell you that Massaponax Creek will influence the way the greens break whenever it flows in the vicinity, although sometimes it is hidden from view.

While it is not a course for raw beginners, it is a thoroughly pleasant test for players of most skill levels.

The opening hole, a medium-length par four, offers a splendid taste of things to come. The dogleg right is lined along its length by mounds and hills. The huge two-tiered green is guarded by a gaping crescent-shaped bunker.

The 2nd hole, rated the toughest on the track, is an imposing par five that winds like a Z-shaped lightning bolt; virtually everybody needs at least three shots to reach the pear-shaped green. The fairway is split by a marshy wetland just beyond the landing area for your tee shot and then jogs sharply to the right. The ideal place for your lay-up second is in the vicinity of the 100-yard marker. The

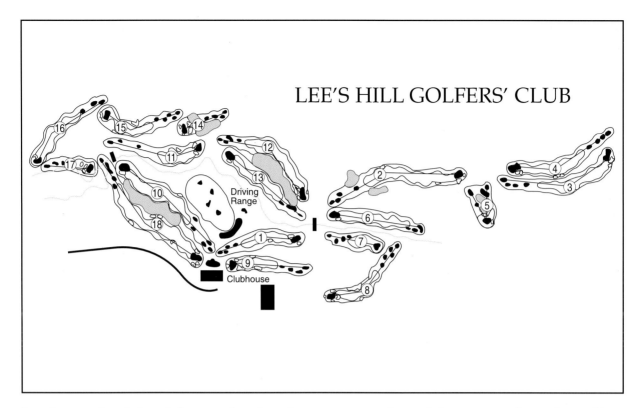

bunker to the right of that marker is to be avoided. The 3rd also is a par five but is considerably more generous than its predecessor. It's a gentle dogleg left and, while cutting too much of the dogleg can result in tree trouble, a solid drive will put long and medium hitters in a position to go for it in two.

Don't breathe easy yet. The long par-four #4 is rated the number-three handicap hole and, for my money, may actually be the most difficult hole on Lee's Hill. The hole is a dogleg right with a steep hill and trees along the right length, a pair of fairway bunkers on the left about driving distance, and a fairway that slopes to the left. The thin, narrow green is elevated, with that steep hill to the right and a pair of greenside bunkers to the left. Anything to the left of the bunkers will careen down a severe hill, possibly reaching the unfriendly and unyielding forest. This hole surrenders pars grudgingly, and produces a wide

array of much larger numbers for golfers given to imprecise shots.

The par-four #8 is a short, tight little devil, a dogleg right that features natural wetlands along both sides, not to mention abundant trees and mounds. Two big, strategically placed fairway bunkers require your tee shot to find the short grass or face punishing difficulties. The irregularly shaped green, with an intersecting ridge, is surrounded by bunkers, and failure to get close to the flag can make three or more putts the rule more than the exception.

The locals will tell you that on a dry day with a favorable wind, the short par-four #9 can be reached in one shot by a lot of players. Most play it with a long iron and a wedge or sand iron.

The back nine opens and closes with a pair of very solid double-dogleg par fives that caress the banks of a small lake. On #10, the lake is in play up the entire left side. The lake, a series of mounds, and a hungry bunker guard the two-tiered green, which is shaped like a chubby "7". The 11th, 12th, and 13th holes are back-to-back par fours, followed by the splendid little par-three #14. The ghost of Robert E. Lee may well be looking down from the hill on which his headquarters was located. The enormous rolling green is protected by four bunkers, and your tee shot must carry an expanse of natural wetland and marsh. Pin placement will dictate club selection, and the most common advice you'll hear is "Don't be short!"

The 15th hole is rated the easiest on Lee's Hill, but it is a treacherous and challenging little par-four dogleg right that yields as many double and triple bogeys as it does birdies. It's only a little over 300 yards—only 256 yards for women—but it is fraught with trouble. Many players use something other than a driver for their tee shots. A drive that drifts too far to the left can catch a fairway bunker or rough and be left with a forced carry over a tongue of marsh that guards the left front of the green; a shot to the right that fails to clear the huge fairway bunker will be left with a blind shot to the V-shaped green; and a brazen drive that cuts the dogleg but fails to stop in the fairway can run all the way into the wetland. Almost everybody plays this hole better the second time around.

The 16th is a fine par four with a split fairway and an extremely narrow approach to the green. The par-three #17 is well protected by three little bunkers in front and a creek behind the tiered, shallow green.

The finishing hole, a long double-dogleg par five, is rated the second-toughest on the course—and with good reason. It plays more than 600 yards from the back tees and just under 500 yards for women. The lake to the left is in play on your tee shot and your second, and there are trees, mounds, marsh, and bunkers to the right. The first question is how much of the lake to bite off on your tee shot. The big green is relatively easy to hit, but its generous size often makes getting on easier than getting close.

Lee's Hill Golfers' Club is a thoroughly pleasant and challenging test of the game. Because of its location—in a residential area of Fredericksburg—it draws less outside play than a lot of courses closer to Washington, D.C., or Richmond, but it's well worth the drive if you're in the area, and it is worth a detour if you're anywhere in the Virginias.

Lee's Hill

HOLE NUMBER	Ra	Sl	1	2	3	4	5	6	7	8	9	OUT	10	11	12	13	14	15	16	17	18	IN	TOT
CANNON	72.4	128	403	579	510	446	150	357	209	372	316	3342	554	374	440	386	195	345	410	183	605	3492	6834
RIFLE	69.7	120	362	558	479	411	140	340	184	351	278	3103	522	336	390	350	166	318	378	161	544	3165	6268
SABER	68.2	117	346	550	468	391	117	316	167	334	240	2929	511	325	381	341	140	302	337	139	520	2996	5925
PAR			4	5	5	4	3	4	3	4	4	36	5	4	4	4	3	4	4	3	5	36	72
HANDICAP			7	1	5	3	17	11	13	9	15		4	12	6	10	16	18	8	14	2		
PISTOL	69.2	115	304	450	435	352	73	282	121	251	201	2469	444	266	336	267	106	256	315	114	491	2595	5064

Abundant water, sand, and trees—evident here around the par-three 7th green—are just a few of the natural and man-made hazards that combine to make Locust Hill a challenging golf course.

LOCUST HILL GOLF COURSE

St. Andrews Drive, Charles Town, West Virginia (From I-81 take Route 51 east for 9 miles to St. Andrews Drive on right; from Route 9 or 340, take Route 51 west for about 2 miles to St. Andrews Drive on left.)
Phone: (304) 728-7300

Architect: Guy Rando   Year opened: 1993

Course rating/Slope rating:
Black - 73.5/128   Gray - 67.9/117
White - 70.7/122   Red - 72.0/120

Charles Town, West Virginia, sits in the middle of the northeastern knob of the state, which is bordered to the south and west by Virginia and to the north and east by Maryland. It's that part of West Virginia that pinches the Maryland panhandle so tightly against Pennsylvania that it almost disappears. For years people from Baltimore and Washington have trekked out to Charles Town for the races or have stopped by because of its proximity to historic Harpers Ferry. But today there is another reason for golfers from the city or visitors from anywhere to travel to Charles Town: Locust Hill Golf Course.

When you drive up to the clubhouse, Locust Hill gives the impression of being flat and open, but that first image proves to be a figment of your imagination. In reality it is a splendid piece of interesting land on which architect Guy Rando has created a superior golf course. So far it's an undiscovered gem. For some reason, not many players have even heard of it. But it's worth discovering. It is long and demanding, more than 7,000 yards long from the back tees. Taming it requires both skill and cunning. Timidity is not the way to approach Locust Hill. The golf course is a difficult but fair test for all but the newest of players.

For women, it is an exceptional challenge. Rando took special pains to enhance the playability of the course from the front markers, giving women an interesting and unique look at several holes while not diminishing their perspective on the course. On the par-three #16, for example, men face a forced carry across a small lake of from 173 to 132 yards, depending on which markers are in play. For women he constructed an island for the tee box in order to create a 98-yard shot that is all carry to the green, skillfully providing women with a shot that is similar to but more playable than the one presented to men.

The greens, ranging from large to huge, are generally well protected by bunkers, mounds, trees, and natural rock formations. The putting surfaces are replete with ridges, tiers, and humps and require as much skill as you can muster. The general rule is that approach shots that get close will be rewarded; shots that are not close can easily require three- and four-putts to finish.

Rando cleverly incorporated Mother Nature's handiwork into the design of Locust Hill. Instead of bulldozing out many of the huge boulders that dotted the terrain, he left them in place to punish

LOCUST HILL GOLF COURSE

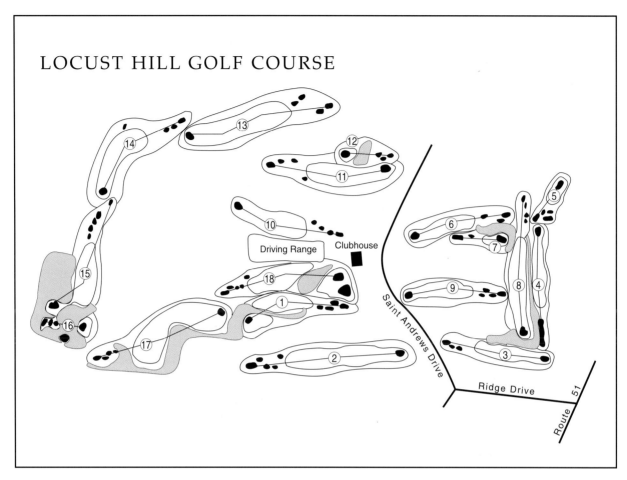

errant shots; towering ancient trees reach out like giant hands to slap down wayward golf balls. The 11th green and the 12th tee are in the shadow of a Civil War-era plantation house that was once the scene of a bloody skirmish and for which the course is named. (Close examination will reveal bullet holes in the bricks.)

The par-five #2 is rated the toughest hole on the course for men and women. What you see from the tee is what you get: a loooong, straight hole that will take you three shots to get home. Players who tend to hit left to right must beware the tight out-of-bounds along the entire right length of the hole. The green, in the shape of an inverted pear, is bisected diagonally by a devilish little ridge.

The par-three #5 is a splendid little one-shot hole with a panoply of tee boxes that

gives it a different look from day to day and from round to round. The irregularly shaped three-tiered green is sculpted from the side of a hill, with the right side giving way to an almost vertical slope that feeds into a pair of tough bunkers.

The next hole is a wonderful example of how Rando has put the natural terrain to work for him. The approach to the dog-leg-left par-four #6 is littered with clusters of weathered old trees and scrub brush, along with imposing boulders that can ricochet your golf ball into another area code. The 7th (a par three) and the 8th (a short but extremely tight par five) both feature greens protected by abundant water. The 8th is also well bunkered.

The front side finishes with a tricky little short par four. The key is where you place your tee shot. The ideal shot is straight down the middle, avoiding a gnarly stand of trees that lurks to the left. The green is fronted by a pair of trees that stand like sentries guarding the entrance. If you have failed to leave yourself a straight approach directly through the eye of the needle, you face some strategic decision making. Playing under the trees risks sending your golf ball into a minefield of boulders. Anything other than a high, soft shot—preferably with some backspin—risks skidding off the back of the putting surface.

The long par-four #11 plays straight up a substantial hill to an elevated green. It's rated the second-toughest hole on the course for men and the number-four handicap hole for women (because of the break they get in the length of it). Most second shots provide a view of the flagstick, but the putting surface remains hidden. To the left rear of the big, rolling irregularly shaped green—in the shade of the venerable old trees—is the skeleton of the Civil War-era plantation house, Locust Hill. The front porch feels like it is almost up to the fringe.

The 13th is a long par five featuring a split fairway and a green that is guarded by trees and four greenside bunkers. The par-four #14 is a severe dogleg left with a blind tee shot that plays up a hill and then back down to the green. Your tee shot, which does not necessarily require the services of a driver, should be aimed right at the marker flag, and if you can put a little right-to-left action on it, so much the better.

The 15th green is virtually an island, connected to the mainland by a thin strip of land just about wide enough for a pair of golf carts to pass each other. The 16th is an extremely attractive par three that's all carry across a lake. Your tee shot on the shortish par-five #17 must avoid the dimple of the lake on the right side that protrudes into the fairway about where long hitters might think about landing. Stay left or stay short of the water.

The par-four #18 is a splendid finisher. A long tee shot is required in order to set up a makable approach across the water that guards the front of the big, rolling multileveled green.

Locust Hill is not the kind of golf course that engenders a sigh of relief when you're finished, nor does it evoke strong emotions while you're playing it, but once finished there is little doubt that you have encountered a fine layout that leaves a feeling of satisfaction and pleasure. If you live in the area or visit regularly, Locust Hill is the kind of golf course you might well like to play several times.

Locust Hill

HOLE NUMBER	Ra	Sl	1	2	3	4	5	6	7	8	9	OUT	10	11	12	13	14	15	16	17	18	IN	TOT
BLACK	73.5	128	428	588	396	416	178	376	183	507	370	3442	390	439	181	555	432	424	173	514	455	3563	7005
WHITE	70.7	122	401	563	375	381	152	344	170	471	315	3172	353	420	150	522	377	348	147	474	431	3222	6394
GRAY	67.9	117	375	531	351	345	128	287	160	452	294	2923	317	335	120	470	337	304	132	446	388	2849	5772
HANDICAP (m)			5	1	7	3	15	17	11	9	13		18	2	14	10	8	4	12	16	6		
PAR			4	5	4	4	3	4	3	5	4	36	4	4	3	5	4	4	3	5	4	36	72
RED	72.0	120	333	501	313	320	110	268	129	407	256	2637	275	283	109	452	239	236	98	414	369	2475	5112
HANDICAP (w)			3	1	7	5	13	17	15	9	11		12	4	18	6	16	8	14	10	2		

The par-three 11th green on Oglebay Park's Speidel Course is nestled at the base of a hill between a pair of bunkers. Club selection is critical.

OGLEBAY PARK

Wheeling, West Virginia (From I-70, take the exit marked Oglebay Park and follow the signs.)
Phone: (800) 752-9436 or (304) 243-4141

Speidel Course architect: Robert Trent Jones Sr.   Year opened: 1971
Crispin Course architect: Robert Biery   Year opened: 1928

Speidel Course rating/Slope rating:
Gold - 73.5/137   White - 69.2/126
Blue - 71.6/129   Red - 69.7/120

Crispin Course rating/Slope rating:
Blue 66.6/109   White 65.1/108
Red 68.4/103

This lovely and inviting mountain facility is a remarkable example of the success that can result from a public-private partnership. Oglebay Park (they pronounce it "OGLE-bee") is a Wheeling municipal park, but head pro Karen Waialae underscores that it is "self-sustaining," adding, "All of our funds come from what we generate in fees, the hotel, that sort of thing." The goal, she said, is to make it a premier golf venue that provides a broad range of golf for all players, from pros to those high handicappers who may only play a few times a year. The plans include fifty-four holes of golf on three courses, a golf academy, and practice facilities, as well as the other resort amenities.

As we went to press, a new eighteen-hole golf course designed by Arnold Palmer was well on the way toward becoming a reality, scheduled for completion in the summer of 1999. A preview look during construction revealed a long, sporting, spectacular mountain golf course that will challenge even the best players. Palmer's bold and ambitious design will complement the classical elegance of Robert Trent Jones's Speidel Course and the old-fashioned charm and peculiarity of the Crispin Course.

The park has long been a popular favorite with Wheeling-area residents, drawing regulars from Ohio and Pennsylvania as well. It is now expected to become a nationally known golf complex, able to compete on its merits with the best in the country.

Speidel Course

This course is an example of Robert Trent Jones Sr.'s golf-course architecture at its very best, and it clearly demonstrates that he is every bit as much at home in the mountains as in the marshy lowlands of Virginia's Tidewater or on the windblown linksland of Ireland's Kerry coast. The Speidel Course is in sharp contrast to some of Jones's flatland golf courses, such as the Gold Course at the Golden Horseshoe, yet at the same time his philosophy of how the game should be played comes through on virtually every hole. Robert Trent Jones Sr. is reluctant to make any hole too easy. For example, rarely does he provide much bailout

OGLEBAY SPEIDEL GOLF COURSE

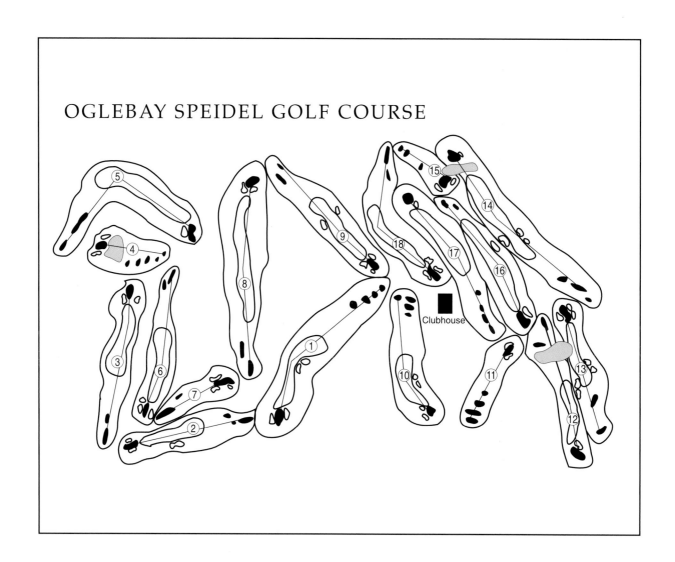

Speidel Course

HOLE NUMBER	Ra	Sl	1	2	3	4	5	6	7	8	9	OUT	10	11	12	13	14	15	16	17	18	IN	TOT
GOLD	73.5	137	484	384	449	192	508	420	233	514	412	3596	335	214	391	378	579	158	435	456	458	3404	7000
BLUE	71.6	129	442	380	412	148	499	399	202	493	400	3375	335	198	379	378	536	158	398	432	416	3230	6605
WHITE	69.2	126	411	342	374	124	446	387	161	465	385	3095	319	162	345	278	500	139	398	414	396	2951	6046
PAR			4	4	4	3	5	4	3	5	4	36	4	3	4	4	5	3	4	4	4	35	71
HANDICAP			1	13	5	17	7	9	15	3	11		16	12	10	14	2	18	8	4	6		
RED	69.7	120	377	319	355	94	378	360	131	431	358	2803	297	129	325	258	360	91	355	266	357	2438	5241

room on his par threes, rarely does he give you a short par five that's anything but a risk-reward situation with the extremes favoring the risk side of the equation, and rarely does he design greens that are anything but replete with subtle and not-so-subtle contours and undulations.

Jones takes special pains with his par threes. On virtually every one of his golf courses you can expect one-shot holes that are difficult, clever, aesthetically pleasing, visually intimidating, daunting, awesomely treacherous, or all of the above. The Speidel Course is no exception.

The moderately sized greens range from merely fast when the weather is cool and moist to blisteringly quick when the weather gets hot and dry. The golf course itself plays uphill, downhill, or sidehill on virtually every hole, every shot, and every putt. Flat stances and level lies are more the exception than the rule. Even veteran mountain players are impressed; flatlanders will come away breathless.

The LPGA staged an annual tournament at Oglebay Park's Speidel Course for a dozen years in the 1970s and '80s for twelve years. "It gave the girls fits," said Waialae. "They weren't used to this after playing in flat places like Florida and Arizona."

It's a long, difficult course for most average women players and, in fact, several new tee boxes are being constructed to shorten the forward markers and make them a little more forgiving, "but without compromising the integrity of the golf course," emphasized Dick Moore, operations manager and PGA pro. That change will give women the options of playing the forward markers or—for the better, lower-handicap women—of moving back and playing a slightly longer set of tees.

The opening hole presents a panoramic view of the surrounding mountains and forest from an elevated set of terraced tees. It's a long par-four dogleg left with bunkers at the left bend of the dogleg. Two more par fours get you well into the heart of the Speidel Course: the medium-length, downhill #2 and the long #3 with its steep uphill approach to the green. In fact, on your second shot you can usually see the flag, but you can't see the putting surface.

The tees on the breathtakingly beautiful par-three #3 serve as an amphitheater for the forested mountains, with abundant flowers in spring and an artist's palette of color in the autumn. Don't let the view interrupt your concentration. The hole plays from a steeply elevated series of tees to a small green far below. The angle of the approach makes the green appear even smaller than it really is, nestled behind a pond with an embankment studded with trees arcing behind it. The verdant mountains tower in the distance, and care must be taken not to be distracted by the scenery. Club selection here is critical.

A wonderful par-five dogleg right follows. Big hitters can challenge the trees along the right side and try to cut enough of the dogleg to have a shot at the flag in two. Note that in the landing area the fairway is sloped precariously down the hill. The green is perched on a hillside platform that will reject an approach that comes short or right. The par-four #6 plays downhill all the way. The approach to the long, thin green must be precise. The green is about 45 yards from front to back and, in an unusual and subtle design twist, the contours run from front to back. It is possible to be at the opposite end of the green from the pin and have a putt that's not only tremendously long but that also has two, three, or four breaks in it as it traverses the length of the putting surface.

Three long, demanding holes finish the front side. The 7th is the longest par three on the track and plays uphill. As if that's not tough enough, Jones has constructed a nasty little a drop-off to the right. The tight par-five #8 plays to a green that's hooked to the right and guarded by bunkers and trees. The par-four #9 is two different golf holes. From the forward markers the hole is a gentle dogleg right that plays slightly uphill on your drive; from the back markers it plays from elevated tees straight to the green.

The back nine begins with another panoramic tee placement at the top of a hill playing down into a valley. The short par-four dogleg left then requires an uphill shot to the green. You may want to think of hitting something other than a driver here. The 11th is another lovely and challenging par three by Robert Trent Jones Sr. The hole is a glorious test of golfing skill and a feast for the eye. It demands a long tee shot with a steep vertical drop to a small green protected by a severe, unforgiving hill to the left and a deep bunker to the right front.

A pair of interesting par fours follow in succession. The 12th hole is intimidating from the tees, especially for women. Female golfers must hit a long drive and carry a wide lake with no bailout room. Everybody hits to a precarious hilltop landing area that's constricted on the right by a hill and on the left by a bunker. The tee shot on the next hole is comparatively forgiving, but the ribbon of green is long enough to land a small plane, just under 50 yards from front to back.

The 14th is a huge par five that's tightly out of bounds to the right, and there's nothing you want to hit out of on the left.

Your tee shot must thread its way through a trio of fairway bunkers. A small pond caresses the front of the green and provides virtually no escape route on any side. Dick Moore related the story of one of the LPGA pros one year who was among the tournament leaders on Sunday at #14. "She put her second nicely in front of the pond," Moore said. "She then chili-dipped her third into the water, skulled her next shot out of bounds over the green, and chunked the next one back into the water. I think she walked away with an eleven."

A trio of par fours follows the watery, sandy par-three #15 to complete the round. Your drive on the long #16 is to a hilltop, and then the approach is steeply downhill to the green. The long par-four #17 is a dogleg left that plays around a hill. And #18 is a lovely closer that will test your nerve and your skill. It's a sharp dogleg left with a line of pines blocking a view of the green from the tee boxes. The conservative play is to hit an iron or fairway wood to the bend in the dogleg and then negotiate a long approach to the green. The bold play is to hit your drive over the pines and leave yourself anything from a sand wedge to an eight iron in to the pin. The green is devilishly difficult. "When I was here in the evening to close up," said Dick Moore with a smile, looking over the 18th green from the clubhouse restaurant, "some of us would sit up here and watch the last groups play in, and we'd bet on who'd sink it, who'd two-putt, and so on. Three putts was never a bad bet."

For some reason the Speidel Course has not gotten very much national press lately. Perhaps that is because of all the new golf courses being constructed in the Virginias. Perhaps golf publications just don't have much to say about venerable old courses that have been around for decades. But it is no exaggeration to say that the Speidel Course ranks among the very best courses in West Virginia and in the region.

Crispin Course

This little golf course has garnered sneers and scorn from some golfers and golf writers, many of whom may never even have played it. They are automatically put off by its length—only 5,627 yards from the back tees and a mere 4,993 from the forward markers—and they proceed under the assumption that it's a pitch-and-putt goat track and should simply be ignored. It's too easy, they postulate. It's not worthy of the time to play it. They are wrong—on all counts! Yep. It's short. That's the way they built them in the 1920s. Yep. It's easy, by today's standards. Nope. It doesn't have planked bunkers, sculpted greens, and fairways lined with man-made mounds. But therein lies its uniqueness.

It is a throwback to another era, a vestige of days when few people owned golf clubs, when only a few companies made golf balls, when golf shoes were a custom-made luxury for only the very rich, and when golf itself was considered an odd and somewhat decadent pastime. Today golf is accessible to a wide segment of the population, but there are too few reminders of the way things used to be. This is one of them.

The Crispin Course is an absolutely charming little piece of golf history there for the sampling. It is unlike almost any other golf course in the country. It's not a big, blustering, belligerent modern golf course; it's a quirky, peculiar oddity, far removed from those immaculate modern designs that we're all accustomed to and that fill the pages of every golf magazine. It's a look backward, a key to our golfing past. It is thoroughly charming in its old-fashioned way. And for students of the game, it serves as a living textbook of where the game was and how far it has come.

The first nine holes opened in 1928, the tail end of the Roaring Twenties, the age of jazz and flappers and sequins and boas. The economic and social events that led to the Great Depression were taking shape. The country was in a period of transition. And there, in the mountains outside Wheeling, West Virginia, a golf course was hewn out of the hills and forests. It was very sophisticated for its day, if primitive by the standards of today's earth-moving exercises. What emerged was a golf course set among forested hills and grassy glens. The greens range from tiny to minuscule. In fact, the only smaller greens I've ever encountered are at the Spotswood Course, the executive course designed by Robert Trent Jones Sr. at The Golden Horseshoe in Williamsburg.

Time passed and events changed the face of America. The country was plunged into the economic bleakness of the Great Depression. And in the years immediately following, projects were undertaken to get the country back on its feet. The administration of Franklin D. Roosevelt pushed legislation to put people to work on public projects. Crispin's architecturally intriguing stone clubhouse was built as a WPA project and has become a community landmark. "The big bands would all come to play in the big room there, and everybody would drive up the mountain on Saturday night. If

The tiny 3rd green on Oglebay Park's Crispin Course, with the even smaller 7th in the distance, is a reminder of how golf courses were built before the Great Depression.

you weren't there on Saturday night, you were nowhere," said a retired executive who used to caddy at the Crispin Course as a boy during World War II.

The second nine was built after the Great Depression and, as if to reflect the new optimism in the country, the greens were bigger, the fairways wider and more level, and the holes more forgiving.

They didn't use much sand in those days unless there was a source of sand nearby; needless to say, they didn't have much sand in the mountains around Wheeling. From a playing perspective, the front side is the better and more interesting nine, although each in its own way offers a glimpse of the past. By any standard it is a pretty course. It requires shot making, and it is utterly charming.

The outgoing nine is the older side and consists of three par threes, three par fours, and three par fives. Two of the par fives are short enough that they can be ego-boosters for even medium hitters who may attempt to go for the greens in two. The most notable holes include #2, a lovely par three that plays slightly downhill along a hillside, with a steep right-to-left slope all the way from tee to green. The wee green is missed about as often as it's hit from 174 yards away. The par-five #4 plays downhill and is reachable in two shots except for women, who must propel their golf balls 472 yards from tee to

green, the same length as from the men's white markers. The 7th is a lovely, long downhill par three. The minute green looks about as big as a handkerchief from the tee boxes. The 8th is a par five and would have been a monster in 1928. It's more than 550 yards from the back tees and plays across a pond and then straight uphill. The approach crests the hill and must find a tiny green at the base of the hill. Toughest hole on the card.

On the back nine, the 11th is a short, tricky par four. It's an uphill hole playing to a green that's hooked behind a pair of tall, canopied trees that make floating a shot onto the putting surface nearly impossible. The 13th is a long, pretty par three that plays from elevated tees to a green at the base of the hill. The course finishes with three short par fours, with the final hole playing up a hill from the tees and then downhill to the green.

The Crispin Course has critics who berate it as being out of step and not worth playing. The other side, however, can be argued with passion. Those who claim that it's too easy, too short, too old-fashioned, or too tame have no reverence for the origins, history, and heritage of the sport. To paraphrase a Native American proverb: It is impossible to know where you are going if you do not know where you have been. If for no other reason, that makes the Crispin Course worth playing.

Crispin Course

HOLE NUMBER	Ra	Sl	1	2	3	4	5	6	7	8	9	OUT	10	11	12	13	14	15	16	17	18	IN	TOT
BLUE	66.6	109	280	174	350	491	89	314	190	551	490	2929	152	351	472	192	351	334	240	272	334	2698	5627
WHITE	65.1	108	264	162	330	472	89	301	181	530	480	2809	140	336	462	182	340	320	220	260	315	2575	5384
PAR			4	3	4	5	3	4	3	5	5	36	3	4	5	3	4	4	4	4	4	35	71
HANDICAP			15	9	11	5	17	7	13	1	3			16	2	8	12	6	4	18	14	10	
RED	68.4	103	240	156	312	472	89	275	170	461	454	2629	121	310	414	179	325	310	184	250	272	2364	4993

The back nine at the Olde Mill Golf Club opens with a pair of spectacular par fours that play beside a portion of the sixty-five-acre lake that comes into play on more than half the holes on this Ellis Maples design.

OLDE MILL GOLF CLUB

Laurel Fork, Virginia (From I-81, take I-77 to Route 58 east for about 18 miles; golf course sign is on the right)
Phone: (800) 753-5005 or (540) 398-2211

Architect: Ellis Maples   Year opened: 1972

Course rating/Slope rating:
Blue - 72.7/127   Gold (men) - 66.2/116
White - 69.5/122   Gold (women) - 76.2/142
Red - 70.4/134

If the Olde Mill Golf Club is not the most unknown spectacular golf course in the Virginias, it is certainly in the top two or three. When it opened in 1972, it firmly established Ellis Maples, already a well-known golf-course architect, as one of the premier designers of mountain golf courses in the world. (Maples' more famous Devil's Knob course opened at Wintergreen five years later.)

Maples took what nature gave him and enhanced it, using the terrain and all it offered to generate the character and temperament of the golf course. And what a wonderful temperament it is. To play it once is to want to play it again and again. The mountains and hills are its foundation; the trees and rocks are fundamental to its personality; and the water is its very soul. "There's no question that what people remember is the lake," said head pro Hagen Giles. "We've got a sixty-five-acre lake that weaves through a lot of the golf course." In fact, water—in the form of that lake or a series of meandering creeks—comes into play on fourteen of the eighteen holes.

The course is not the most difficult or demanding in the Virginias. It does not offer the brutal intimidation or extremes of difficulty of, say, Stonehouse, Royal New Kent, or the Gold Course at the Golden Horseshoe. But that's not what Ellis Maples set out to build. What he did build is fair and enjoyable from both a golfing and an aesthetic perspective. The setting is simply breathtaking, with the distant Blue Ridge Mountains changing shades and hues as you observe them during your round.

There are an enormous number of courses that offer pleasurable golf in a serene setting, but this is one of those rare golf courses that you can fall in love with. It's the kind of course that you wish were closer to home so you could join it and play it regularly. This is the kind of course that, like a good friend, you'd like to know intimately.

This is not a golf course for beginners, but while low handicappers will enjoy the back tees (at 6,833 yards), higher-handicap players will have a fine time with the shorter markers. The course features three sets of tees that are rated and sloped for men and two sets for women. Female golfers should be warned that the gold markers are rated a daunting 76.2 and are sloped 142 for women; they will test even those planning a run at the LPGA to their

limit. Most women will find the red tees provide a very satisfying round.

In general the golf course is tight and hilly. All of the greens are on the small side and offer a plentitude of subtle contours, tiers, levels, and breaks. That said, they are true and generally receptive and will reward precise shot making.

The 1st hole provides a panorama of what's to come. It tees from the vicinity of the clubhouse, which sits on a mountain-top, and plays steeply downhill to a slender fairway far below. The well-bunkered green is hooked behind the lake, which comes into play along the left side of the fairway for about the last third of the hole.

The short 3rd hole is devilish, a severe dogleg right around a corner of the lake. The fairway is compressed between the hazard and a pine-studded hill, and it

narrows precipitously as it gets closer to the green. The putting surface is a peninsula, surrounded by water on three sides and offering precious little bailout room to the left. It is a risk-reward hole. A well-placed drive can leave a short chip to the pin; a tee shot that fails to clear the lake can drown any thoughts of a par or birdie. While it is not rated among the most difficult holes on the course, regulars say it yields at least as many bogeys and doubles as it does pars and birdies.

The short par-five #5 is a dogleg left with a blind tee shot. The hidden danger, unseen from the tees, is that the fairway is canted steeply right to left, and a little tongue of the lake intrudes into the fairway directly in front of the green. The danger of going for it in two is that your second shot must carry all the way to the puny putting surface.

150

The 7th hole is a tough par five that plays uphill. It's rated the second-toughest hole on the golf course. Your tee shot must thread its way between the bunkers that guard both sides of the fairway. There's an indentation in front of the elevated green and a large greenside bunker directly in front of the putting surface.

The outward side finishes with a cute, short par four that tees off dramatically downhill. It's a sharp dogleg right, and most players will find a driver puts them through the fairway, possibly into one of several fairway bunkers, and leaves a tough, if not impossible, approach. Those brave souls who try to launch a fairway wood or long iron over the four sentry-like pines that stand at the right corner of the dogleg can easily find the lake. The green is perched on a hillside shelf across the lake from the landing area.

The medium-length par-four #10 is the Olde Mill's signature hole. From the terraced tee boxes on the side of the mountain, you launch your drive into space, across the lake far below, to a stingy landing area. The green is then back up an incline between a pair of large sand traps. A pair of short par fours can enhance your score as you head toward the most distant point from the clubhouse.

The toughest hole on the card is the long, tight, par-five #13, a dogleg right with the lake along most of its left length and an inhospitable rock-strewn hill to the right. Any shot that strays from the

fairway is in some measure of trouble; the degree of the trouble is dependent on how errant the shot. The smallish, elevated green is protected by four gaping, steep-faced bunkers that require a high, soft approach.

The pretty par-three #14 is all carry over a corner of the lake, although there is a little room to chicken out to the right. One of the creeks that splash and roll through the golf course plays around the par-four #15 and intersects the par-four #16 in front of the green.

The finisher is a par five that's reachable in two. Your drive is through a chute of trees to the left and a steep, unfriendly hill to the right. It's a gentle dogleg right uphill to the green, with a pair of bushy old trees blocking the entrance to the green and splitting the fairway. It looks easier on the card than it plays.

Despite its remote location in Laurel Fork, Virginia—south-southwest of Roanoke and north of Mount Airy, North Carolina—it is well worth a detour if you find yourself in southwestern Virginia, northwestern North Carolina, or southern West Virginia. It is a fine golfing experience. The golf course itself is well maintained, and the whole facility is superbly managed. In addition, the scenery—both from the golf course and as you drive to it—is unparalleled.

"I've been here ten years," head pro Giles said. "It's certainly a beautiful place to come to work each day."

Olde Mill

HOLE	Ra	Sl	1	2	3	4	5	6	7	8	9	OUT	10	11	12	13	14	15	16	17	18	IN	TOT
BLUE	72.7	127	440	162	379	378	524	413	511	188	390	3385	371	388	386	580	178	460	394	197	494	3448	6833
WHITE	69.5	122	395	134	325	356	454	378	471	164	363	3040	338	348	356	549	156	423	368	163	444	3145	6185
GOLD	66.2 (m)/76.2 (w)	116 (m)/142 (w)	380	128	264	287	405	334	419	143	318	2678	265	311	305	507	123	408	308	119	429	2775	5453
HCP (m)			7	18	13	11	3	5	2	15	9		14	12	10	1	17	4	8	16	6		
PAR			4	3	4	4	5	4	5	3	4	36	4	4	4	5	3	4	4	3	5	36	72
RED	70.4	134	286	119	245	281	397	263	407	139	312	2449	261	301	261	452	111	266	277	115	383	2427	4876

The par-four #17 at Raspberry Falls Golf & Hunt Club is lined with bunkers from the bend in the dogleg all the way to the elevated green.

RASPBERRY FALLS GOLF & HUNT CLUB

Leesburg, Virginia (Take either the Dulles Toll Road or Route 7 west to Route 15 north; the entrance is about 3 miles on the left.)
Phone: (703) 779-2555

Architect: Gary Player   Year opened: 1996

Course rating/Slope rating:
Black - 74.3/134   White - (men) 66.4/114
Gold - 72.2/129   Blue (women) - 76.4/133
Blue - (men) 69.8/126   White (women) - 71.7/124
Raspberry - 68.0/115

Raspberry Falls Golf & Hunt Club describes itself as an upscale daily-fee golf course set on what was once one of Virginia's most productive eighteenth-century plantations. It is little short of a brilliant example of golf-course design, coupled with the amenities of a first-rate country club. Gary Player has created a golf course that stands among the best in the country, and each year as it matures it simply gets better and better. The course plays among rolling hills, rocky outcroppings, ancient trees, and streams, but if there is one thing that will stick in your mind long after you've played Raspberry Falls, it will be the bunkering.

On every hole, Player the architect has called on the enormous experience and institutional memory of Player the champion. In his heyday he was one of the greatest sand players that ever lifted a sand wedge, and he has deliberately and systematically challenged the sand skills of all who venture forth into his realm. Player has used what is known as a "stacked sod" technique for creating many of his sand hazards, thus imparting the feel of a Scottish or Irish links course to this design. It also presents the golfer with enormous vertical lips over which almost every sand shot must be played.

There are dozens of them—not dropped in haphazardly, but brilliantly and often devilishly placed. Some are there more to create elements of visual intimidation than to catch stray golf balls; others will come into play if an unfortunate golfer experiences a lapse in concentration or fails to execute his or her shot properly. Player has even given some of the bunkers names such as "Deep Cotton," "Player's Prison," "Grant's Tomb," and "Satan's Revenge." The best advice is to avoid them. The reality is that very few players will succeed in staying out of the sand for eighteen holes, and anybody who's that good should be playing the back tees (which present a nearly 7,200-yard monster) and should be thinking about getting a PGA card.

The opening hole sets the stage. It's a straightaway, medium-length par four with a trio of fairway bunkers eager to catch any tee shot that drifts to the right. The approach to the irregularly shaped, slightly elevated green must clear a thin but treacherous sand trap that Player has dubbed "Deep Cotton." The little bunker

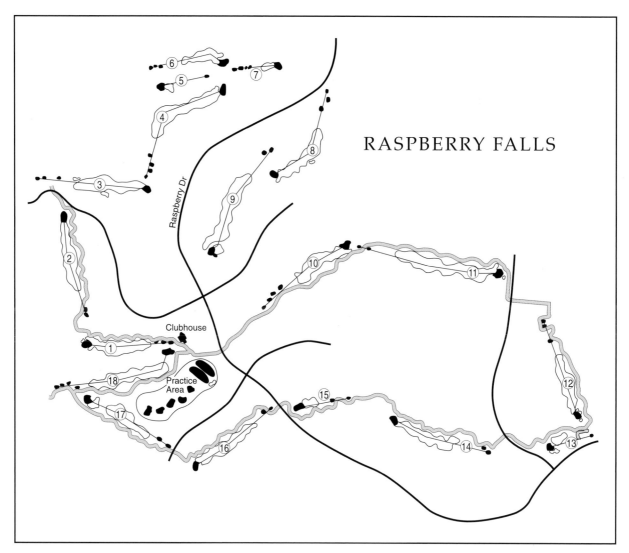

RASPBERRY FALLS

at the back of the green is often a reminder to the nervous sand player that an overeager shot can easily be propelled from Deep Cotton to deep trouble.

The long, tight par-four 3rd is rated the second-most-difficult hole on the front nine. It plays downhill from an elevated series of tees and measures more than 400 yards from all but the forward markers. Your long approach is to a rolling, undulating green shaped like a three-leaf clover, with the leaf in front canted back down the fairway toward you. The par-five 4th hole is a huge dogleg right, and only the bravest or the longest hitters will

try to carry the enormous bunker that extends almost from the tee boxes to the point at which the hole turns right. There is lots of room off the tee, but the hole narrows as you near the smallish green.

The par-three #5—the first of the four brilliant, if sometimes daunting, one-shot holes on Raspberry Falls—ranges in length from a testing 204 yards from the championship tees to 83 yards for women. It's rated the easiest hole on the course, but before you whine about its lack of challenge, consider taking your par or birdie and walking away happy, because you're in for some seriously demanding golf for the rest of the round. Even the holes rated easy will give you something to stiffen your spine. And the three holes at the turn—#9, #10, and #11—are the three toughest on the course. So if you can shoot low numbers on #6, #7, and #8, do it, because bogeys, double bogeys, and worse lurk just up ahead.

The tee shot is everything on the short par-four #6. A shot that's too long can run through the fairway and into the rough. If you are merely strong or if you really muscle it, the shot can find a nasty, strategically placed bunker from which it's almost impossible to score well. A shot that aims at the open front of the green and comes up short or drifts to the right will be penalized by rocks and scrub brush. The green is guarded by a snarling bunker named "Ford's Theater."

The 9th hole is justifiably rated the most difficult on the front side. Unlike many of the longer holes on Raspberry Falls, which provide a generous landing area from the tee, this par five requires an accurate tee shot because of sand to the left and hazards to the right. But that's just the tip of the iceberg. The bulk of the trouble is around the green, which will require a serious risk assessment before you think about going for it in two. It goes without saying that Player has provided well-placed sand traps, but this hole also presents a small but hungry stream that meanders across the fairway and edges the front of the green. The putting surface extends almost to a rock wall, dubbed "The Citadel," which creates a buffer between the elevated green and the water hazard. Be aware that if you elect to go for it in two and come up short, your ball can end up in the next area code; if you land your shot too crisply on the putting surface, it will skip off the back into one of

the bunkers or into a collection area between them. One eleven handicapper playing from the gold-tee markers said, "Three wood. Three iron. Wedge close. One putt. That's the theory."

The par-four #10 is deceptively lovely, with the lake that caresses the green shimmering in the distance as you tee off. Avoid the cluster of fairway bunkers to the right, but the key here is to place your drive in a position to successfully approach the green, which is a peninsula on the lake. The lake itself is in play on the left from the point where the fairway doglegs right all the way to the green. If you have to bail out, there's room to the right front.

The 11th hole is simply a monster par five, nearly 600 yards from the back tees to a wide, shallow green guarded by—you guessed it!—three enormous bunkers, the front one ominously named "Grant's Tomb." Length is the key here, but once you're safely on the putting surface, you will find that the green is relatively flat.

Take a breather on the par-three #12, which appears much harder to the eye than it is. The Saharan waste area that runs from tee to green should not come into play, but you must take enough club to clear the little stream and marshy area in front of the green and to avoid the treacherous little amoeba-shaped bunker that abuts the putting surface.

The 16th and 17th are just very solid golf holes. Sixteen is a straightaway, unpretentious par four, save for the desertlike peril known as "Myrtle Beach" that sits directly in front of the elevated green. If you land in it, you generally have a blind shot out of it. The stacked-sod face is taller than Michael Jordan (The first time I was unlucky enough to get into it, I failed to get out on my first two attempts and ended up chipping it back into the fairway and hitting over it to the green). The 17th hole, also a par four, features a treed ridge to the left and four gaping bunkers on the right side of the fairway. That leads to a slightly elevated green wedged between two bunkers.

The par-five #18, designed in the shape of a J, presents a spectacular panorama from the elevated tees. The left side of the fairway is protected by trees, a stream, and marshy rough. Most players try to lay their second shots directly in front of the stream that cuts across the fairway adjacent to the green. The banks of the stream on both sides are severely beveled toward the water. The hourglass-shaped green is extremely difficult to approach and yields birdies unwillingly. Nonetheless, once finished, you know you've played a superior golf course by any standard.

Gary Player has used his substantial knowledge of the game from a player's perspective in working out the placement of the ladies' tees, in many cases presenting women with the same type of approach shots as men. For example, on the first hole most women will outdrive most men, but nearly everybody—men and women—will be faced with a medium- to short-iron approach; on the short par-four #6, virtually every player will use a very lofted club for their second shot. It is a testament to Player's sophistication as a designer that he does not simply present women with a drive and a fairway wood on virtually every par four—a feature that has, arguably, been an architectural error on many courses laid out before the 1970s and '80s.

It was always acknowledged that women played golf, and a few of the old-timers—designers such as Donald Ross and Harry Colt—took pains with the placement of the women's tees. But a few modern architects—such as Player, Mark McCumber, Arnold Palmer, and Rees Jones—have entered a new dimension and have taken special pains to make their courses challenging and fair to women as well as to male players of all levels of ability, both in tee-box placement and in anticipation of the kind of second shots that will be played.

Raspberry Falls succeeds extremely well in its stated goal of being a daily-fee golf course that feels like a private country club. The course itself is painstakingly maintained. The clubhouse is top-notch. The pro-shop staff is knowledgeable and friendly. The bag-and-cart crew and the starters all strive to afford players a good golf experience. The amount of repeat play is testimony to the popularity and excellence of Raspberry Falls and, even if you live far away, it is worth a detour if you're anywhere around Washington, D.C., or Leesburg, Virginia.

Raspberry Falls

HOLE	Ra	SI	1	2	3	4	5	6	7	8	9	OUT	10	11	12	13	14	15	16	17	18	IN	TOT
BLACK	74.3	134	385	428	479	549	204	333	192	443	529	3542	462	590	432	184	431	220	411	369	550	3649	7191
GOLD	72.2	129	358	397	445	529	182	316	176	409	498	3308	426	570	413	171	412	200	384	342	539	3457	6765
BLUE	69.8 (m)/76.4 (w)	126 (m)/133 (w)	316	375	428	498	138	293	160	265	479	3052	384	542	396	158	390	184	354	301	535	3244	6296
PAR			4	4	4	5	3	4	3	4	5	36	4	5	4	3	4	3	4	4	5	36	72
HCP			12	10	4	6	18	14	16	8	2		3	1	9	13	7	15	11	17	5		
WHITE	66.4 (m)/71.7 (w)	114 (m)/124 (w)	273	336	411	467	119	270	150	331	420	2777	332	445	352	133	334	158	319	275	451	2799	5576
RASP	68.0	115	241	300	378	416	83	210	131	260	390	2409	288	405	289	108	292	132	265	258	418	2445	4854

RESTON NATIONAL GOLF COURSE

11875 Sunrise Valley Drive, Reston, Virginia (Take Dulles Airport Toll Road from the Washington Beltway or I-66 to exit 12, Reston Parkway south to second stoplight; turn left; golf-course entrance is one block on the right.)

Phone: (703) 620-9333

Architect: Ed Ault   Year opened: 1968

Course rating/Slope rating:
Back tees - 72.9/126   Middle tees - 71.4/123
Forward tees - 74.3/132

The day John F. Kennedy took the oath of office, what is now Reston, Virginia, was an amalgam of rich farmlands, pastures, trees, creeks, and marsh; it was a rural stretch of land without a name between the Washington, D.C., suburb of Vienna, Virginia, and the sleepy, remote village of Herndon. Reston is a "planned" community in the mold of New York's Levittown, Long Island, with a set number of apartments, townhouses, single-family homes, schools, stores, and the like. When the town of Reston was still on the drawing board, two golf courses were envisioned—one public, the other private. Ed Ault was commissioned to design both. What is now Reston National Golf Course was originally earmarked to be the private club; its sibling about two miles north is now the private country club.

Reston National is a mature old golf course, laid out among hills, trees, and townhouses. It is a long, testing track that provides a superior golfing experience for players of all levels. It plays to a par 71 for men and a par 72 for women, and even low handicappers will have to use almost every club in the bag. Typical of Ed Ault golf courses, it presents a different look and feel to men and women. For example, the par-five #2 is rated the third-most-dif-

ficult hole on the course for women, and it's rated the easiest for men. The par-three #16, in contrast, is rated the easiest hole on the course for women, while it is the number-five-stroke hole for men.

The round begins with a gentle par four, rendered even friendlier in that it plays down a hill and features little trouble off the tee. The biggest problem approaching the large green is that a tee shot that drifts too far to the right can be blocked by a stand of towering old trees in the vicinity of the green.

The par-five #2 offers tremendous scoring opportunities. It is reachable in two shots for even moderate hitters, and even though the drive is blind, there is really little to cause you difficulty from the tee. For women, however, it's a 426-yard headache. Women's tee shots must crest the hill in order to set up a solid approach. The green, which sits on a little plateau, is guarded on the right and left by small but frequently hit sand traps.

The one-shot 3rd hole is superbly bunkered and demands that the player select enough club to carry all the way to the putting surface. The par-four #4 is one of the tighter holes on the front nine, with trees and out-of-bounds along its left length and a forest to the right. The dogleg right par-five #5 plays into a valley,

In spring, dogwoods bloom behind the green on Reston National's long, difficult par-four 17th hole.

across a stream, and then back uphill to a large and tricky green.

The finishing three holes on the outward nine are a trio of splendid par fours, rated more difficult for men than women, but anybody walking away with three pars will be well satisfied. The 7th is a dogleg left with a lake in play to the left along most of its length. A yawning fairway bunker at the point where the hole changes direction is just waiting to catch a wayward tee shot. The 8th hole, which is blind from the tee, is a gentle dogleg right and is uphill for most of its length. Any shot to the right is almost guaranteed trouble and may well result in a penalty stroke. The green is undulating and well guarded. The 9th hole is also a dogleg right and tempts long hitters to cut a substantial chunk out of it, but it's longer than it looks, and the trees to the right will make for a difficult approach if your drive isn't long enough to clear them.

The 10th is a long, tight par four for men rated the number-one handicap hole; it's a very scorable par five for women. What you see from the tee is what you get: it's down a substantial hill with lots of trees lining both sides of the fairway and playing to one of the smallest greens on Reston National.

The 12th, 13th, and 14th holes again provide a wonderful trio of par fours, which then lead to the superb par-five #15, a dogleg right that is fraught with peril down its right side and that plays to a green that's button-hooked behind a greedy and unpleasant bunker.

The long par-four #17 is a trough with a treed ridge along its left length and a hill along the right. Straight tee shots will provide good results and present an excellent approach to the green; hooks and slices will not produce happy consequences. The hole plays to an elevated green and more often than not into the prevailing westerly wind. As with many of Ed Ault's holes, you see exactly what is required of you from the tee, so the only issue becomes execution and club selection.

The 18th is a lovely finisher with no less than eight bunkers in play. It's the sandiest hole on the course but is designed in such a way that a well-struck drive will land in the middle of a quintet of sand traps. The big green requires a close approach to stay out of three-putt range, but it offers a good scoring opportunity for men and women at the end of the round.

Architect Ed Ault favors an interesting but fair mix of holes—long and short, tight and relatively open—in his designs. While Reston National is far from the most difficult course built by Ault, it is a fine and representative example of his work. There are a few blind shots, a good measure of sand and water, and more than enough trees to punish errant hits. But there is nothing tricked-up or contrived in Ault's courses. They require solid shot making and course management to score. In this case, the par threes are especially good, ranging from moderately short to long and tough, with well-guarded greens and interesting tee-box placements.

While most of the greens are ample and undulating, they are generally not cut particularly fast, although an accurate read and a true putting stroke will yield generous rewards. If there is a problem with Reston National, it is that it is an extremely popular course located in the shadow of the nation's capital, and as a result it can be very crowded—with slow play to match—especially on summer weekends. On the other hand, if you reserve your tee time and arrange to play on a weekday—Monday through Thursday are optimal—you are in for a very pleasant round.

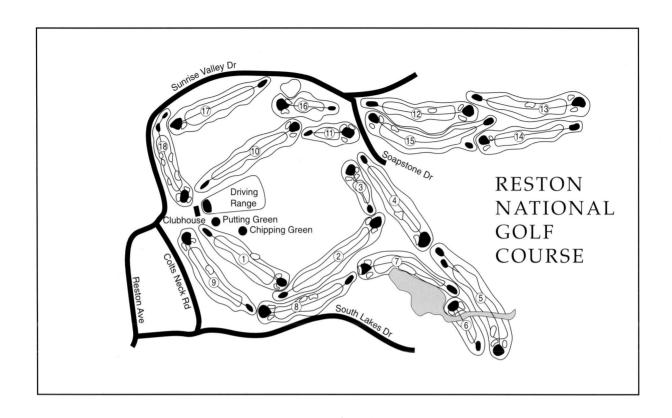

Reston National

HOLE NUMBER	Ra	Sl	1	2	3	4	5	6	7	8	9	OUT	10	11	12	13	14	15	16	17	18	IN	TOT
BACK	72.9	126	394	516	184	423	515	208	422	389	414	3465	459	175	426	447	378	529	204	416	372	3406	6871
MID	71.4	123	373	487	166	411	499	183	405	374	397	3295	439	160	408	416	358	500	192	380	358	3211	6506
PAR (m)			4	5	3	4	5	3	4	4	4	36	4	3	4	4	4	5	3	4	4	35	71
HANDICAP (m)			14	18	16	8	10	12	4	2	6		1	17	7	3	11	13	5	9	15		
FOR	74.3	132	351	426	147	399	477	127	386	360	380	3053	418	144	395	393	338	435	142	319	299	2883	5936
PAR (w)			4	5	3	4	5	3	4	4	4	36	5	3	4	4	4	5	3	4	4	36	72
HANDICAP (w)			13	3	15	11	1	17	5	7	9		4	16	8	10	12	2	18	6	14		

ROYAL NEW KENT

3001 Bailey Road, Providence Forge, Virginia (Take I-64 to exit 214 and follow Route 155 south for about 2½ miles; turn left at the Royal New Kent entrance.)
Phone: (804) 966-7023

Architect: Mike Strantz   Year opened: 1996

Course rating/Slope rating:
Gold - 74.9/144   White - 70.8/135
Black - 73.1/141   Green - 72.0/130

Royal New Kent is a part of the Legends Group of Myrtle Beach, South Carolina, which owns and operates a series of golf courses in Virginia and the Carolinas. This is the younger of two Legends courses in the Williamsburg area, and despite its youth, it has spawned an enormous amount of attention from the golf press and the public. This course and its sibling, Stonehouse, have golfers talking from Boston to Miami and from Atlanta to San Francisco. To cite just a few of the achievements of architect Mike Strantz and this golf course, it ranked fourteenth on *Golf & Travel*'s 1998 list of "America's 40 best public golf courses," and *Golf Digest* dubbed it "best new upscale course".

Strantz used to work for Tom Fazio's design company and has adopted and adapted some of Fazio's techniques. Some might argue that he has taken some of them to entirely new strata. From the moment you drive into the parking lot, you know you are in for a unique golfing experience. From the first glimpse of it, it is clear that this is a daunting and intimidating golf course that presents its moonscape to you on the first tee and doesn't let up until you're safely across the lake and having a cold one in the bar after your round. This relentless and demanding golf course favors players who can

put the ball where they want on every single shot and with every club they carry.

The course is set up to look like a Scottish or Irish links course, and in fact Strantz has succeeded remarkably well from the visual perspective. The first hole has the appearance of The Old Course at Ballybunion in Ireland's County Kerry or of Royal Portrush in Northern Ireland's County Antrim. But the appearance is deceiving for anyone who has played true links golf on the windblown, hard-packed coastal sand dunes and crags of Scotland or Ireland, and it might mislead those who have not had the experience to believe they are about to embark on a comparable venture. The fact remains that there is no linksland in Virginia, and it is a geological impossibility to try to re-create it without something like the holodeck simulator on TV's *Deep Space Nine*. While Strantz has created a marvelous design hybrid, Royal New Kent is not a links golf course. Links courses are very specific types of institutions. They are coastal and are hewn out of the sandy, largely treeless seaside landscapes generally associated with the British Isles and Ireland. Links golf courses exhibit a bounty of gorse and heather, rocks and dunes, and winds and rain. The sandy soil of true linksland drains almost miraculously,

The two-tiered 10th green on Royal New Kent is protected in front by an expanse of marshy wetland and a huge wraparound bunker. The back tier is almost as high above the front tier as the flagstick.

which is not the case with any of the golf courses in the Williamsburg area of Virginia, including Royal New Kent.

With great creativity and artistry Strantz has explored some entirely new design territory at Royal New Kent. The course is utterly brilliant in its conception and is an engineering marvel in the final product. That Ballybunion look-alike opening hole is just a prelude of things to come. The opener is a nothing short of awesome to the eye as you stand there pondering your future. It's a par four on which you launch your drive from terraced tees that unveil a severe dogleg left. The blind tee shot plays through a trough and must be far enough to pass the mountain on the left that hides the two-tiered green perched like a vulture at the top of a hill. Avoid the massive bunker on the right side. If you get in it, the bunker is about 12 feet below the putting surface.

The 2nd hole is a horseshoe-shaped par five. Your tee shot must clear a creek in the middle of a stretch of knee-high rough, and rocks. The landing area raises the curtain on the green, which sits on a shelf above and across a basin of deep grass, mounds, moguls, and brush that forms the center of the horseshoe. The long par-three #3 plays across more unplayable foliage, rocks, and wetlands to an elevated, two-tiered hourglass-shaped green. There's trouble in every direction except to the back, with a steep slope to the left that will cascade your golf ball into a pair of bunkers and another to the right that can reject your ball into the unplayable morass.

Most of what you see from the 4th tee—except the forward markers that actually glimpse the fairway—is an enormous bunker that looks like the footprint of some three-toed monster. There's a lot more room over the hills to the left than meets the eye. The second shot then plays uphill over a ridge that intersects the hole about midway from tee to green to an elevated putting surface that may or may not be visible, depending on the placement of your drive.

The drive is critical on the long, tight par-five #5. The shot must thread the needle between two fairway bunkers left and another pair to the right. The ball must stop just short of the three big bunkers that divide the fairway. Your shot over those bunkers is to the more elevated part of the hole, but safely on the upper fairway the green opens up.

The most difficult hole on this most difficult of golf courses is #6. It's steeply uphill from the tees, and around the bend of the left dogleg it's uphill to the multi-tiered, elevated green perched atop the hill. Royal New Kent's own literature describes it as the "most difficult green on the course," quite a statement indeed, given the difficulty of the greens here in general.

The long par-three #7 plays to a long, skinny, and highly contoured green with a creek guarding the left front and deep bunkers guarding the right rear. That's followed by a treacherous dogleg-right par four with a creek to the left and hillside bunkers to the right. If your tee shot is not precise, you may have a blind or partially blind shot uphill to the domed green. The front nine finishes with a medium-length par-four dogleg right that demands a long carry from the tees to clear the creek. That creek extends the length of the hole and lurks at the base of the hill on which the green is poised. An approach shot that's short will kick right and, barring divine intervention, drop into the water.

The back nine opens with a solid three-shot par five with a generous landing area for your tee shot. The hole then tightens and toughens all the way to the exaggerated two-tiered green. Your second shot must avoid the enormous bunker to the left. The approach to the green is almost a 90-degree angle to the left. The green sits across an expanse of marshy wetland and is squeezed vise-like by a wraparound bunker. The green's top tier is a good six feet above the lower tier.

A long uphill par four with abundant scrub and rocks and an equally inhospitable par three lead to two short par fours. The 13th is a dogleg right to a long, narrow, turtleback green. The key is to avoid the four hillside bunkers that seem to beckon from the tee boxes. There is ample room to the left once you clear the wasteland of deep rough between the tees and the short grass. The second of the short par fours again requires a tee shot—probably not a driver—across deep rough and nasty hills to a broad landing area that's the bottom of an hourglass. The second shot is blind to a hilltop green that is the top of the hourglass. The neck of the hourglass is pinched by perils. The green hides behind seven sand traps; the three in front are big enough to bury a Buick.

The 15th is a long par three to an enormous green. It may be the most difficult tee shot on the course for women. Number 16 is a brutally long par-four dogleg left. The long par-five #17 requires two well-hit setup shots to give you a reasonable look at the extremely narrow green with a hill behind it and a creek in front.

The finish at Royal New Kent is every bit as intimidating as the start. Eighteen is a long par four that tees off across an expanse of water to a green surrounded by water hazards in the front, the back, and to the right. A creek runs into the lake to the rear of the green and creates almost an island of the putting surface. The course's yardage book notes that "this hole can destroy a great round"—a claim that verges on understatement; or it can simply compound the felonious assault this golf course can inflict on anybody's game.

This is simply not a course for beginners. Period. Don't waste your money. Several pros and golf people in the area advise that for all women but those with single-digit handicaps, the course is almost unplayable. They noted that two of four par threes play in excess of 150 yards (and both are all carry) and that all of the par fives are more than 400 yards from the forward markers.

The Legends Group is paving the way for high-tech, futuristic golf. Every golf cart has a GPS (Global Positioning Satellite) receiver that will tell you such information as how far you are from the pin. And since you often can't see the pin, that information is very useful to know. In fact, without the GPS system you can get completely lost.

ROYAL NEW KENT GOLF COURSE

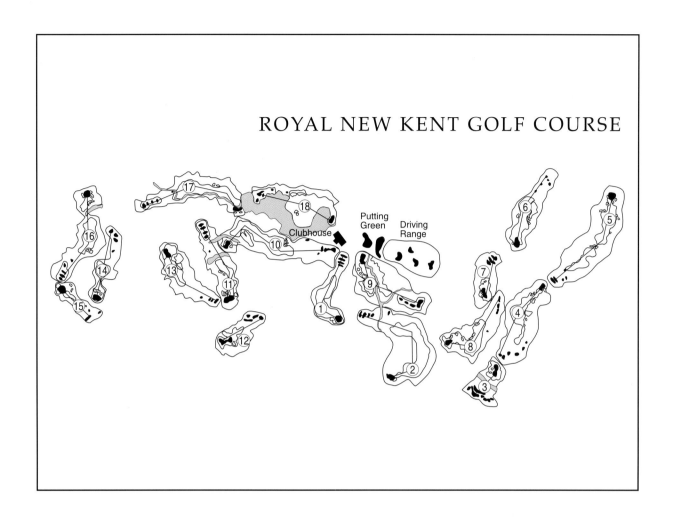

Royal New Kent

HOLE NUMBER	Ra	Sl	1	2	3	4	5	6	7	8	9	OUT	10	11	12	13	14	15	16	17	18	IN	TOT
GOLD	74.9	144	396	537	176	431	576	404	186	403	379	3488	567	401	202	366	333	229	459	537	403	3497	6985
BLACK	73.1	141	378	512	160	381	541	392	173	386	337	3260	546	378	176	346	330	208	442	509	386	3321	6581
WHITE	70.8	135	354	489	156	334	526	347	157	364	311	3048	537	354	166	334	311	182	412	484	351	3131	6179
PAR			4	5	3	4	5	4	3	4	4	36	5	4	3	4	4	3	4	5	4	36	72
HANDICAP			7	5	17	3	11	1	15	9	13			6	8	14	16	18	12	2	10	4	
GREEN	72.0	130	222	424	144	297	495	299	135	232	305	2553	475	285	151	297	256	158	374	406	276	2678	5231

The 8th hole on Shenvalee's Olde Course, with the Blue Ridge Mountains behind it like a stage set, is a short par five that many players can reach in two shots.

THE SHENVALEE GOLF RESORT

New Market, Virginia (Take I-81 to exit 264, Route 11; go east about 1 mile; entrance is on your left.)
Phone: (540) 740-3181 Fax: (540) 740-8931

Architects: Rod Smith and Ed Ault   Years opened: 1927, 1963, 1992

Course rating/Slope rating: Creek/Miller
Blue - 71.5/120   Black - 69.1/115
Red -65.0/102

Course rating/ Slope rating: Miller/Olde
Blue - 70.1/119   Black - 70.1/119
Red - 65.1/104

Course rating/ Slope rating: Olde/Creek
Blue - 70.0/117   Black - 70.0/117
Red - 65.2/103

What the twenty-seven holes that make up The Shenvalee Golf Resort lack in difficulty or championship caliber, they compensate for with history and charm. The Shenvalee originally opened in 1927 as a nine-hole playground for the wealthy upper crust fleeing Washington, D.C., in search of cooler temperatures in the steamy summer months. The Olde Course was opened amid much fanfare, with the legendary Bobby Jones presiding. The old-fashioned golf course—a short, tight little track with tiny greens—was hewn out of the hilly land once used for farming by men with picks, shovels, and wagons pulled by horses. The original resort hotel was created by expanding the plantation house once owned by Thomas Lord Fairfax (a significant name in the history of Virginia) in the 1740s.

When the second nine was added in the early 1960s, the Olde Course was updated. The minuscule greens were enlarged to merely small; some fairways were widened; and several holes were lengthened. Nonetheless, to this day the Olde Course still maintains some of its old-fashioned charm and character, a reminder of what the game was in our not-too-distant past. The third nine was opened in 1992, bringing the facility to its current status. The Miller and Creek courses are far more challenging, if not as amusing from a historical perspective, and if you are given an option of the best eighteen to play as one golf course, this is the combo to pick.

While there are a handful of extremely interesting holes, The Shenvalee is not going to hold much allure for the single-digit handicapper. However, if there is a resort facility that is ideally suited to the mid- to high handicapper who wants a satisfying but unintimidating golf experience, this is it. Golfers who have passed beyond the beginner phase but who have yet to acquire the skill level to enjoy a championship track to the fullest should make a note of The Shenvalee. Even beginners will find this a superb way to improve their games. And the setting is simply lovely, with breathtaking views of the Blue Ridge Mountains at every turn.

For the most part, the greens are on the slow side, in pretty good shape and generally flat but true. With the exception of #4 on the Creek Course, the par fives are all fairly short and offer great birdie opportunities. For a low-handicap player whose chipping and putting are solid, these twenty-seven holes can provide a wonderful boost to your ego.

The short Olde nine (only 3,030 yards from the back markers) is a step back in time. It reminds me of some of the wonderful little nine-hole golf courses that dot the English and Irish countryside. The straight par-four #2 features a small pond that guards the green and can catch a drive that's too bold. It can be played with a long iron and a wedge. The par-five #3 can easily be reached in two shots and affords a fine eagle or birdie opportunity.

The 8th hole is distracting in its loveliness, with the Blue Ridge Mountains hanging like a stage set behind the green. It's a steeply downhill par five with a very tight out-of-bounds along the left side. The green is up a short incline from the point at which most lay-ups will land, with the putting surface pitched back toward the fairway. Even though the greens tend to be slow, this is a good hole on which to keep your approach below the flag.

The 9th hole, far and away the best hole on the Olde Course, is arguably the most interesting of Shenvalee's twenty-seven holes. It's a short, tricky par four, a severe dogleg left with a blind tee shot. The drive must be kept to the left of the two giant, ancient trees in the middle of the fairway.

However, a shot that drifts too far left will find deep rough if it stays in bounds. To the right of those trees, the fairway drops away to the right at a severe angle. The approach to the green is all uphill. Once safely on, the challenge diminishes.

The opening hole on the Miller nine, a short par five, is an excellent scoring hole, short enough to be reached with fair ease in two shots. The tee shot is blind, and all of the trouble is in the vicinity of the elevated green. The approach to the green is guarded by a pair of ponds. The green itself is surrounded by bunkers, with a stand of pines framing the back. A bold second shot that doesn't reach the putting surface is likely wet or sandy.

The par-four #2 is one of the truly superior holes on the track, although its handicap rating would lead one to believe that it's easier than it actually is. It's a longish dogleg right with a green that's protected by water and sand. The optimal tee shot hugs the line of trees along the right side of the fairway, cresting the hill and opening the putting surface for your approach.

The par-three #3 is an aesthetically pleasing one-shot hole across a lake to a wide, shallow green. The par-four #6 holds the top ranking for difficulty on the Miller Course. It's a long, well-bunkered dogleg right that demands precision off the tee and on the approach. The sand traps around the green are among the best on the entire layout. The par-three #8 is especially taxing for women in that it plays straight uphill and makes the 138 yards from the red markers seem more like 150 yards. Women can see the flag from their tee box, but they cannot see the putting surface.

The Creek Course is the longest of the three nines. The 4th hole is the longest and most difficult par five at The Shenvalee, stretching 570 yards from the back tees. It requires a long drive but features a generous landing area. Your lay-up second must be played well left of the second gaping fairway bunker in order to open up the green for your chip. From about midway between tee and green, the fairway slopes sharply to the right and feeds into a grassy gully that should be avoided.

The par-four #5 is a gentle dogleg left with a creek running along the left side from tee to green. The green is surrounded by three large sand traps. The par-four #6 is a severe dogleg right with water on both sides of the fairway. Really big hitters can consider biting off a goodly amount of the lake to the right and leaving only a sand wedge or lob wedge to the flag, but it's a longer shot than it appears from the tee boxes. Many a good player has found the water and suffered a bogey or worse for taking the risk of clearing the lake.

The dogleg-left par-four #9 is rated the toughest hole on the Creek Course for men, but it's considered one of the easier holes for women. The back markers are more than 100 yards longer than the red tees. The biggest problem on the approach is the little bunker that lies in wait directly in front of the putting surface and gobbles up shots that are intended to land short and run up to the flagstick. A high, soft approach is best.

The Shenvalee Resort is one of those courses that would not be included in this volume if the book were only about the toughest championship golf courses in the Virginias. But this is among the very best layouts in the two states for holiday or occasional golfers, for players who are learning the game, for seniors, and even for mid-handicappers who want an enjoyable track in a wonderful setting. In addition, it's an exceptional golfing value.

Creek and Miller Course*

HOLE NUMBER	Ra	SI	1	2	3	4	5	6	7	8	9	OUT	10	11	12	13	14	15	16	17	18	IN	TOT
BLUE	71.5	120	417	434	191	570	405	344	145	385	451	3342	507	426	185	331	502	441	353	205	317	3267	6609
BLACK	69.1	115	405	338	176	553	380	320	130	365	434	3101	467	'406	169	296	486	414	331	195	302	3066	6167
PAR (m)			4	4	3	5	4	4	3	4	4	35	5	4	3	4	5	4	4	3	4	36	71
HANDICAP (m)			11	7	15	3	5	9	17	13	1		14	12	4	8	10	2	6	16	18		
RED	65.0	102	295	310	145	438	300	230	84	268	350	2420	414	286	80	173	360	338	278	138	270	2337	4757
PAR (w)			4	4	3	5	4	4	3	4	5	36	5	4	3	3	5	4	4	3	4	35	71

Olde Course

HOLE NUMBER	1	2	3	4	5	6	7	8	9	TOT
BLUE	320	326	464	195	400	151	338	465	375	3030
BLACK	310	310	450	185	345	145	330	455	350	2880
HANDICAP (m)	8	7	6	4	2	9	5	3	1	
PAR	4	4	5	3	4	3	4	5	4	36
RED	261	283	343	158	290	134	292	350	230	2341
HANDICAP (w)	7	6	4	5	1	9	2	3	8	

*Shenvalee mixes its nines each day to form three different eighteen hole courses. This reflects the most challenging eighteen.

The par-three #8 hole at Stonehouse is typical of what you can expect from architect Mike Strantz. It features large, deep bunkers, exaggerated contours, and a gigantic, multitiered green.

STONEHOUSE

9540 Old Stage Road, Toano, Virginia (From I-64, take exit 227; go north about ¼ mile to the Stonehouse entrance on the right.)
Phone: (804) 566-1138

Architect: Mike Strantz   Year opened: 1996

Course rating/Slope rating:
Gold - 75.0/140   White - 71.4/133
Black - 73.3/136   Green - 69.1/121

Stonehouse is one of two much-discussed, extremely difficult new golf courses built in Virginia by The Legends Group of Myrtle Beach, South Carolina. The course is the brainchild of golf-course architect Mike Strantz, who was with Tom Fazio's design firm before leaving to become an artist and now incorporates his art into his golf-course design. He spent three months walking the terrain to give him a feel for the land and then, as explained by head pro Tom Farris, he "drew the pictures for how he wanted the holes to look. I've seen some of the drawings, and it's amazing how close those drawings are to what has come about."

Artistically, Strantz may well have rendered golf-course pictures to rival Whistler or Gainsborough, but what translated from the easel to the golf course is Dali or Picasso on a bad day. What Strantz has created is one vengeful, unrelenting golf course. It certainly ranks among the toughest, most demanding daily-fee golf courses in the Virginias, and a case can be made that it's among the toughest in the country. Some golfers who have played it argue that it verges on being so difficult as to be unplayable, certainly for the average golfer. Others protest that it causes so many lost balls and delays that five-hour rounds are routine. One local club pro who did not want his name used said, "You see people lining up to play it once because they've heard so much about it. You don't see them lining up to play it a second time."

On the other hand, a couple of guys from Olney, Maryland—one with a seven handicap and the other with a ten—said they just love it and play it at least two or three times a season. *Golf Digest* sides with them and named it "Best New Upscale Course" in 1996.

Stonehouse is a mountain-style golf course with tremendous contours and variations in elevation, something of a surprise given the fact that it's only a few miles from the relatively flat Tidewater region of Virginia and Williamsburg. Blind tee shots abound. The greens are generally enormous and tough, with lots of breaks and bends, ridges, gullies, crowns, bowls, and tiers. The course demands a level of accuracy and finesse—both from the tee and on the approach to the greens—that simply makes it too difficult for beginners. In fact, men who carry handicaps beyond the teens might be well advised to consider another venue.

Unlike Royal New Kent—the other Legends course nearby and also a Mike Strantz design—women are given a substantial break in yardage on Stonehouse

171

and in some cases might even find a couple of holes too easy. The par-three #3, for example, plays only 82 yards from the front markers. Overall, there are just under 1,900 yards of difference between the championship tees and the forward tees. Women are well advised not to complain too much. Take the birdies where you find them, because this golf course is rife with bogey opportunities as well.

There are only three par fives on this par-71 course, all long and demanding. The 4th hole is a good three-shot exercise from the men's tees. The drive is blind and must clear the hill and bunkers to the right. Aim right for the marker pole. That will produce a lay-up just short of the creek in front of the putting surface. This is one of the holes that gives women a huge advantage. It's only 353 yards from the forward markers, so two very big hits can offer a reasonable look at a good score. The 7th is again blind from the tees. The hole is a double dogleg in the shape of a lightning bolt. Staying to the right is imperative. Everything to the left is more trouble than a Sherpa can get you out of, if it's not a penalty or a lost ball. The green is guarded on the right by a mammoth bunker. The only par five on the back is a test of accuracy. The drive on #13 is through a chute; from the back tees it looks like a tunnel. The hole does not reward sheer length as much as it does the ability to avoid the long grass and find a flat stance. From tee to green the margin of error is zero.

Strantz devoted much care and attention to the par threes on Stonehouse. "Don't miss any of the par threes to the left," admonished pro Tom Farris with a grin. "Bad things can happen if you do." That's a gross understatement of the trouble you can get into with shots that fail to find the putting surface. Rocks, bushes, gnarled scrubby trees, pines, marshy areas, and sand are but a few of the difficulties lurking around virtually all of the greens at Stonehouse, but especially the par threes.

The 3rd is a fine downhill one-shot hole that's only 82 yards from the forward markers. The putting surface on #8 is actually two greens on two separate tiers. Club selection is critical because it's 55 yards from the front to the back of this giant. The 15th and 17th holes are both as difficult as they are picturesque. Both are surrounded by nothing but trouble, and you can probably count on a penalty stroke if you miss the green. For women, #17 is extremely difficult, requiring a carry of nearly 150 yards.

What architect and artist Mike Strantz has done with his par fours proves just how tough he can make them. The easiest of the eleven par fours is difficult; the hardest of them almost defies description. The 1st hole is a super opener. The blind tee shot plays downhill to a green that looks like a chubby boomerang tucked in a little grassy basin. The 5th hole also features a blind tee shot that requires you to aim at the marker. Do not miss to the right! The trouble includes a Saharan bunker, nasty hills, and dense forest. Even if you find your ball, you have almost no chance of finding the green on your second shot. The green is protected by a handful of unkind little pot bunkers.

The dogleg-left #9 is a short par four that probably requires something other than a driver off the tee for everybody. It's a blind shot with ample opportunity to find trouble. A tee shot that's too long is likely to catch the serpentine bunker that extends from about 150 yards out right around the right side of the green. The

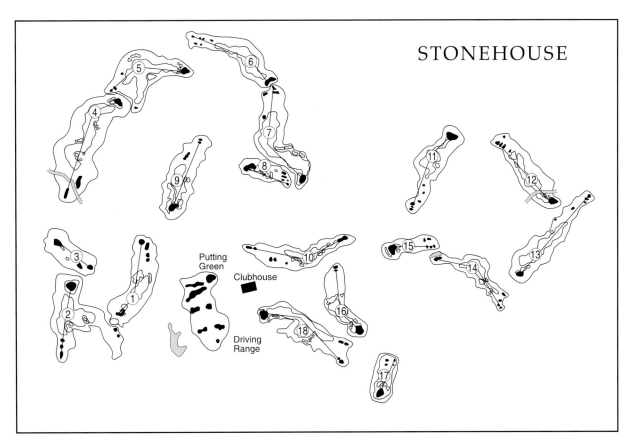

STONEHOUSE

Putting
Green

Clubhouse

Driving
Range

hole funnels down to the green with only a few yards of clear space between the desert on the right and two greenside bunkers on the left. The green features tremendous undulation, including a basin that encompasses the right-rear quadrant of the putting surface.

The back nine opens with a dogleg left par four that plays to a fairly generous landing area from the tees, although you must avoid the four fairway bunkers to the right front of the tee boxes. The interesting green is shaped like a saddle, with deep and unforgiving grass bunkers on the right and left protecting most of the 48 feet in depth. "Mike told me that he designed this to be a long bump and run," said pro Tom Farris, noting that only the most precise wedge or short iron has a chance of holding this green. The 11th hole is made up of three hills and two valleys.

Your drive must clear five crossing bunkers that look like the toe prints of some golf course monster trying to claw its way up the hill. The 12th is an extremely narrow hole that plays down a grassy gully with bunkers on both sides. A creek intersects the fairway about 75 yards from the green, which is at the base of a cliff.

Of all the holes about which people talk on Stonehouse, none gets more attention than #14. It is sheer intimidation, and although not rated the toughest hole, it arguably ought to be. Despite the appearance that you've got room to bail out to the right on your blind tee shot, stay left off the tee if you want a chance to glimpse the green on your second shot. The green is tucked down a steep hill and behind a pair of hills that give the impression that your approach is down a gun barrel with a V-shaped sight right at the end. The two-tiered green—one of the smallest on the golf course—is also protected on the right and rear by a creek.

The 18th is a fine finisher that might let you wrap up your round with a par. It offers a substantial landing area for your drive, but if you get on the downslope, you can drift into the waste area that wedges its way into the fairway and forms a buffer in front of the green.

As with the other Legends courses, Stonehouse is state of the art. Each golf cart is equipped with a GPS receiver, a satellite positioning device that tells you the exact distance from your golf cart to the flag, as well as giving you a computerized look at each hole and green as you play them. What it will not tell you is how to keep your ball in the fairway or how to find it when it's buried in the deep rough or mishit into the scrub, rocks, or creeks.

The deluxe new clubhouse opened in the spring of 1998.

Stonehouse

HOLE	Ra	Sl	1	2	3	4	5	6	7	8	9	OUT	10	11	12	13	14	15	16	17	18	IN	TOT
GOLD	75.0	140	401	426	204	584	431	435	536	177	382	3576	456	418	402	529	407	187	363	172	453	3387	6963
BLACK	73.3	136	382	369	174	530	399	417	510	168	364	3313	437	401	395	512	387	168	346	161	431	3238	6551
WHITE	71.4	133	342	341	163	486	374	391	506	156	306	3065	382	383	387	496	367	151	305	159	416	3046	6111
PAR			4	4	3	5	4	4	5	3	4	36	4	4	4	5	4	3	4	3	4	35	71
HCP			13	5	7	15	3	1	9	11	17		4	10	8	12	6	18	16	14	2		
GREEN	69.1	121	314	306	82	353	301	351	385	102	271	2465	266	287	333	433	351	122	288	149	391	2620	5085

STONELEIGH GOLF CLUB

35279 Prestwick Court, Roundhill, Virginia (From the Capital Beltway, take the Dulles Toll Road to its end at Leesburg, then follow Route 7 west for about 15 miles. The golf course is visible from the highway on the left.)
Phone: (540) 589-1402

Architect: Lisa Maki   Year opened: 1993

Course rating/Slope rating:
Blue - 72.6/136   White - 70.1/119
Red - 69.9/118

Stoneleigh Golf Club is steeped in the history of Virginia. The old stone manor house that dominates the eye as you drive up to the bag drop and pro shop dates to 1750, before Virginian Thomas Jefferson penned the Declaration of Independence. Canadian architect Lisa Maki took enormous pains to turn this wonderful, rolling piece of rural Blue Ridge Mountain land into a golf course. The upper portions of it were once a dairy farm; the lower portions were an apple orchard, whose remaining trees still infuse the landscape with their blossoms and their scent in spring. In the land-loving tradition of Dr. Alister MacKenzie and Donald Ross, Maki has caressed and enhanced what nature put there. Like some Scottish and Irish courses, ancient fieldstone fences border and intersect the field of play. They are an integral part of the design of nine of the eighteen holes. However, unlike most courses in Ireland and Scotland, players are allowed relief if the walls interfere with a player's stance or swing.

The greens are generous, but many are as undulating as the surrounding countryside. Maki also generously employs the plateaued, or turtleback, style of green construction so much favored by Donald Ross. The course features an abundance of water, blind tee shots, strategically placed bunkers, and unfriendly forests. The par fives offer good scoring opportunities.

For one of the only female golf-course architects in the business, Lisa Maki has been kinder to the men who play her course here than to the women. Stoneleigh is a real challenge for women, despite what could be argued is a misleading course rating and slope from the front markers. If there is any place women receive a slight advantage, it is on the par threes.

The course opens with a pair of excellent par fours. The 1st hole features a blind tee shot with the wide, shallow green protected in front by one of those fieldstone walls. The 2nd hole, a slight dogleg left, is short but plays up a substantial hill that mitigates the yardage on the scorecard. The green is a multitiered monster. The 3rd hole is a short par five that is reachable in two for almost everybody, save for the fact that about 120 yards from the green the hole doglegs severely to the right. The out-of-bounds line hugs the left side of the hole; the right is pitched down into a grassy gully. The optimal tee shot is left center. Going for it in two requires a long carry across the dogleg, which is festooned with trees and

The par-five #15 at Stoneleigh is a double dogleg with the green tucked directly behind the lake.

moguls. The hilly green encourages approach shots that come in softly. Shots that are hot and left will cascade into a little collection area. Shots too far right will find all manner of trouble.

The par-five #5 can also be reached by two solid shots, although at 416 yards from the red markers, it's a three-shot hole for almost every woman who plays it. Like #3, #5 features a severe dogleg right and a big undulating green protected in front by a gully and a gaping bunker. The short par-four dogleg-right #7 is one of Stoneleigh's more interesting holes. The elevated tee boxes play to a well-protected green that sits down in a valley. The locals say there are two ways to play it: go for it or play a long to medium iron over the two sand traps that edge the right side of the fairway and denote the point at which the dogleg goes to the right. The green itself is sculpted from the side of a steep hill. This is a hole that virtually everybody plays better the second time they face it.

The 8th hole is rated the second toughest on the course for men, the number-one handicap hole for women, and it is simply a brute. It plays from a tiered set of tee boxes down a terraced fairway. A rock wall intersects the fairway about driving distance; a creek bordered by a marshy area crosses the fairway in front of the big elevated green. The creek creates an optical illusion of being closer to the green than it really is, so it's easy to underclub, clearing the creek but leaving a delicate little chip. Scoring requires both length and precision on the drive and the approach.

The short par-four #9 features a dogleg left of almost 90 degrees. An iron is the preferred driving club, although care must be taken to hit it far enough to open the green, which is tightly guarded by trees from along the left side of the hole from tee to green.

The toughest hole on the golf course for men is the dogleg-right par-four #12 (It's only 315 yards for women and is rated the number-two handicap hole). It's about as tight a tee shot as you'll face here—water and wetland guard the left, and a rock wall protects the right and intrudes into the fairway in front of the green. Anything to the right will render the green totally obscured by tall trees.

The 13th and 14th—a solid par three and a long par four, respectively—set up the wonderful par-five #15, a double dogleg if you play it by the scorecard. But it's reachable in two for if you've hit a big drive into the fairly generous landing area. Just don't play your tee shot too far left or it can leave an impossible second. The green is tucked behind a pond that laps right up to the front apron. If the water makes your knees a little weak, there is ample room to lay up to the left. The hole can be an easy birdie or a tough bogey.

The par-three #16—with its big, multi-tiered green—and the par-four #17 offer good scoring opportunities before you tackle the short par-five #18. This hole is a snap if you can hit a long, accurate tee shot. If you can't, there is a cornucopia of trouble waiting on all sides. To the right are trees and a steep-sided ridge; to the left there's water, marshy rough, and a series of those fieldstone walls. In fact, the green sits between two of them, both fully capable of sending your golf ball in directions you never imagined possible.

If there is a generality about Stoneleigh Golf Club, it is that few, if any, golfers who play it come away neutral. The design and character of the course engender strong feelings—some people simply love it, others dislike it intensely. I tend to like the course and believe that Lisa Maki has created a demanding, clever, and intensely pleasing test of the game. As with many great golf courses, shot making is rewarded, length is an asset, a good eye and equally good touch with the putter will yield pars and birdies, and errant, wild, or imprecise shots will be punished.

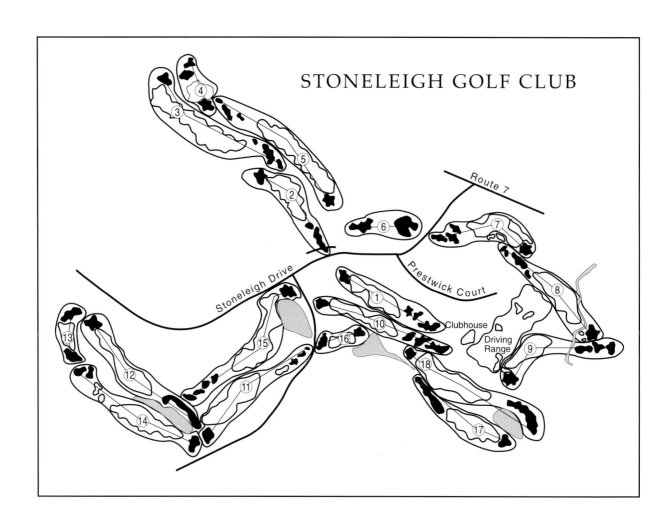

Stoneleigh

HOLE NUMBER	Ra	Sl	1	2	3	4	5	6	7	8	9	OUT	10	11	12	13	14	15	16	17	18	IN	TOT
BLUE	72.6	136	401	336	514	197	529	223	342	456	354	3352	372	441	422	170	457	502	168	357	487	3376	6728
WHITE	70.1	119	361	328	474	178	495	193	326	408	325	3088	340	378	408	167	421	458	151	337	460	3120	6208
HANDICAP (m)			8	10	4	14	6	16	18	2	12		11	9	1	13	5	3	17	15	7		
PAR			4	4	5	3	5	3	4	4	4	36	4	4	4	3	4	5	3	4	5	36	72
RED	69.9	118	259	204	386	100	416	143	247	347	222	2324	267	305	315	120	362	376	109	282	327	2463	4787
HANDICAP (w)			9	3	5	17	7	15	13	1	11		10	12	2	16	8	4	18	14	6		

THE TIDES

Irvington, Virginia (From Fredericksburg, take Route 3 south to Route 200 south; for the Tartan Course, turn right at Route 646, and for the Golden Eagle Course, turn left at Route 646, or from I-64, take Route 33 to Route 3 north to Route 200 north; for the Tartan Course, turn left at Route 646, and for the Golden Eagle Course, turn right at Route 646.)

Phone: (800) 248-4337 (resort),
(804) 438-4337 (Tartan) or (804) 438-5501 (Golden Eagle)

Tartan Course architect: Sir Guy Campbell   Year opened: 1959
Golden Eagle Course architect: George W. Cobb   Year opened: 1976

Tartan Course rating/Slope rating:

Black - 71.7/125	Blue (women) - 76.1/134
Blue (men) - 70.2/123	White (women) - 71.7/121
White (men) - 67.7/116	Green - 69.2/116

Golden Eagle Course rating/Slope rating:

Gold 74.3/134	White 69.1/124
Green 72.3/130	Red 70.9/126

The thoroughly charming, venerable Virginia institution that is known as The Tides has been—as it describes itself—"a retreat for ladies and gentlemen" since immediately after World War II. In the late 1950s golf was added to the other genteel pastimes available to guests, including boating, fishing, tennis, and the general pampering for which the place was famous. The Stephens family, the resort's owners, commissioned renowned Scotsman Sir Guy Campbell, the resident architect at the Royal and Ancient Golf Links in St. Andrews, Scotland, to sojourn to the New World to build nine lovely holes. George W. Cobb, the brilliant golf-course designer based in Augusta, Georgia, finished the second nine at the Tartan Course in the early 1970s, keeping very much to the British feel conferred on the original holes by Sir Guy.

Golf expanded in the mid-1970s, when Cobb was brought back to build the Golden Eagle Golf Course, which has been tapped as one of the ten best in Virginia by *Golf Digest* and has hosted scores of local, state, and regional tournaments, including the Virginia State Amateur Championship in 1987, 1991, and 1998; the Mid-Atlantic Women's Championship in 1995; and the Mid-Atlantic PGA Section Championship in 1997.

While the resort offers a wide variety of other amenities, The Tides should be listed high among golf venues in the Virginias. It is far enough away from the beaten path that the courses are rarely jammed, the pace is pleasant, the golf facilities are immaculately maintained, and the people are friendly.

The par-four 15th hole at The Tides' Tartan Course exemplifies the lush, wooded feel of the parkland golf courses of architect Sir Guy Campbell's native Scotland.

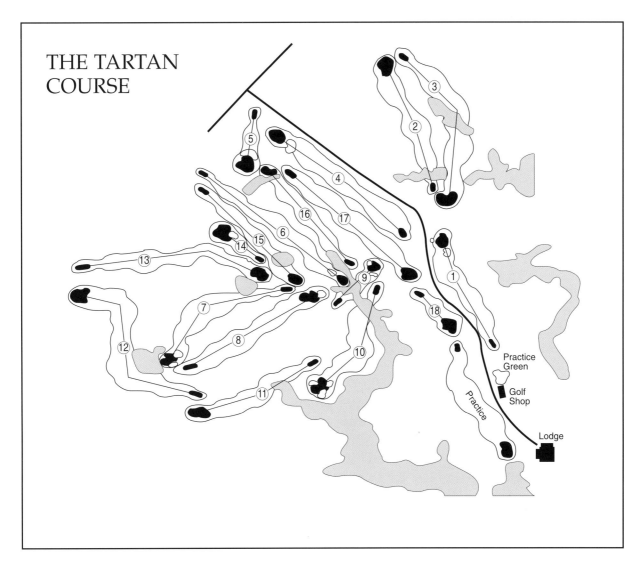

THE TARTAN COURSE

Tartan Course

The Tartan Course has been something of a work in progress since the late 1950s. The first nine opened in 1959, the design of Scottish architect Sir Guy Campbell. The second nine was completed in 1972 under the watchful eye of George W. Cobb, who managed to maintain the feel and flavor of the European design imported by Campbell. Its latest face-lift was completed in 1988, when three new holes were added and other updates and modifications were implemented to make the course more playable.

The design is classical and quintessentially Scottish. Its character and personality conjure up images of what the British and Irish call "parkland" golf course; not the daunting seaside links courses so much associated with Scotland and Ireland, but the more gentle inland courses laid out among the hills, trees, and streams where the green smells of the woods infuse with the subtle aroma of peat smoke. British and Irish parkland golf courses are rustic and not as meticulously manicured as their American counterparts, and therein lies a good measure of their charm, a charm that you can experience firsthand on the Tartan Course. It comes as close as any American course I've played to re-creating the pleasures of, for example, such Irish favorites as the Mallow Golf Club in County Cork, the Golf Course at Shannon Airport, or the Kenmare Golf Club in County Kerry.

It's a fair test of the game in a glorious setting. The greens are generally ample, the fairways rolling, and the water and woods always ready to snag a shot that strays too far from the short grass. In fact, trees and water form a natural partnership that enhances the experience of the golf course. Water comes into play on eleven holes. Trees come into play everywhere.

The course has more than the average number of memorable holes. The long par-five #3 is rated the toughest hole on the course for both men and women. It's a dogleg right that requires a drive that comes up short of a water hazard. Your tee shot is blind, and unless you hit your drive far enough, your lay-up across the bend in the dogleg is blind as well. It's a good 250 yards from the water's edge to the putting surface across an indentation in front of the green. The 4th is a fairly straight, long par four with branches of the towering old pines constricting the entrance to the green.

The short par-five #6 is a risk-reward hole, and those big hitters who want to get on in two need to consider that they're playing to one of the smallest and most difficult greens to approach. Water arcs around it like a horseshoe, pinching the opening to the putting surface. The green is slightly domed and will reject an imprecise shot, probably into the water. The front nine finishes with a lovely little par three. You tee off from a high hilltop and across a little arm of a lake to a two-tiered hillside green slightly lower than the level of the tee boxes.

That's followed by a spectacular short par four. The blind drive is across water and marsh for all but the most forward markers. It plays to a landing area at the turn of the dogleg right and then requires a precise downhill approach to a green that's guarded by a pair of towering old deciduous trees to the right and two sand traps to the left. The twelfth is a Z-shaped par five that plays around a lake to the right on your drive. Your lay-up second then plays to the corner of the left dogleg. Going for it in two is a high-risk gambit. It's almost impossible to hit your shot high enough to clear the stand of trees behind which the big green is positioned.

The Tartan Course's signature hole is #15, a moderate-length par four. The hole curves to the left along the path of a streambed that creates a hazard along the left length of it. A small pond is in play from about 130 yards out to the left front

Tartan Course

HOLE	Ra	Sl	1	2	3	4	5	6	7	8	9	OUT	10	11	12	13	14	15	16	17	18	IN	TOT
BLACK	71.7	125	368	451	553	446	174	479	392	425	143	3431	349	361	525	380	180	371	362	491	136	3155	6586
BLUE	70.2 (m)/76.1 (w)	123 (m)/134 (w)	349	431	541	418	159	472	367	417	134	3288	327	349	511	372	163	345	345	479	129	3020	6308
WHITE	67.7 (m)/71.7 (w)	116 (m)/121 (w)	283	286	507	398	146	425	314	383	125	2867	308	289	415	360	147	331	301	468	122	2741	5608
HCP (m)			13	3	1	7	17	5	11	9	15		10	12	2	8	14	4	16	6	18		
PAR			4	4	5	4	3	5	4	4	3	35	4	4	5	4	3	4	4	5	3	36	72
GREEN	69.2	116	277	280	443	331	118	416	307	375	118	2665	260	282	410	305	92	292	295	406	114	2456	5121
HCP (w)			11	3	1	9	15	5	7	13	17		12	14	2	6	16	8	10	4	18		

of the small, plateaued green. Any shot that drifts left or comes up short will run sharply downhill toward the water. There is a little bailout room to the right. The 16th is a short par four that plays from hilltop to hilltop to a hilltop green. There is a hidden hazard: a small pond to the left front of the green, very much in play if your approach fails to find the putting surface.

As with the front nine, the back finishes with a par three. Your short-iron tee shot plays to an interesting and tricky green that's shaped something like inverted Mickey Mouse ears, with an indentation between the two. A birdie depends on whether you land on the proper ear.

The Tartan Course is part of a growing trend in its approach to what tees golfers should play, especially in its approach to women golfers. No more are women relegated to one set of tees and, in fact, the traditional "red tees" have disappeared completely. The scorecard recommends that low-single-digit-handicap men play the black markers, teens play blue, and those above that play white. But unlike other courses, it recommends that women go by their handicaps as well, that low-single-digit women play the blue markers, women with handicaps of 4 to 22 play the whites, and others play the green tees. It provides a very satisfying round for everybody, especially players who have not encountered the golf course before, and it is an especially good test for women.

The Tartan Course is not a monster test or a course you're likely to see on television, but it is delightful, mature, classically designed, and carefully maintained. And while it is in the shadow of the more famous Golden Eagle, it is a hidden jewel that should not be overlooked. In

discussing regional courses with several pros at other clubs, they were surprisingly lavish in their praise for the Tartan Course. "It's a great course," said Ben Thompson, golf director at the Colonial Golf Course just outside Williamsburg. "It's challenging. It's fun to play. And it's fair."

Golden Eagle Course

George W. Cobb has a wonderful knack for designing memorable golf courses, and the Golden Eagle ranks among his most memorable. This is a golf course you will always recall fondly, even after playing it only once. There's good reason it has hosted so many regional and state tournaments. There's equally good reason that so many guests return season after season to The Tides just to play it. It's not tricky. It's not gimmicky. It's just straight-forward good golf.

The course features long holes with plenty of water, hills, trees, and generally small, well-bunkered greens that yield up birdies only grudgingly. It is a good test for everybody, and an exceptionally well-thought-out test for women. The forward tee placement is anything but haphazard. It is well considered and executed. The nearly 7,000 yards across which the championship markers play will examine the skill and cunning of even the most accomplished pros. Good club players will be well satisfied to shoot their handicaps from the green tees. And even mid- and high-handicap players will enjoy the course from the white markers. It is simply a superior golf course from every perspective.

The course itself is maintained beautifully, and its reputation as a superb golfing venue is well deserved. Typical of

Both the par-four #9 (left) and the par-four #18 (right) at the Golden Eagle Course at The Tides require precision approaches to hillside greens perched above the lake around which the course is built.

George Cobb golf courses, the holes provide a rich and complicated pattern that combines to form the overall design. All but one of the par fives is extremely long. The par fours offer a wonderful mix of structures and lengths. And the par threes are tough, ranging in length from long to moderate.

A medium-length par four takes you out, with a blind tee shot that plays severely uphill on your drive. The 2nd is the shortest of the par fives and presents a good scoring opportunity. The gentle dogleg left is tight off the tee and requires a drive that splits the fairway for a look at getting on in two.

The brilliant, if belligerent, 5th hole is the toughest on the course. It is a long par four that tees off across a large lake. How much of the lake you bite off determines how long your second shot will be. It's a sharp dogleg left, with the fairway pinched by the lake and a marshy pond at about the midway point between tee and green. Your approach to the green must also steer clear of the water that comes back into play to the front and left of the putting surface; the green is constructed on a peninsula out into the water. This hole is a doozy that can render a very satisfying par or send your score soaring into double- or triple-bogie range very easily.

The long par-five #6 tees off uphill to a very tight landing area. Your second shot then heads back down toward a green guarded by four bunkers on the left and three on the right, creating a funnel to the putting surface. The 7th is a long par four on which you drive through a chute of trees to a fairway that is canted sharply left to right. Keep your drive left of center.

The outgoing side finishes with a magnificent hole, an acute dogleg right that gives you a notion of what you'll face on #18. This par four plays to a green on a shelf above a lake. Your tee shot needs to be to the water's edge and, even with a good drive, your approach shot is a long carry. The green is scoop-shaped, with the back bowl sloped back toward the water and the front half relatively flat.

The 10th is another lovely George Cobb par four, a dogleg left where a blind tee shot from the back markers plays to a fairly narrow landing area. The women's tees were splendidly redesigned in the mid-1990s and placed in a position to straighten the dogleg substantially, but without compromising the integrity of the hole. A large, leafy tree on the left and a big bunker on the right team up to tighten the women's tee shot and demand a straight hit to a more slender landing zone than the men face. Once safely in the short grass, the green is then fairly open and receptive. The par-three #14 is rated the easiest hole on the course, but the long and thin green—sloped with varying degrees of severity to the right and with abundant sand—makes it a challenge.

The long, extremely tight par-four #15 tees off across a creek and then plays uphill to a small green. The hole is lined with trees to the left and forest and bunkers to the right. The fairway is canted from right to left, and anything left of center tends to roll toward trouble. The par-five #16 is a solid three-shot hole. Your drive is over a hill into a little valley. Your second is uphill across an expanse of mounds and moguls. That second shot needs to stop just in front of the entrance to the green, which is constricted by a series of bunkers right and left. The demanding par-three #17 plays uphill to a well-guarded green. While women get a substantial break in length, their tee shot must traverse a more acute uphill angle.

The Golden Eagle's wonderful finishing hole looks like another ordinary short dogleg-right par four from the tees. Once you get to the landing area, the hole reveals itself to be a watery challenge. From the landing zone in front of the lake you face a long uphill carry to the steeply elevated and contoured green. There is precious little room for error in front. From the green the look back across the lake and down the fairway creates a wonderful memory of a fine test of golf, a memory that is destined to linger for a long time to come.

THE GOLDEN EAGLE GOLF COURSE

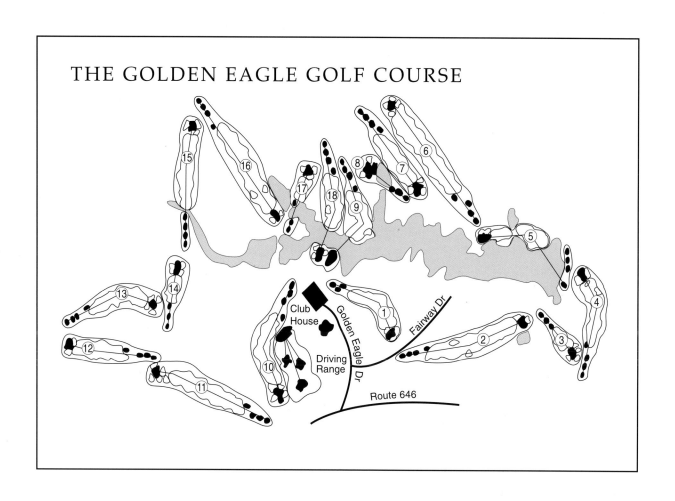

Golden Eagle Course

HOLE NUMBER	Ra	Sl	1	2	3	4	5	6	7	8	9	OUT	10	11	12	13	14	15	16	17	18	IN	TOT
GOLD	74.3	134	406	486	200	361	463	571	400	175	411	3473	445	529	369	383	180	430	569	205	380	3490	6963
GREEN	72.3	130	389	460	179	340	428	543	373	149	384	3245	421	503	337	364	149	411	530	192	359	3266	6511
WHITE	69.1	124	350	423	160	315	412	503	340	126	358	2987	388	474	304	342	108	374	493	166	328	2977	5964
HANDICAP (m)			7	9	15	17	1	5	11	13	3		10	8	16	14	18	4	2	6	12		
PAR			4	5	3	4	4	5	4	3	4	36	4	5	4	4	3	4	5	3	4	36	72
RED	70.9	126	330	415	115	268	360	471	305	112	305	2681	259	463	265	297	98	340	356	112	290	2580	5261
HANDICAP (w)			9	7	15	13	1	5	11	17	3			10	4	14	12	18	8	2	16	6	

VIRGINIA OAKS

14313 Lee Highway, Gainesville, Virginia (From I-66, take Route 29 for about ¾-mile and turn left at the sign.)
Phone: (703) 551-2103

Architect: P. B. Dye   Year opened: 1995

Course rating/Slope rating:
Gold - 73.5/133   White (men) - 69.8/125
Blue - 71.5/130   White (women) - 75.0/135
Red - 72.0/115

Virginia Oaks has received a flood of favorable publicity since it opened, winning praise for its design and accessibility. It is one of a slew of new daily-fee golf courses that are sprouting up in northern Virginia within easy driving distance of the Washington, D.C., metropolitan area. These new courses are well designed, well maintained, and upscale in their price structure, and they offer many of the same amenities as country clubs (such as advance booking for tee times). Many have been developed in conjunction with residential real-estate communities as well, and such is the case with Virginia Oaks.

The course provides four sets of tees, three of which are rated and sloped for men and two of which are rated and sloped for women, although only a scant number of women will be very eager to play the white markers, with their rating of 75.0 and a slope of 135. The course is a par 72 for men and a par 71 for women playing the forward markers.

Virginia Oaks features several signature elements of architect P. B. Dye, such as blind tee shots, of which there are many. He also takes delight in intimidating golfers with abundant visual distractions: water, topographical changes, stands of trees, massive bunkers or clustered bunkers,

mounds, moguls, and rocks are all part of his arsenal of optical threats. Of course, the threats are very real if your shot is extremely errant or astray. The design technique is especially apparent from the tees on the #8, #9, #13, and #16. He uses the same technique on the approach on #3, #6, #14, and #18. When P. B. Dye wants to intimidate you on the approach to a green, he is among the best in the business.

In addition to his optical challenges, Dye likes heavily contoured and mounded fairways, sometimes to such an extreme that finding a flat stance is difficult, even if you've hit a good golf shot. He also places his undulating greens on hillside shelves or on hilltop plateaus. Like the Scottish architect Donald Ross, Dye rarely presents the player with much opportunity to approach his greens with a bump-and-run shot.

Holes of note—and there are many of them—include the par-four opener, on which the approach to the green is blocked with a mound about 35 yards from the putting surface, out of which a bunker has been scooped. A finger of marshy wetland intersects the second fairway in front of the green, which sits on a shelf well above the hazard, making for a difficult approach shot to the par-four hole.

The par-five #3 at Virginia Oaks, an example of architect P. B. Dye's best work, can be reached by many players in two shots, but an imprecise shot is destined to find deep rough or sand.

The 3rd is a very interesting, picturesque short par five with a blind tee shot that plays to the crest of a hill. The red tees are more than 200 yards ahead of the men's tees, and the result is a testing par four for women. Your approach to the shallow, wide green is hard. A ridge splits the fairway, creating two distinct elevations, from greenside to about 100 yards out. The upper portion of the fairway, which is only about 15 yards wide, allows you a look at the putting surface; the lower part of the fairway, which is even skinnier than the high ground, provides only a glimpse of the flag. It's a pretty hole, with Lake Manassas peeking through the trees along the right length of it. The best way to play the hole is to leave your lay-up about 100 yards from the green and bring it in high and soft.

The 6th is a long, straight, tight par five

rated the toughest hole on the golf course for men and women. It will be a solid three-shot hole for all but the biggest hitters. P. B. Dye has exercised his ability to create optical threats near the green by using two huge bunkers to intersect the fairway about 50 yards in front of the green. This creates a basin of grass beyond the sand and below the elevated putting surface. The enormous kidney-shaped green slopes precariously from left to right and back toward the fairway.

From the tee boxes on #8, it appears that sand is everywhere. The clustered bunkers that give the impression of unavoidable sand are less in play than might be imagined unless you really boot your drive; nonetheless, the eye tells you your tee shot is across the sands of the Kalahari. The 9th is a short par three with an island green surrounded by rocks. If

188

the water doesn't intimidate you, the rocks will.

The back nine opens with a huge par five in the shape of a question mark. Do not give in to the natural tendency to keep your ball to the right. The tee shot is sharply downhill, and then the heavily mounded, sculpted, and tortured hole curves to the left, narrows, and climbs steeply toward an elevated and tricky multilevel green. It's rated the second-toughest hole on the course, and an argument could be made that it's tougher than that.

The 12th features elements of visual intimidation along its entire length. The drive on this short par four is across a pond and club selection is critical. The green is surrounded by dangers that are seen and other, even more menacing dangers that are not. What you see from the landing area is a pair of mounds out of which big bunkers have been scooped. They shield most of the green from view on your approach. A tongue of water, invisible on your approach, laps at the right edge of the putting surface, and only a high, soft approach shot will stand a chance of getting close to the pin on this extremely shallow green.

The 13th is a par four with a blind tee shot that plays uphill and then back down to a green that is strangled in front with trouble to either side and almost no way to run the ball up onto the multitiered putting surface. The difficult par-four #14

is a dogleg right with a tight out-of-bounds to the right as the dogleg bends. The out-of-bounds continues to hug the remainder of the right length of the hole. The uphill fairway to the green is a runway with trouble to the right and a grassy precipice to the left out of which extrication is difficult, if possible at all. The hourglass-shaped green is only about a dozen yards wide at its waist. The 16th is a long dogleg right par four with water in play from tee to green. The tee shot is across a pond that looks bigger and more threatening than it really is. The water plays along the right side right up to the putting surface.

The 17th is a long par four with a big bunker smack-dab across the fairway about 130 yards from the green. The finisher on Virginia Oaks is a long straight par five with a minefield of bunkers down the right side and one big fellow directly in front of the landing area for your tee shot. Most of the trouble is near the green. A little finger of a hill intrudes back into the fairway about 50 yards from the green, a smaller version of the ridge that split the fairway on the 3rd hole. A lake is then in play to the left.

In all, Virginia Oaks is an enjoyable and challenging golf course. It's advisable to book in advance, especially on weekends, as this a very popular golf course with local players.

Virginia Oaks

HOLE	Ra	SI	1	2	3	4	5	6	7	8	9	OUT	10	11	12	13	14	15	16	17	18	IN	TOT
GOLD	73.5	133	412	444	471	432	205	525	336	392	135	3352	621	223	310	414	428	120	446	469	545	3576	6928
BLUE	71.5	130	378	424	446	406	175	515	315	361	125	3145	581	195	290	370	404	110	426	425	522	3323	6468
WHITE	69.8 (m)/75.0 (w)	125 (m)/135 (w)	356	402	419	390	140	480	295	341	114	2937	557	170	280	352	363	101	406	390	505	3124	6061
PAR (b)			4	4	5	4	3	5	4	4	3	36	5	3	4	4	4	3	4	4	5	36	72
HCP			11	3	7	5	15	1	17	9	13		2	14	16	12	6	18	8	10	4		
RED	72.0	115	334	324	268	340	98	426	235	289	80	2394	466	112	205	294	330	72	261	315	403	2458	4852
PAR (f)			4	4	4	4	3	5	4	4	3	35	5	3	4	4	4	3	4	4	5	36	71

The lovely par-three #16 at Williamsburg National requires a forced carry across a strip of marsh and a creek to a large undulating green.

WILLIAMSBURG NATIONAL GOLF CLUB

3700 Centerville Road, Williamsburg, Virginia (From I-64, take exit 234 to Route 60 east; follow Route 60 about ½-mile to Route 614, Centerville Road, and turn right; stay on Centerville Road for about 5 miles to the entrance sign on the left.)
Phone: (800) 826-5732 or (757) 258-9642

Architect: Jim Lipe Year opened: 1995

Course rating/Slope rating:
Black - 72.9/126 White - 67.7/114
Blue - 70.3/117 Green - 68.3/112

Jack Nicklaus did not design Williamsburg National personally, but it bears his stamp. Jim Lipe is part of the design team at Nicklaus Design Associates, and from the moment you tee off on the 1st hole until you putt out on the tough par-four 18th, you know you've played a Nicklaus golf course, or at least a course that's well within chipping distance of the Nicklaus name. You'd expect big greens with myriad overt and subtle contours and breaks, at least one very short and deceptively difficult par four, strategically placed bunkers, abundant water hazards—both natural and man-made—and a hole with a split or double fairway. Williamsburg National has everything but the double-fairway hole. The greens are especially good, well maintained, and true, though not lightning fast.

Of special interest are the par threes. There's not a bad one on the track; they are well designed and well executed; they are visually interesting as well as presenting a good golfing challenge; and they offer a splendid variety of shot-making options for men and women. The 8th, 10th, and 16th holes all require the tee shot to carry water, marsh, or wetlands. The 16th is a splendid one-shot hole with

elevated, terraced tees yielding to a green hewn out of the forest below. Your tee shot must carry an environmentally protected wetland and creek caressing the hillock on which the tricky putting surface is constructed. For the timid, there's a little bailout room to the right front.

Lipe has constructed a pair of typical Jack Nicklaus-style short, tough par fours, one on each nine. On the front side it's the 2nd hole, and on the back it's the 14th. The characteristics of these holes include deceptive lengths that lull players unfamiliar with the Nicklaus penchant for these uncanny little creations into a false sense of security. That inner peace can be quickly demolished when the player discovers the difficulties and perils concealed within the hole. At Williamsburg National, on #2 there is a steep indentation in the fairway just beyond the 150-yard marker. Any approach to the green from within that indentation is to be avoided. It lets you see the flag but not the putting surface, and the chip is very tricky and demanding.

From the scorecard #15 looks as if you ought to be able to drive it on a good day. In the flesh—or, more properly, on the grass—the hole reveals itself to be far more challenging than its yardage would

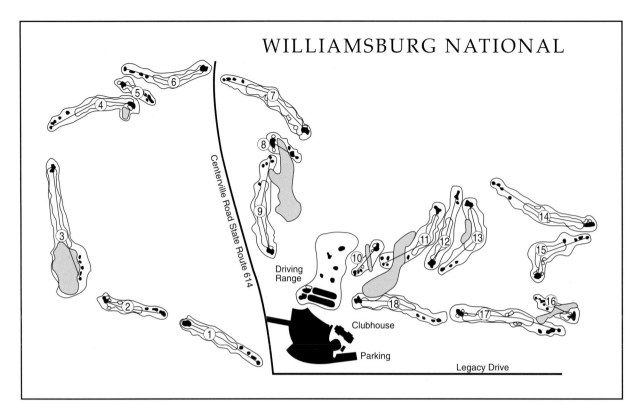

indicate. It's an acute dogleg left with a huge multi-trunked tree and a pair of gaping bunkers in the path of a direct hit from the tee boxes to an elevated green. The hole plays uphill. It's a blind shot for men, but for women it's a great scoring opportunity because players can both see the green and maneuver a tee shot into easy chipping position from the forward markers. There is a trough in front of the green, and a shot that lands between the apron of the green and the 100-yard marker stands a good chance of facing an unpleasant uphill chip.

Jack Nicklaus golf courses usually feature at least one massively long par five, the kind Jack used to eat up in his prime, when he was one of the longest hitters ever to pick up a club. The par-five #3 is such a hole. It starts with an intimidating tee shot. Everybody must carry an expanse of water to put the ball in play, but the landing area is generous and the green is easily approachable.

The 4th is rated the toughest hole on the course. It's a par four, a gentle dogleg right, but what you can't see from the tee is that the green is guarded by a marshy wetland and pond. There's a bunker in front of the putting surface, more to keep balls from rolling back into the lake than to punish errant shots. Long hitters can reach the par-five #7 in two shots, although at 402 yards it's a long ride for women. There's a bit of an optical illusion near the green: the bunker to the right looks like a greenside sand trap from the fairway, but it's about 25 yards short of the putting surface. The big bunker to the left is greenside. You can make the green in two by just clearing the right bunker and rolling it up.

The front side finishes with a big par-four dogleg left. Men tee off across water; women play from the dry side of the hole. For men the tee shot is blind; women get a glimpse of the green. The hole plays uphill, and then the approach is downhill to the putting surface. This is a fine golf hole on which tee shots must stay to the right side of the fairway in order to be in scoring position. Shots that stray too far left will be blocked out by towering ancient trees.

The back nine is as pleasing to the eye as it is enjoyable to play. The 11th is a splendid par four that starts with a blind tee shot from an elevated series of tees across a tree-filled gulch. Women do not have to carry the wasteland. It's a dogleg left, a demanding hole, but the landing area is actually more generous than your eye would suggest from the tee boxes. The 12th is a medium-length par four with a blind tee shot over the crest of a hill. From the landing area it's a straight approach to a gently elevated green that slopes left. There's a grassy collection area to the left front to catch shots that come up a little short.

The 13th is an excellent golf hole—a long, tough, tight par four that doglegs sharply to the left. The fairway slopes left into unpleasant rough that then drops sharply into a scrubby, rock-strewn ravine. Keep your tee shot right of center, but beware: the out-of-bounds is close to the fairway at the right elbow of the dogleg. The closer you get to the green, the narrower the fairway becomes, to the point that it almost disappears beyond the 150-yard marker. The green plays uphill on your approach. There are no bunkers around the long, narrow green,

but it is on the top of a hill, and any shot that ventures near the collar risks running substantially away from the target into one of several deep collection areas.

The par-five #14 offers a fine scoring opportunity for men. Lipe has made the par fives on Williamsburg National tougher for women than for men, all of them more than 400 yards from the forward markers. This hole is a gentle dogleg left that requires a right-to-left shot beyond the fairway bunker on the left, which then sets up the perfect approach to the green on your second. It's just the kind of hole Nicklaus loved as a player. The approach is down a short incline and back up to the putting surface.

The last two holes on the back nine provide a solid finish that can make or break your round. The 17th, a long par five, features elevated tees and a blind tee shot with a tightly constricted entrance to the green. The 18th is a solid par four that plays to a well-bunkered, elevated green tucked behind a grassy vale.

Overall, Williamsburg National is a good test for low handicappers, but it's not so intimidating or overwhelming that mid- to high-handicap golfers can't enjoy it. The four sets of tees are well designed to present a varied look at the golf course and to let golfers play to their ability.

As we go to press, a second eighteen holes is under construction at Williamsburg National.

Williamsburg National

HOLE NUMBER	Ra	SI	1	2	3	4	5	6	7	8	9	OUT	10	11	12	13	14	15	16	17	18	IN	TOT
BLACK	72.9	126	430	322	583	449	175	429	530	138	455	3511	177	412	396	417	506	354	202	532	446	3442	6953
BLUE	70.3	117	400	302	560	409	149	388	478	122	435	3243	161	384	365	387	472	321	179	491	408	3168	6411
WHITE	67.7	114	368	272	551	370	140	344	430	113	416	3004	146	370	337	338	435	280	161	466	363	2896	5900
PAR			4	4	5	4	3	4	5	3	4	36	3	4	4	4	5	4	3	5	4	36	72
HANDICAP			7	13	5	1	15	11	9	17	3		14	10	18	4	16	12	6	8	2		
GREEN	68.3	112	324	227	475	328	109	321	402	97	324	2607	144	211	321	302	435	222	123	428	329	2515	5122

Brooding trees and large bunkers line the par-four 2nd hole at Wintergreen's Devils Knob. A ski chalet overlooks the back of the green.

WINTERGREEN

Wintergreen, Virginia (from I-95 or I-81, take I-64 to exit 107, route 250 west; follow route 250 west to route 151 south; follow that for about 14½ miles; the entrance to Stoney Creek is on the right; to get to Devils Knob go another mile or so to the entrance to Wintergreen and follow the winding road to the top of the mountain.)
Phone: (804) 325-2200

Devils Knob Architect: Ellis Maples   Year opened: 1977
Stoney Creek Architect: Rees Jones   Year opened: 1988

Devils Knob course rating/Slope rating:
Blue - 72.4/126   White - 69.8/119
Red - 68.6/118

Stoney Creek course rating/Slope rating:
Championship - 74.0/132   Middle - 71.6/121
Back - 72.6/126   Senior - 69.2/118
Forward - 71.0/125

In the winter, the Wintergreen complex is one of Virginia's most popular ski resorts. In the summer, Wintergreen is home to a pair of spectacular golf courses as different in personality and character as are the architects who designed them. Overall, Wintergreen's golfing facilities rank among the state's best, forty-five holes in all, the Devils Knob eighteen laid out high in the Blue Ridge Mountains with simply breathtaking vistas and views at every turn, and Stoney Creek's twenty-seven holes far below in the valley that looks up to the towering mountains that surround it.

The newest nine was opened at Stoney Creek in 1998 after more than a year of careful and painstaking construction aimed at maintaining the character and integrity of the original eighteen.

While Devils Knob and Stoney Creek are both under the Wintergreen umbrella, they are so different and so unique that both deserve to be played. Stoney Creek tends to get more publicity because more

tournaments and major golf outings are held there, but when it comes to mountain golf, Devils Knob is a superior challenge.

Devils Knob at Wintergreen

At 3,800 feet, Devils Knob is the highest golf course in Virginia, having been laid out along a series of mountain ridges. It is a tight, testing track rivaling such legendary mountain golf courses as Eagle-Vail in Colorado or the Banff Springs course in Alberta for both scenic beauty and golfing challenge. It is a quintessential example of mountain golf. The fairways are rolling and contoured. The rough is difficult, if not impossible. The greens are firm and tough. Add to that the visual distractions offered by the panorama of the Blue Ridge Mountains in every direction and frequent glimpses of the Shenandoah and Rockfish Valleys in the distance below, and keeping your focus on the back nine is especially difficult.

Devils Knob is short, playing only to a

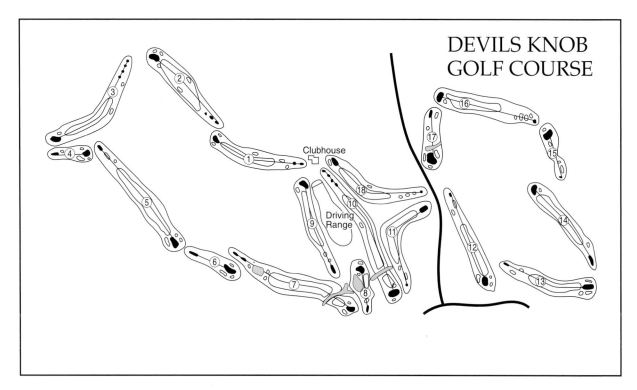

par of 70, but what it lacks in length it more than compensates for with tightness and trouble. There are two par fives on the outward nine and only one on the back. Be warned that the greens are full of subtlety and require a keen eye and a skilled touch. This is a fine test of the game for women, requiring female golfers to exercise virtually every club they carry and to manufacture a few shots as well. As with many mountain golf courses, naked aggression is often rewarded less than accuracy and course management.

The pair of par fours that start your round are solid but scorable holes: a gentle dogleg right followed by an gentle dogleg left. The first green is on the small side, but affords a straight-on approach. "This is one of several greens on which you don't want to be long," said one of the assistant pros. The back apron abuts a steep hill that feeds an overly aggressive approach right into the trees behind the green.

The par-four #3 is a monster, a long and tight dogleg right that plays downhill from tee to green. After the initial distraction of the view of the valley floor miles away and a couple thousand feet below, the difficulty at hand is evident. The elevated tee boxes reveal a ribbon of fairway lined by towering old trees on both sides. Your tee shot must stay just to the right of the fairway bunker at the turn of the dogleg. The pear-shaped green is slightly elevated, with a gaping bunker eager to catch an approach shot that is short or to the right.

The par-five #5 is reachable in two for long hitters, but any ball that ventures too far from the short grass is likely to find unforgiving trouble. From the tees the tree-lined fairway looks about as wide as a country lane. The long oval-shaped green angles to the right and is severely bunkered as any green on the course. Pine trees shield the right side and can come into play if your lay-up second shot is not kept to the left of the big unfriendly fairway bunker about 70 yards in front of the putting surface.

A pair of par threes brackets the toughest hole on the golf course for both men and women. The par-five #7 is a double dogleg that measures 600 yards from the back tees. Men's tee shots must clear a small pond to a minuscule landing area. Your second shot plays uphill to a stream that intersects the fairway in front of the green. While women get a substantial break on the yardage, the red tee markers are nestled right next to the forest on the left, exacerbating the first dogleg and demanding a precise tee shot. The putting surface is tucked behind a bunker and trees.

The finisher on the front nine is a gentle dogleg-right par four that plays uphill through a chute of trees and rocks. The men's tee boxes are elevated, but the ladies must drive from the base of the hill that presents a blind shot to a small landing area. The hilltop green is tiered and tricky and yields one-putts only grudgingly and with the help of a very accurate approach shot.

The 10th hole, the only par five on the back, is a solid three-shot test for all but the Tiger Woods and Davis Love III type of players. It's rated the number-two handicap hole, the toughest on the inward nine. A small stream intersects the fairway about 50 yards in front of the green and must be avoided on your lay-up. The

par-four #11 is a severe dogleg right that plays to a well-treed landing area. It's possible to cut the dogleg, but a shot that drifts too far right will be jailed by trees or will shoot out of bounds.

A trio of par fours—all medium-length—presents good scoring opportunities as you head to the final four holes. Note that there is a small path through the trees and brush behind the championship tees on the 14th hole. About 20 yards down the footpath is an unsurpassed view of the Shenandoah Valley and the surrounding Blue Ridge Mountain peaks. It's worth a few seconds to take a look, and it's a must if you happened to carry a camera along.

The long par-four #16 is a signature hole at Devils Knob, playing downhill from a series of tiered tee boxes. It's another one of those holes that's tightly cramped with trees along both sides and that opens a spectacular vista as you descend from the tees toward the green. The green itself is protected by a huge bunker to the left front and an unforgiving hill directly behind the putting surface.

The par-three #17 is a lovely little hole playing from elevated tees and across a small pond to a long, thin, and tightly trapped green. And the par-four #18—a dogleg right—requires players to negotiate over or around a pair of strategically located trees that protrudes into the fairway and blocks clear access to the elevated green.

Devils Knob

HOLE NUMBER	Ra	Sl	1	2	3	4	5	6	7	8	9	OUT	10	11	12	13	14	15	16	17	18	IN	TOT
CHAMP	72.4	126	398	392	478	146	525	200	600	166	402	3307	574	305	354	372	378	185	408	173	430	3269	6576
REG	69.8	119	378	359	461	125	484	180	560	132	340	3019	550	355	329	328	344	124	388	171	395	2984	6003
PAR			4	4	4	3	5	3	5	3	4	35	5	4	4	4	4	3	4	3	4	35	70
HANDICAP			9	11	3	17	7	13	1	15	5		2	6	14	10	12	18	8	16	4		
FOR	68.6	118	303	312	378	116	438	154	497	102	287	2589	476	286	240	300	287	108	344	115	356	2512	5101

The par-three 16th hole at Wintergreen's Stoney Creek typifies the demanding golf and the spectacular beauty of this championship course designed by Rees Jones.

Stoney Creek at Wintergreen

This is an elegant and demanding championship golf course laid out in a verdant valley surrounded by towering mountains. Rees Jones has skillfully bordered most fairways with mounds and moguls, said to be a miniature reflection of the mountains themselves. Some of the club's members argue that the big mountain that seems to brood over most of the front nine also has an impact on the way the greens roll. One of the assistant pros opined that that's more lore than reality.

In general, your game plan should revolve around a strong start. The front nine is more open and scorable than the tighter, tougher back.

Stoney Creek opens with a very solid par-five dogleg left. The fairway dips into a valley about 150 yards in front of the green, and the valley is intersected by a stream in front of the deep but scrawny putting surface. A ridge from front to back divides the green.

The 2nd, 3rd, and 4th holes—all par fours—demand accuracy and caution. There's a stream on the left side of the 2nd hole from about the midpoint to the green, and there is water to the right on the 3rd and 4th holes. The long, tight 4th is J-shaped, with the well-bunkered green hooked behind a tongue of Lake Monocan and nestled among towering trees. An approach that fails to find and hold the putting surface is more likely than not destined to land in trouble. Justifiably, the 4th is rated the toughest hole on the side for women. The shortish par-four #6 requires a drive that is kept far enough to the right to take out of play a huge old tree that lives on the left center of the fairway.

The toughest hole on Stoney Creek for men is the long, tight, par-four #7. Your tee shot must stay in the fairway just left of the fairway bunkers on the right side. The long approach then plays through a chute of trees to the hilly, undulating, and difficult green. The pretty par-three #8 then leads to the photogenic par-five #9. The green is hidden by trees until you reach the turn of the dogleg right, but the approach is fairly clear and the hole presents a good opportunity to finish the side with a birdie or par.

The par-four #10 is a dogleg right and is about as tight a hole as you can imagine. The sizable green is relatively hospitable despite the hungry bunkers around it. Take enough club. A long approach will not punish you as severely as one that's short or to either side.

The par-three #12 is tougher than it looks and more demanding than its handicap rating would foretell. The green is hewn out of the dense forest, with Stoney Creek itself in play down the left side from tee to green. The putting surface is well bunkered and surrounded by a range of those hills, mounds, and moguls that Rees Jones found so attractive. The par-five dogleg-left #13 is rated the toughest hole on the course for women. The landing area for your tee shot is fairly generous, but the hole narrows the closer to the green you get. Seven sand traps and unpleasant mounds surround the green. Accuracy from 100 yards or closer will reap rewards.

The par-four #14 is a treacherous driving hole whose approach to the green is choked by trees and sand. On the par-four #15, beware of the stream that crosses the fairway diagonally in front of the ridged, undulating green. The long par-three #16 presents a club-selection challenge in that the green is well below the elevated tees and the wind can have an enormous influence on what the golf ball does once it's airborne.

The par-five #17 and the long, testing par-four #18—rated the toughest hole on the side on the men's card—are simply grand finishers. The approach to the long, narrow 17th green is a daunting test, with trees jutting into the fairway on the left and an octet of bunkers caressing the putting surface like a pearl necklace. The dogleg-left #18 requires a tee shot that avoids the trees to the left and comes to rest immediately adjacent to the fairway bunker denoting the point at which the dogleg turns. A serpentine waste bunker with three grassy islands within its confines protects the left from about 100 yards out to the green.

Individually, Devils Knob and Stoney Creek are worth a detour. They are both fine examples of golf-course design, management, and maintenance. Together they are not only worth a long detour but also are well worth regular return visits.

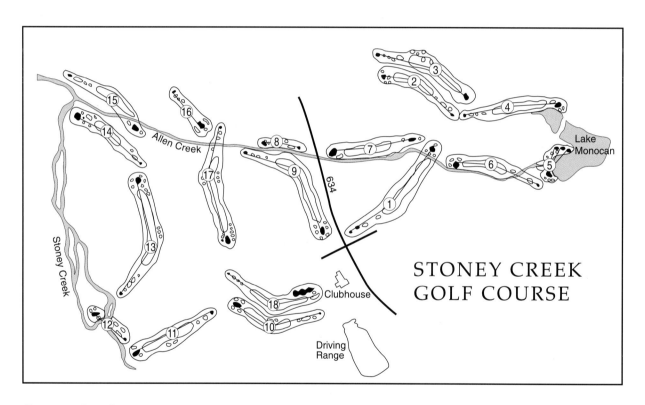

Stoney Creek

HOLE NUMBER	Ra	Sl	1	2	3	4	5	6	7	8	9	OUT	10	11	12	13	14	15	16	17	18	IN	TOT
CHAMP	74.0	132	552	375	447	420	175	380	413	181	536	3479	440	396	179	575	358	405	200	515	458	3526	7005
BACK	72.6	126	535	355	434	410	165	364	401	175	513	3352	415	388	165	545	342	392	200	500	441	3388	6740
MID	71.6	121	497	330	406	380	150	354	391	165	483	3156	398	377	155	501	333	355	181	481	404	3185	6341
SENIOR	69.2	118	487	283	383	352	144	339	363	138	428	2917	398	346	130	489	320	350	134	475	398	3040	5957
HANDICAP (m)			7	15	5	3	17	9	1	13	11		6	18	14	4	12	8	16	10	2		
PAR			5	4	4	4	3	4	4	3	5	36	4	4	3	5	4	4	3	5	4	36	72
FOR	71.0	125	425	256	340	346	115	315	333	134	420	2684	375	341	126	464	290	317	115	418	370	2816	5500
HANDICAP (w)			6	14	8	2	18	12	4	16	10		3	9	15	1	13	11	17	7	5		

COURSES BY REGION

**Northern Virginia
(Washington, D.C., area)**

Algonkian
Brambleton
Bristow Manor
Lansdowne
Raspberry Falls
Reston National
Stoneleigh
Virginia Oaks

**Northern Shenandoah
(Virginia and West Virginia)**

Cacapon State Park (W.Va.)
Caverns Country Club (Va.)
Locust Hill (W.Va.)
Shenvalee (Va.)

Central Virginia

Augustine
The Gauntlet at Curtis Park
Lee's Hill
Wintergreen

Southeastern Virginia

Colonial
Ford's Colony
Golden Horseshoe
Kiln Creek
Kingsmill
Royal New Kent
Stonehouse
The Tides
Williamsburg National

Southwestern Virginia

Hanging Rock
The Homestead
Olde Mill

**West Virginia
(north and west)**

Canaan Valley State Park
Hawthorne Valley
Lakeview Resort
Oglebay Park

**West Virginia
(south and central)**

Glade Springs
The Greenbrier

COURSES BY ARCHITECT

Ault, Brian   Mountainview Course (Lakeview Resort)

Ault, Ed   Algonkian
Reston National
Shenvalee

Biery, Robert   Crispin Course (Oglebay Park)

Breeden, Russell   Hanging Rock

Campbell, Sir Guy   Tartan Course (The Tides)

Clark, Tom   Kiln Creek
Woods Course (Kingsmill)

Cobb, George   Glade Springs
Golden Eagle Course (The Tides)
Tartan Course (rework Sir Guy
    Campbell's original)

Cornish, Geoffrey   Canaan Valley State Park

Dye, P. B.   The Gauntlet at Curtis Park
Virginia Oaks

Dye, Pete   River Course (Kingsmill)

Flynn, William S.   Cascades (The Homestead)

George, Lester   Colonial

Gordon, Hank   Brambleton

Jones, Rees   Green Course (Golden Horseshoe)
Stoney Creek (Wintergreen)

Jones, Robert Trent, Jr.   Lansdowne

Jones, Robert Trent, Sr.   Cacapon State Park
Gold Course (Golden Horseshoe)
Lower Cascades (The Homestead)
Speidel Course (Oglebay Park)

Killian, Ken	Bristow Manor
Lipe, Jim	Williamsburg National
Love, Bill	Lee's Hill
Maki, Lisa	Stoneleigh
Maples, Dan	White & Red Course (Ford's Colony) Blue & Gold Course (Ford's Colony)
Maples, Ellis	Olde Mill Devil's Knob (Wintergreen)
Macdonald, C. B.	Old White Course (The Greenbrier, with S. J. Raynor)
Nicklaus, Jack	Greenbrier Course (rework George O'Neil's original)
O'Neil, George	Greenbrier Course
Palmer, Arnold	Plantation Course (Kingsmill)
Player, Gary	Hawthorne Valley Raspberry Falls
Purdy, Mal	Caverns Country Club
Rando, Guy	Locust Hill
Raynor, S. J.	Old White Course (The Greenbrier, with C. B. Macdonald)
Robinson, Jim	Lakeview Course (Lakeview Resort)
Ross, Donald	The Old Course (The Homestead)
Smith, Rod	Shenvalee
Strantz, Mike	Royal New Kent Stonehouse
Wilson, Dick	Lakeside Course (The Greenbrier)

MOST WOMAN-FRIENDLY COURSES

Algonkian

Brambleton

Cacapon
Canaan Valley
Colonial

Ford's Colony, White & Red Course

Glade Springs
Golden Horseshoe, Green Course
The Greenbrier, Old White Course
The Greenbrier, Lakeside Course

The Homestead, The Old Course
The Homestead, Cascades

Kiln Creek
Kingsmill, Plantation Course
Kingsmill, Woods Course

Lansdowne
Lee's Hill
Locust Hill

Oglebay Park, Speidel Course
Oglebay Park, Crispin Course
Olde Mill

Reston National

The Shenvalee

The Tides, Tartan Course
The Tides, Golden Eagle

Williamsburg National
Wintergreen, Devils Knob
Wintergreen, Stoney Creek

BEST COURSES FOR BEGINNERS

Brambleton

Golden Horseshoe, Spotswood Course

The Greenbrier, Lakeside Course

The Homestead, The Old Course

Kingsmill, Plantation Course

Oglebay Park, Crispin Course

The Shenvalee